MW00829859

A Thank you from
Kedar (Suma knows
how much I wanted
this book) ☺

And Then One Day

NASEERUDDIN SHAH

And Then One Day

A Memoir

HAMISH HAMILTON
an imprint of
PENGUIN BOOKS

HAMISH HAMILTON
Published by the Penguin Group
Penguin Books India Pvt. Ltd, 7th Floor, Infinity Tower C, DLF Cyber City,
Gurgaon 122 002, Haryana, India
Penguin Group (USA) Inc., 375 Hudson Street, New York, New York 10014, USA
Penguin Group (Canada), 90 Eglinton Avenue East, Suite 700,
Toronto, Ontario, M4P 2Y3, Canada
Penguin Books Ltd, 80 Strand, London WC2R 0RL, England
Penguin Ireland, 25 St Stephen's Green, Dublin 2, Ireland
(a division of Penguin Books Ltd)
Penguin Group (Australia), 707 Collins Street, Melbourne, Victoria 3008, Australia
Penguin Group (NZ), 67 Apollo Drive, Rosedale, Auckland 0632, New Zealand
Penguin Books (South Africa) (Pty) Ltd, Block D, Rosebank Office Park,
181 Jan Smuts Avenue, Parktown North, Johannesburg 2193, South Africa

Penguin Books Ltd, Registered Offices: 80 Strand, London WC2R 0RL, England

First published in Hamish Hamilton by Penguin Books India 2014

Copyright © Naseeruddin Shah 2014

Words and music from 'Time' © Pink Floyd Music Publishers Ltd administered by Imagem (UK) Ltd.

All rights reserved

10 9 8 7 6 5 4 3 2

The views and opinions expressed in this book are the author's own and the facts are as reported by him which have been verified to the extent possible, and the publishers are not in any way liable for the same.

ISBN 9780670087648

For sale in the Indian Subcontinent only

Typeset in Adobe Caslon Pro by Ram Das Lal, New Delhi
Printed at Thomson Press India Ltd, New Delhi

This book is sold subject to the condition that it shall not, by way of trade or otherwise, be lent, resold, hired out, or otherwise circulated without the publisher's prior written consent in any form of binding or cover other than that in which it is published and without a similar condition including this condition being imposed on the subsequent purchaser and without limiting the rights under copyright reserved above, no part of this publication may be reproduced, stored in or introduced into a retrieval system, or transmitted in any form or by any means (electronic, mechanical, photocopying, recording or otherwise), without the prior written permission of both the copyright owner and the above-mentioned publisher of this book.

A PENGUIN RANDOM HOUSE COMPANY

For my sons Imaad and Vivaan, the only two of my family who don't appear in this book . . .

. . . and for Dulha bhai and Apa bi, who might finally have understood.

'. . . and then one day you find
ten years have got behind you,
no one told you when to run,
you missed the starting gun'

— Pink Floyd, 'Time', Dark Side of the Moon

Contents

Preface and acknowledgements   xi

'All that David Copperfield kind of crap'   1

The boy from Sardhana and Shah Tandoori, London   7

St Joseph's Film Institute, Nainital   17

Heroes, villains and dolls   22

Cricket, my second, er . . . third love   33

Through the looking glass, sort of   41

Mr Shakespeare and St Anselm ride to the rescue   48

Back to their roots   63

The girl in the tent and the miracle at St Paul's   69

The road less travelled   77

Prodigal   93

The Aligarh University absurdists   103

The woman with the sun in her hair   111

Heeba, gift of God   123

School of drama, tragedy and heartbreak   128

The penny drops in super slo-mo   145

Film, only a director's medium?	161
Zoo story	169
And introducing . . .	185
The churning	209
Of admen and film-makers	225
Breeng the shit	241
New wave or old hat?	254
Poor theatre, moneyed film	275
Search for a voice	292
Finding my spot	304
Epilogue	316

Preface and acknowledgements

There were two strong motivations for saying yes to a big budget Hollywood film in the year 2002. They were: a) I would get to meet Sean Connery, who I had long adored, and b) I was promised an amount of money which if not totally obscene was definitely pretty vulgar. So vulgar in fact that with a couple of weeks' per diem I purchased a laptop and hired a man to teach me how to switch it on.

Through a bone-wrenchingly boring six-month shoot, not knowing what else to do with the machine I started typing, 'I was born in . . .' and so forth and continued for about twenty-five pages. There are many reasons, not the least being indolence and self-doubt, why the final thing emerges a dozen or so years after I started on it. I got bored of it, abandoned it, re-engaged with it a year or so later, and then again a year or so later and so on.

Most of it was written during shootings, sitting in a trailer awaiting the next shot, then transferring it on to a pen drive, more than once losing the pen drive and having to start all over again. Ergo the travails I endured have nothing whatsoever to do with writer's block or anything of the sort, granted that some passages proved tough to write about and my threshold of boredom is rather low I am told; it all had to do with the question of the intrinsic worth of such a book. I felt very much like writing it but not at all sure I wanted anyone to read it. I decided, for my own amusement, to write about incidents I could recall and I need hardly testify I really took my time over it, double-checking facts with my two brothers—the only reliable witnesses. I was also pretty certain that some of my contemporaries' versions of later incidents would vary drastically from mine, but as I said, it was great fun comprehensively reliving those days. I never thought anyone would read about them though.

Then one day I handed over about half the final manuscript to Ramachandra Guha, of whom I had by then sufficiently overcome my awe to consider a friend. His exhortation to me to finish the job I never thought I would is why I must thank him first of all. His positive response to my output and insistence on ridding the text of superfluities, slang, swear words and exclamation marks (which crept in nonetheless, sorry Ram!) galvanized me into finishing the rest of it in one-twelfth the time it had taken me to write the rest.

What this book will mean to anyone I have no clue but I had to get it out of my system, and for helping me do that, warm thanks go to David Godwin of Godwin Associates, Chiki Sarkar, the head of Penguin India publications, and the wonderful Nandini Mehta and Jaishree Ram Mohan, who edited the manuscript. Their encouragement and support were invaluable even though my dearest wish that anyone proving that he/she consistently came last in class be given a free copy of the book did not find much merit in their eyes. Many thanks to my favourite performers for generously providing me the photos I needed, and the associates who helped me get through to them.

A warm hug to the teachers and friends I have been

fortunate to encounter—all the remarkable men and women who had so much they wished to share and unstintingly did.

And lastly a big fat slobbery kiss to the jewel of my existence, Ratna, queen of her species, who while doing so much else has also steadfastly, through thick and thin, better and worse, for richer and for poorer, in sickness and in health held my hand and propped me up for well-nigh forty years. May her tribe increase.

'All that David Copperfield
kind of crap'

I was born in Barabanki, a small town near Lucknow, in July
of the year 1949 or maybe it was August of the year 1950.
No one including Ammi (Farrukh Sultan, my mother) was
later ever quite sure which. Her saying 'tum ramzaan mein
paida hue thhe' wasn't much help in figuring it out either.
Smallpox then was a scourge, typhoid a killer, malaria and
cholera rampant. Children often never made it out of their
infancy, or more frequently lost a year or two on falling ill
or on failing their final exams; so a child's date of birth was
invariably amended, and registered at school time as being
a year or two later than it actually was. To provide for either
eventuality or perhaps simple absent-mindedness made Baba
(Aley Mohammed Shah, my father) register my year of birth
as 1950. Why July 20th was altered to August 16th, however,
is a mystery and I've had quite a bit of fun with the wise ones
who took it upon themselves to figure out my astrological
chart. Consequently, I am whichever age it suits me to be on
any particular day. While it doesn't make me feel a whole lot
younger, it just seems like something to do.

Baba had had a peripatetic life before finally settling down
to serve the British government in the Provincial Civil Service

1

when Freedom's dawn, Independence and Partition hit the country. Not wanting to take any chances, he stayed on in India. Two of his brothers left, as did several of my mother's siblings; he had seven, she had ten. My oldest brother Zaheer was two, the one after him, Zameer, newly born; and I hadn't yet arrived so we didn't have much say in the matter, but doubtless we would all have backed the decision: none of us has been much of a gambler. Apart from the fact that Baba possessed no property in India and thus could not in any conscience claim any across the border, leaving a secure job and starting a new life when somewhat past his prime must have been less appealing to him than staying on in this newly independent 'Hindu country'. He was never one to rock any boats and he figured we'd do all right here. As it happened, he was not wrong in his assessment of our future chances in India.

As an infant I seem to remember travelling continuously by car down tree-lined, practically empty highways. Provincial Civil Service officers saw a fair amount of road on their 'inspection' tours to places not yet connected by rail, and lodged in 'dak' or 'inspection' bungalows built for that purpose. These once splendid mansions, alike in their sprawling colonial isolation, all featured mirrored hat-stands and battered cane furniture on gloomy, pillared verandahs overlooking unkempt gardens and lawns. And I still know the smell of those places: the musty drawing rooms (I always puzzled over why they are called 'drawing' rooms—until a chance visit to Blair Castle in Pitlochry explained it; they were the rooms ladies would 'withdraw' to while the men drank their brandy and threw bread rolls at each other) with the then ubiquitous mounted-head tiger/leopard skins strung over dead fireplaces, ancient copies of *Reader's Digest* on undusted mantels. Insipid food in cavernous dining rooms with Ammi not cooking or serving, and looking pretty unsure about it all. The odour of damp and peeling plaster everywhere, and fetid air in the thickly curtained bedrooms. There were also frequent transfers from town to town in UP necessitating long train journeys, always including endless hours of sitting on our luggage at strangely deserted railway stations awaiting our connection.

The earliest thing I can recall doing is sitting in someone's (not either of my parents') lap and watching a performance which I couldn't identify then and still can't, but which was probably a 'nautanki' by an itinerant theatre troupe, or a Ram Leela, the kind of show performed in the open or in makeshift tents. What has stayed burned into my mind is the thickly painted face of a person up there I got mesmerized by— dancing on top of a very high platform, his face alight, his eyes darting like agitated snakes. A singular rush of excitement coursed through me whenever, body contorting and eyeballs slithering, he looked towards me, which seemed to be most of the time. I remember absolutely nothing else from this day, I must have been about two, and I sometimes do wonder if this is a memory I have invented. Even so, it's become absolutely real and given me a great deal, but something tells me it must have happened. It could even have been a circus and he a clown, but at that moment he seemed to be touching the sky. It was only of course my own minuscule size at the time which made me perceive him as such, but this vision has stayed stuck in the forefront of my consciousness, because that day this man, whoever he was, handed me the most valuable thing I've ever received: the gift of wonder—complete terror combined with the deepest fascination and envy. I wanted to be up there with him forever, I knew that for sure. Mr Yann Martel in his hallucinatory hagiography of the boy Pi puts it the way I wish I could: 'first wonder goes deepest; wonder after that fits in the impression made by the first'. Perhaps that's why in my mind I connect actors and clowns very closely, and sometimes the distinction blurs with great clarity.

I also remember standing on the balcony of one of these inspection bungalows and peeing on someone reading a newspaper below, feeling pretty sure he'd never know where it was coming from. As it happened, he not only figured out where it came from, he also turned out to be Baba's superior. I sometimes wonder if this was one of the incidents that made my father reassess my worth. For some reason I also remember a guy puking all over Baba's gun case on a bus ride down from Nainital to Haldwani. The stain remained on that canvas cover for years, until Baba sold the gun, stained case and all. There is also a memory of riding pillion on a bicycle on a deserted stretch of road and being asked to move aside by two uniformed cops on motorcycles, Zameer getting a fishbone stuck in his throat, and Baba smashing a couple of plates at the dinner table because they weren't clean. Funny, the kind of things that stick in one's mind, like 'dust on honey' as someone said. And then there are things unforgettable like getting butted to the ground by a baby goat I was trying to be affectionate to, or running to the handpump to replenish the almost empty bottle of lemonade with water, tripping and carrying the scar of that on my left palm still, or Zaheer driving Ammi's sewing machine needle through my finger after assuring me it would get stitched.

I was always told I was my father's favourite, words that would come back to haunt me later. Ammi gave birth to five sons, the three of us survived. Baba often confessed that he dearly wanted a daughter. He was never to have one. So when it was my turn to arrive, he must have fervently prayed and hoped, only to be disappointed yet again. He probably overcompensated by indulging me greatly for the first few years of my life. When I awoke he would carry me on his back to the bathroom and tend to me. Evidently I was spoiled rotten at that stage; Zaheer once received a dressing down because I had told on him. In fact looking at some photos of myself at that age I suspect I must have been something of a pest. Baba's large elegant hands and tapering fingers had a warmth I can still feel and I loved his short prickly Hitler-ish moustache scraping my face, but as it happened he and I touched each other less and less in the years that followed.

In an age when girls were married off by fourteen and were expected to start bearing children within the year, Ammi stayed unwed many years longer than was normal. She and Baba were from different branches of the same family, spawned by Agha Syed Mohammed Shah, a soldier of fortune from Paghman, near Kabul, who arrived in India sometime in the first half of the nineteenth century, fought for the British in the 1857 War of Independence and was rewarded with the estate of Sardhana, near Meerut, and the title of Nawab Jan Fishan Khan. My parents had been engaged to each other for a while until Baba, who was then in Kabul, embarked for England. Why exactly he went to either place has never been fully explained, but ostensibly it was as English tutor to the daughter of Amanullah, the exiled Afghan king. My brother has a theory that it was a romance of some kind, something I find intriguing but irreconcilable with my memory of the man. Anyhow, Baba was one of the entourage the king took with him when he had to flee. These royals never even fled without an entourage. The engagement was broken off and Ammi was then assigned for life the role of serving her parents, a somewhat woolly-headed couple unwittingly presiding over the final fall of feudalism in the house of the Sardhana Shahs. She performed the role of selfless daughter to perfection, until Baba fresh from

England and a disastrous marriage to a lady he never ever spoke to anyone about, but with an enviable government job as 'nayab tehsildar', re-entered her life and asked for her hand. He was about forty, she close to thirty, ages at which they should have been grandparents not newlyweds.

The boy from Sardhana and
Shah Tandoori, London

Ammi always told me I had the thickest, blackest hair she'd ever seen on a newborn's head. This was two years after Zameer was born and when Zaheer, one of twins who survived, was three, and well after Ali Ahmed, the eldest born, had succumbed to one of those maladies that got newborns in those days. The trauma of having had to deal with these infant deaths, and now with not one but two howling infants, probably proved taxing for Ammi, and Zameer was sent to Sardhana into the care of one of her younger sisters, Akabi (Rafat Sultan) who had now been cast in the role of selfless daughter. Akabi, tall and strapping, was a somewhat masculine specimen who had to pluck and sometimes clip her facial hair; strong men trembled when her voice did its stuff. She would have been a hard-ass Sergeant Major or the leader of a Mule-train or a Captain of Industry had she been born male and in different circumstances, that assertive and enterprising was she, not to mention sharp-tongued, straightforward, deeply caring and full of fun. A fiery-tempered angel, she was more than a mother to Zameer, who stayed with her till he was almost four. When he came back to live with us in Haldwani, a stud in his left ear which Baba promptly got rid of, he was not only a stranger, he looked, behaved and dressed like a village boy which is what he in fact was. Having spent more time than we had in the sun, his complexion was darker than ours and I daresay he knew it. Initially aloof and withdrawn, always addressing Ammi as 'Apa bi' and Baba as 'Dulha bhai', it took us some time getting used to having him around. Despite still carrying the scars of having been sent away at that age he was, I think, fortunate to have forged the priceless, unbreakable bond he had with Akabi. I myself always sought, and never found, such an equation with an elder.

Zameer and I finally forged our own bonds when Zaheer went away to boarding school at the age of five. This 'Sardhana boy' and I stood waving at the train taking Zaheer away from us and we saw a myriad white hankies waving back. Among the list of compulsory requirements for each departing boy was 'one white handkerchief'. The teacher-escort who had decided this obviously had an acute sense of aesthetics; those white hankies waving from every window is an indelible memory, and though at a different time I suppose this very sight could evoke a giant washing line as well, I still think I've never seen so entrancing a vision, even under the influence of LSD with which I was to repeatedly experiment a couple of decades later. I don't think Zaheer's hanky was among those waving though: the last we saw of him he was crouched on his berth looking frightened, bewildered and terribly angry. I've only seen him look that way on one other occasion since, but I won't talk about that.

The school he was going to was St Joseph's College, Nainital where two years later Zameer and I joined him when Baba was transferred there. Featuring two gloomy Gothic towers in the front, it had seven playing fields, a gymnasium, four tennis courts and many 'Christian Brothers' from Ireland, a forbidding sect of Roman Catholic priests, convinced they were doing this country a monumental favour by just being here. Built sometime in the second half of the nineteenth century as a seminary, hence the abbreviation 'Sem', it was later converted into a school with the brooding atmosphere of self-denial clinging to it still. Nainital's rains, gusty winds and frequent mists probably reminded these Irish adventurers of home, but all it needed was rider-less carriages and giant bats flying around at dusk to complete the picture of Transylvania. Punishments were severe; six of the best with an oiled malacca cane on a winter night was hard and you got some sympathy from your peers, and perhaps admiration if you hadn't flinched, but anything less than that was not to be taken seriously. Rules were inflexible and expulsions common, and we were all judged almost instantaneously and either approved of or consigned to the rubbish heap. For all their inflexible notions, one has to admire the spirit of those intrepid souls a hundred and more years ago, discovering pristine hill locations, some of them difficult to reach even now, and building such awe-inspiring structures in the middle of these wildernesses. No doubt the bricks and mortar were carried by native labour, probably bought very cheap, but it would have to be the unshakeable belief that they came bearing much-needed enlightenment and were spreading the word of the Lord that drove these early missionaries to India. And the legacy they left behind survives.

Baba was an Anglophile. He never left home, even in a one-tractor town like Sardhana, without his hat. For him the Irish and the English were one and the same and he wanted us to have the best education money could buy. Not that he was by any means rich but, having long ago sold his meagre inheritance in Sardhana, had something set aside. He spoke Pushtu and Persian as well as English but never thought it necessary to educate us in the former two, which I hold against him to this day. Totally enamoured of the British, he was determined to have us educated by them, convinced as he was that the 'angrez' were people of their word, deserving to rule whoever they ruled and doing a damn good job of it, and 'angrezi' was the language of the future. His dearest wish was to visit Vilayat again. He even had a special hat kept aside, a real nice Burberry affair, and a natty navy-blue pinstripe suit, which he intended to wear when he disembarked. In a sudden burst of adventurousness, he once toyed with the idea of moving there and opening an Indian restaurant. We even tried picturing ourselves as waiters in this joint, with Ammi doing the cooking. The plan was, however, quickly abandoned. And so the Shah family missed the opportunity of pioneering the Indian restaurant business in England.

My imagination, at the age of three or four, was helped along greatly by Ammi's maternal aunt Nani Baji in Sardhana, sightless and a great storyteller, who would spin for us magical yarns at bedtime. One night after the storytelling session, I had a dream in which I saw ogres and fairies and flying horses and vanishing castles, the kind of things she told us about from the *Tilism-e-hoshruba* fantasies. When I returned, on a magic carpet I think, I saw myself being transported back to my bed through the ventilator in the cavernous room where we slept. When I awoke I saw a shaft of sunlight coming through the ventilator along the exact trajectory I had travelled. The dream was vivid then and still is; this must have been around the same time I saw that man dancing on that platform.

Habib Manzil, my maternal grandparents' house at Sardhana, was as spooky as any haveli of that time. Many deliciously scary rooms lay unused, which none of us had the daring to enter and in any case, apart from curiosity, there was never any reason to. In one of them, among some gigantic trunks, Zameer swears he once saw an old woman who wasn't there walking about carrying a lantern. The vision has remained unexplained but he says it still gives him the shivers to think of it.

The annual visits to Sardhana would bring on intense bouts of hero worship directed at Ammi's three brothers, strutters extraordinaire, invariably leather-jacketed and hatted, almost caressingly handling their weapons, cigarettes dangling stylishly from lips, joie de vivre practically bursting out of them. My own dissatisfaction and impatience with my childhood would grow as I gaped at these three alpha males, their incredible good looks, their rugged attire, their girlfriends; and I started inhabiting an imaginary world in which I was all three combined, and my derring-do made Douglas Fairbanks grin in approval. I invented stories about what I did in the Burma war. I was a flying ace, my Spitfire got shot down by the Japanese, and I then walked all the way home and my legs wore themselves out, which is why I was the shortest of us three, 'This man who we call Baba is actually my younger brother' I'd tell both the Zs, my audience for these narrations. This unending saga became a nightly ritual until, one day, I froze in mid-sentence realizing Baba had overheard. I couldn't read what he felt but he kind of smiled and patted me on the head saying, 'Good! Very good imagination!' That was the end of those stories. I don't know why.

Ammi knew only how to read and write Arabic and thus Urdu. She spoke a little Persian, which Baba spoke fluently, but mostly she'd been conditioned to serve. She always addressed Baba as 'Shah'; he, at least in my hearing, never called her by her name. Cooking, sewing and reciting the Quran were her chief skills but in these departments did she deliver! Her voice, humming-bird soft when she recited aloud, invariably early in the morning when we were struggling to wake up under our quilts or mosquito nets, somehow made waking up easier. The

same voice, however, could change into a tearing hurricane
when she was worked up, which was seldom, but there was no
mistaking it when it happened. Even Baba would retreat when
she was in full swing, because her ire was invariably directed at
him, never at any of us; she left that to him.

Till the end, even though she took enormous pride in my
work and the fact that I took her abroad and even to Rashtrapati
Bhavan with me, and that I would be recognized in most places,
she never really figured me out and after a while stopped trying.
For a long time through my adolescence, when communication
with Baba was at a complete standstill, she would be my only
confidante and comfort. I still keep in my cupboard one of her
dupattas and it carries her smell. The most soothing sensation
I have ever felt in my life is the touch of the breath-warmed
corner of her dupatta on my eyelids. And of course her cooking
was the best in the world. Strangely, she had never learnt to knit,
but countless were the woollen socks she darned and the trouser
seats she reinforced, and the shirt cuffs she either extended or
shortened to suit whoever was to be the recipient of the hand-
me-downs. It was generally myself since I was last in the line
and for a long time the smallest in size. I never got around to
inheriting any of Baba's clothes, though, until he died. Then I
rummaged among his things and took back to Bombay with me
every garment of his that I could lay my hands on. There weren't
many. Through his days of retirement he'd generally wear only
khaki trousers and white shirt, and hat, of course. The trousers
and shirts were too large for me, he was a portly man, but I and
some other actors have worn them often onstage along with a
pair of his shoes, which fitted me perfectly. I couldn't find the
Burberry hat and the pinstripe suit, I suspect they were taken
away by one of the Zs.

For a couple of years after '51, we shifted from Lucknow to
Bareli to Haldwani and finally to Nainital. Poor Zaheer went

into boarding school in '53, and in '54 Zameer and I were put into the nursery in a 'sister' school, St Mary's (Ramnee) Convent, as day scholars, which meant we went home after school.

At Ramnee I was cast as a cobbler in a play called, I think, *The Shoemaker's Shop*. I had to sit on a stool with a little awl before me and go tap-tap-tap in time to a song, 'In the shoemaker's shop, where a tapping never stops tra la la la LAAAAA' and so forth. I fell ill on show day, and so my debut onstage was delayed by quite a few years. I don't remember being particularly broken up about it, but I must have been and maybe what I felt then, though lost in the smoke rings of time, somewhere unknowingly fed the desire to act. I mean, Zameer played a sailor that night in *On the Good Ship Lollipop* and he never felt a similar urge.

The same year I watched a play for the first time, in the Sem concert hall. It was called *Mr Fixit* and has faded from my memory almost entirely but while watching it the only thing I wanted was to be up there with those people. When a long limousine, which I later discovered to be a plywood cutout on wheels, came gliding on to the stage, I was back in the same universe of wonder where I had watched 'that man' dancing on that stage a hundred feet high. And I have since steadfastly believed that the only magic that happens in this world happens on the stage. Films take you captive, they feed you everything on a plate, the legerdemain they create transports you into a state where you may as well be dreaming, but theatre takes you into a world where your imagination is stimulated, your judgement is unimpaired, and thus your enjoyment heightened. It is only in the theatre that there can be this kind of exchange of energies between actor and audience. The finest definition of theatre that I have come across is 'one actor–one audience'. Implying of course that any meaningful interaction between two people anywhere fits the definition of ideal theatre, with the same qualities needed of both participants as are required from them in an actual theatre. Theatre really is a one-on-one experience.

The time to attend real school was approaching; playing with plasticine and singing songs and drawing all day in Ramnee couldn't go on forever. At the year-ending annual function we were given mementoes. I got a book, *Farm Fun*, Zameer got one called *A Name for Kitty*, and we began to gird our loins for this business of living and learning which had now to begin. St Joseph's had always looked ominous, and now we were to enter into its bowels. Zameer being a year ahead of me even in Ramnee was admitted into Class 1, and myself into the higher kindergarten. Zaheer was no longer a boarder this year but reverted to day-scholarship, which was to last only a year for all three of us.

Perhaps Classes 1 and 2 started their term a day or two earlier than the KG did, because I recall Baba enclosing my hand in his, and taking me to my first day in school by myself. It was a cold rainy day, the mist was deep, I was bundled into a Duckback raincoat and rubber cap and I was carrying my bag in my other hand. I've always had ambivalent feelings about mist since. Beautiful yes, but also chilling; and there's nothing ambivalent about my feeling for school bags—I still hate the damn things. The sensation of setting off from home seemed final. I'm not sure if I cried; I don't think I did, I was too terrified. Walking uphill to the school, a mean climb, I don't remember if Baba and I talked, but he must have said something to me. Even though he was a man of very few words, there must have been a time when we talked to each other.

Our teacher in kindergarten was a Miss Brendish who left the next year. My idea of the perfect teacher has always been in the image of Miss Brendish, really kind and really pretty. I think that somewhere in my wife Ratna's collection of memorabilia there exists my report card for this year (1955). It's a very good one and I'm among the achievers. That did not continue to be the case, however; the decline in academic achievement was to be steady. The days of coming and going to and from school that year I don't recall except for having daily to check with Ammi which my left shoe was and which my right; constantly watching my shadow while walking uphill, to check if my hair still looked combed, something it has consistently refused to be for more than one minute even now; and picking up little bits of gravel to compare with the size of my front ('milk') teeth which I was told would fall out and be replaced by 'teeth of stone'.

I also remember flying on one occasion. It was the annual Sports Day prize distribution, and I was applauding listlessly with the others for the unending row of winners filing up to receive their prizes. I don't think I'd taken part in any event, much less won it, when to my astonishment I was suddenly pushed towards the dais by someone behind me who said 'Hey, Shah! Your name—.' Before I knew how or why, I was shaking hands with the chief guest and being handed a gleaming little trophy, which I still have. I have no idea why I got it, and it still bothers me that maybe it was intended for someone else who also didn't hear his name called. I try to go back in time and invent excuses like 'Well, it was probably the sack race or the egg and spoon race. I must have come third or something!' But the niggling doubt persists that I got that cup for doing nothing.

All this reasoning has happened since I turned fortyish; and after being bored to death at the few film award ceremonies

I did attend and becoming privy to the machinations that go on behind the scenes, I began to loathe all competitive awards, particularly those which are an excuse for the film industry to indulge in its annual orgy of mutual jerking-off. The feeling turns even stronger when I look at that cup now. But then, it made me walk on air for a few brief minutes. I was one with the wind, flying down the steep path that led from the school building to the gate, to the cottage nearby where we lived. My feet were not touching the ground, and I didn't need to figure out why this wondrous thing had happened to me. The feeling of being worthwhile and being rewarded was enough. I didn't need to know whether I deserved it or not. That sensation has repeated itself once more since: twenty years later, after my first meeting with Shyam Benegal, when he told me I'd gotten the part in *Nishant*, my first film.

St Joseph's Film Institute, Nainital

1955 ended, and with it memorizing 'Sing Ann sing. Can Ann sing? Ann can sing' and two-ones-are-twos and spending the post-lunch 'siesta hour' ogling Miss Brendish's legs. Education began in the year 1956. But another blow awaited me before the year was out. Baba was nearing the end of his tenure as a government servant, retirement age being fifty then, and had been posted to Ajmer, a scenic town in Rajasthan ringed by the gentle Aravalis, for the remainder of his working life, which actually had ended but now would extend for another ten years. I came to love and look upon Ajmer as the place I belong to; it was where the three of us went after nine months in school. The hallowed tomb of Khwaja Moinuddin Chishti, a Sufi saint from the twelfth–thirteenth century, is in Ajmer and falls under the jurisdiction of the home ministry. Baba was appointed administrator of the shrine with a substantial increase in salary and he celebrated by buying a small two-band Philips radio and putting the three of us into boarding at St Joseph's. I don't remember being too excited at the prospect. It would mean a cold thorny bed by oneself in an enormous dormitory; no more cuddling with Ammi. It would mean polishing one's own shoes and, impossibility of impossibilities, combing one's own hair. I didn't think I'd survive it. As it turned out, I not only survived St Joseph's, I even got the best education money could buy, though not quite in the way Baba had hoped.

We saw a movie or two every week, possibly the only indulgence, apart from walloping the kids, that the Christian Brothers permitted themselves. The movies were generally on Wednesday, and whoever selected the movies really knew his onions. When I catch an old movie on TV now, it is only the really obscure ones I cannot immediately identify. I'd seen them all in school, or I made it my business to find out about them. The selection took in everything from Mickey Mouse to Orson Welles, from the synchronized swimsuits of Esther Williams to the incomprehensible singing of Mario Lanza, from *On the Waterfront* to *Zorro Rides Again*. I'd wake up at night chortling at the memory of Norman Wisdom tripping over his own big feet or Jerry Lewis quite astoundingly going from one state of imbalance into another without falling. I was mesmerized as Spencer Tracy fought off the sharks and brought his big fish home, and cheered when Gary Cooper took on the baddies single-handed. I loved Frank Capra's and Chaplin's whimsical wonders; Laurel & Hardy, though, I never found the least bit amusing. In Elia Kazan's dramas, everyone shouted and cried way too much, I thought; it was decades before I revisited Mr Kazan's work, but there were the John Ford Westerns and the Tarzan films and the Three Stooges. The jaw-dropping special effects of *Tom Thumb* (from the early fifties) I think have never been replicated even with the great god computer, nor have there ever been in movies other deadpan acrobatic enigmas like Buster Keaton, inspired lunatics like The Marx Brothers, or dancers with the panache and skill of Fred Astaire/Ginger Rogers and Gene Kelly/Cyd Charysse. St Joseph's got me irrevocably hooked on movies, and even though my time there was not the happiest in my life, I can never stop being grateful to whoever chose those movies, and I suspect it was one Brother D.F. Burke, whose fondness for doling out physical punishment was legend, and who I still hate with a passion.

There are only a few other memories not of movies. Moments learning to row on the lake in Nainital; Babar (Shah) Mamu, Ammi's youngest brother and ever my hero in real life, scoring a century in a match at the 'flats' and bringing home a huge cup from which he and his teammates drank something, while shouting and laughing a great deal; the spectacle of the Himalayan range from Cheena Peak on a clear winter day; running around the Government grounds, probably one of the most exquisite golf courses in the world, a castle straight out of *Robin Hood* prosaically called Government House looming over it; watching a huge oak struck by lightning cleave right through its middle into two flaming halves right before our astonished eyes; refusing on one of my low days to copy from the blackboard the weekly letter home which always began 'Dear Mum and Dad, I am well and happy', telling the teacher I wanted to write 'I am not well and not happy', and finally settling for 'I am well and not happy'; stealing a box of matches to eat the unburnt match heads, and being caught before I could eat them all.

Hindi movies were taboo, as was talking in Hindi— sometimes, comically enough, even in Hindi class. In my ten years at Sem, we saw just one Hindi movie there, *Schoolmaster*, which was in fact a Tamil film with Sivaji Ganesan, dubbed into Hindi. Over three hours in length, it felt much longer and actually took two evenings to screen, but we were mercilessly subjected to its plodding story and its semaphoric acting to the bitter end. The film-maker had probably emptied his cavernous pockets into the school coffers, provided the students were compelled to sit through his masterwork. There could NOT possibly be another explanation. The gasp of disbelief that greeted the legend 'INTERVAL' when we were expecting the film to end, in fact feeling it should have ended long ago, would, if the film-maker were present, have discouraged him from ever again testing this particular audience for a reaction. But *Schoolmaster* was a small road-bump on a mesmeric journey that St Joseph's and Brother Burke helped me embark on.

And as if this feast of cinema was not enough we were not infrequently allowed a movie in town (ticket prices deducted from our pocket money) if the movie was one of those 'must-sees'. Usually the biblical epics qualified for this category—*The Ten Commandments*, *Ben-Hur*, *King of Kings*—but there were also the then new movies, in 'Cinemascope' which couldn't be screened in school: *The Bridge on the River Kwai*, *Spartacus*, *The Guns of Navarone*, *Witness for the Prosecution*, all of which I gratefully devoured. Thus my film education was in very good shape by the time I left Sem in shame, having failed in Class 9, a cathartic event that was to shape the rest of my life—but of that later.

While Baba had put his money on St Joseph's improving my mind and preparing me to be a good citizen, I was beginning to realize that watching movies was what I enjoyed more than any other activity, and when not watching one, pretending to be in one. That's all I understood of acting at that time, and deeply unsatisfied as I was with being an unremarkable, unattractive, unintelligent, unfriendly type, there was great solace to be found in pretending to be other people. Of course I never ever 'pretended' in public, never even confessed to anyone about it, and conducted all my 'pretending' on my own, but the virus just continued to grow. I have been grappling for years with the question of whether experiencing difficulty dealing with real life is what drives people to become actors. Though it is far from resolved in my head, looking back at some very worthwhile actors I have known closely, almost every one of them seems to conform to this pattern. It does seem like an aberration of behaviour to want to be someone else all the time, and I think it happens to people who, like me, can find no self-worth early in life and thus find fulfilment in hiding behind make-believe.

So while unknown to him, my father's dreams for me were being slowly demolished, I was beginning to zero in on dreams of my own. There was one problem however: no one else thought I had any ability in any field, least of all in acting, and although dramatic activity was plentiful and the school did marvellous annual theatre productions every year, I never so much as got a look-in at any of these events. The teachers' pets got all the parts. I did not even have the satisfaction of being rejected.

Heroes, villains and dolls

The early years at Sem went by uneventfully except that I gradually managed to slip to the bottom of the class, and learnt how to smoke by the time I was in Class 8. I still have the report card for that year too, which proclaims that I stand 50th in a class of 50. I don't know to what I can attribute this decline in academia except that my fascination for Miss Brendish was now replaced with a fascination for Mrs Ludwig, the art teacher who, while seated at her desk, would dangle her shoe ever so tantalizingly on her foot through the class, without ever letting it fall off. Listening to the teachers' intonations, watching the way they gesticulated, the way they dressed, the way some of them tugged at their cuffs, the way they wiped the blackboard, was far more interesting than what they were trying to teach. I excelled in English at times, but that was all. Maths was totally beyond me as were physics and chemistry, and as for trigonometry . . . ! It's kind of bemusing to wonder how come it never occurred to any of my teachers to investigate the curious case of this child who always got the highest marks in the class in English literature and composition, yet failed in grammar.

Much to my envy, both the Zs featured in the school plays. Zaheer, who actually is pretty good and gave me one of my earliest lessons in acting, won 'best actor' a couple of times while the largest part I had was one line in a play called *Matrimonial Agency*. I loved the school plays, sometimes Gilbert and Sullivan operas, *The Gondoliers* and *The Mikado*, and at other times stuff concocted by Brother Greene: *Aladdin & Out!* and *Alibaba & the 40 Black Sheep*. I'd have given my soul to be onstage in these, but Mephistopheles did not turn up to tempt me and in any case singing, even in a chorus, was quite beyond me. And that, coupled with having no handle at all on the art of 'selling myself', made sure I was left out in the cold. My one line in *Matrimonial Agency*, however, vindicated for me the feeling I'd always had that I wouldn't be a complete disaster as an actor. This needs some recounting.

Every time I ever saw a play, and this dates back to *Mr Fixit*, I would, while waiting for the curtain to rise, be intensely intrigued by exactly what was going on behind it. As the years flew past, I learnt it's a welter of confusion, especially in school plays. But at that time I wanted nothing more than to be privy to what was brewing on the other side. And my opportunity came with this skit which our class put up for the Principal's feast. This was Class 8, the year 1961, and I was twelve or eleven, depending on my mood. After being rapidly rejected by Brother Foran for one of the main parts, I was cast as a guy who, having mistaken the matrimonial agency for a pet shop, comes in and says, 'I want one who will bark all day, bite people's noses off, and guard my house from any intruder!' When I was asked, not for the first time in my life, to speak up so everyone could hear, I found myself receding into the depths of the same black despair I had felt when I was five, and afflicted with a stammer which I finally overcame by speaking as fast as I could. Get the thought out before the damn stammer hits, you know ... Speaking in a rush had become a habit, and though I could, even then, deliver 'if you have tears prepare to shed them now—' quite magnificently to myself, if anyone else were around, bewildered squeaks emerged instead of the beautiful waterfall of a voice I imagined I had. But I held on to the role, mainly by virtue of no one else being available; and after being goaded to 'speak up, speak clear, not so nasal, not so fast!' I found, with a bit of practice, I could actually do that in front of people too. It was a monumental discovery.

Now I was actually standing behind the curtain. I was there! I took a long while savouring the feeling that there were people out there who were curious about what we were doing, about what I was doing. I kicked the hem of the curtain to make it billow and make them wonder even more. That's what the inside of a mother's womb must feel like. Warm, safe, comfortable. You have no weight, no cares. The outside world is outside. It can get to you only when you let it. Then the curtain opened. Suddenly, the womb was gone and I was staring into a black void. Never having been onstage before, I was blinded by the intensity of the lighting, but then I felt the boards under my feet, and I took a breath. In the dazzling blackness, dim shapes of heads gradually began to identify themselves. They looked expectant, receptive, not hostile and judgemental, as in life. And every one of them seemed to be looking at me. I had one of the first lines. After, for a few brief seconds, almost submitting to the most intense fear I've ever known, I finally spoke and got it out loud and clear and not garbled and not nasal at all, and they laughed. They had listened and they had responded! And I discovered that no one in the cosmos is more desirous of loving you, for that moment, than an audience is.

I have sometimes tried to explain the sheer alchemy of this moment to indifferent journalists waiting for the 'apt line', or to other actors not so diffident as I was, people who've had no problem being listened to or responded to, and I guess it's not that they can't understand, but that I can't explain it any better. It was the defining moment of my life and made me feel I was of some worth after all. Acceptance and appreciation were things I was not familiar with. And vain though it may sound, it is absolutely true that never again while stepping on to the stage have I ever felt the slightest anxiety. All I have felt is impatience. I can't wait to be up there. And being up there, for the most part I have known only joy, even when subjected to hostile audiences. Because it's not you they are responding to but what you are providing. A 'bad' audience can be turned into a 'good' one by a good performance and vice versa. I have always wondered if it isn't something of an aberration to want people to respond to you and yet to not want it. Anyway, that is also why meeting the audience after a performance is not my favourite activity. The audience often mixes you up with the part you've just played.

The arrival of the December vacation in school was heralded by icy winds and the appearance of our trunks in the quadrangle. These had lain since March, when we'd all arrived, in the box room, a huge mysterious room below the study hall, which was kept locked through the year. The day of departure was a day of celebration. 'No more Hindi, no more French, no more sitting on the hard old bench!' Till next March, that is. Then the bus ride down to Kathgodam, the nearest railway station, catch the train to Bareli (then spelt 'Bareilly' like 'Cawnpore'), change at Bareli for Delhi. An overnight journey, and finally chugging in over the Jamuna bridge past the ramparts of the Old Fort and into Old Delhi station and parental embraces, followed by warm toast and tea in a pot in the station refreshment room. And then the final leg of the journey to Ajmer, arriving there normally in the dead of night; and the tonga ride home, perched precariously on our trunks all the while. The horse would invariably crap on the way (an ability I've always envied, to be able to do that while running full pelt) and the smell of horse dung is inextricably woven in my mind with the feeling of coming home. I love the smell, and it is definitely responsible for my love of horses.

There wasn't a whole lot to do in Ajmer during the hols. The Sunday morning English matinee was allowed us but other outings were uncommon, and with Baba being the kind of person he was, so was socializing. We visited and were visited by maybe one family, the Capoors, Mrs Capoor being the most beautiful vision of a woman I have ever seen in my life, but even them we saw only on festivals or weddings or suchlike. Spotting Mrs Capoor taking a walk while we were cycling past would make our respective day. Playing cricket was our only pastime, and our most, and only, prized possessions were a bat, a ball and a set of stumps. None of us ever became terribly proficient at the game despite playing it every day in every vacation. There was, however, always one thing to look forward to apart from the Sunday movie in Prabhat Talkies, and that was the annual visit to Sardhana, which Baba abhorred, but which Ammi insisted on, and generally with good reason, as one or other of her sisters and/or brothers would be getting married.

These weddings were monumental affairs. Uncles, aunts and cousins of all varieties from all over the country, from Pakistan and even further, would descend, the celebrations were unending, and the feasts and the flare-ups massive. I don't remember dancing girls but qawwalis went on into the night, and the wind-up gramophone (my introduction to Hindi film music) would blare non-stop. Guns and fireworks went off and antique swords flashed about. Presiding over all this

would be Ammi's parents, Agha Habib Shah and Naushaba
Begum. Until later stricken by paralysis and heartbreak at his
warring sons and getting reduced to a pathetic sideshow, he
was a gargantuan figure, his great quilted coat engulfing all
three of us. She was a tall, slim, elegantly turned out hard-
faced lady with twinkling eyes, who smoked asthma cigarettes.
The lands they owned were still to be divided and fought over
by their children, so the estates were still enormous, but the
picnics and shikars and mango-eating contests were to be
among the last indulged in. Habib Shah owned the Meerut-
Sardhana Roadways, a fleet of three buses which plied the
sixteen miles between these two places, and brought bagfuls
of loose change every evening. Sardhana still does not have
a railway station and Nana's fleet of buses is long gone, like
the lands and the houses, all gradually sold or lying around in
states of dilapidation. The last useful function any of the buses
performed was to provide us children with a great space to
play in, in its remains. The Meerut–Sardhana route today has
scores of buses going up and down, but the Shahs blew their
chance to control it long ago.

Ammi had four brothers, two of whom left at Partition and
two (the eldest and the youngest) stayed behind. The eldest,
Agha Mohiuddin (Agha Mamu) by now a Superintendent
of Police, was a trained lawyer, a 'Hafiz-e-Quran' and had
served in the navy before joining the police. The youngest,
Shahabuddin Babar (Shah Mamu), was a lovable rogue who
was never to amount to anything, but has stayed my idol always.
Of the two who went to Pakistan one, Saeeduddin Khalid
(Chand Mamu), later returned in order to manage the lands,
as the old man was now losing interest in all that, and wanted
to conserve all his energy exclusively for 'shikar'. I've seen
him come home with a bag of ten blackbuck, an endangered
species today. 'Shikar' in fact was to figure very prominently

in my definition of Ammi's three siblings (the fourth I never met) and these three tigers for me were the personification of manhood, so when the dazzle of their personalities later faded, their fallibility and fall from grace was sobering to see. But at that time these square-jawed studs walked among the stars for me; all three of them handsome, humorous, hot-tempered, tall, tough and temperamental, quick to take offence, crack shots with a gun, fast and effective with their fists, seemingly invincible, indestructible people, with an unending capacity for enjoyment.

Though Agha Mamu the cop always felt he had to live up to his reputation of 'Dacoit killer of UP' and very consciously assumed the kind of awesome personality you'd find it tough to feel affection for—in fact who you'd wet your pants at the approach of—the other two when they were young were real cool creatures who laughed and loved a lot. I've seen Chand Mamu drop two flying partridges with two shots in succession, and I've seen Shah Mamu wrestle a wounded blackbuck to the ground single-handed. They couldn't do a thing wrong, even if they had the hideously arrogant habit of reaching out and backhanding any unwary pedestrian or cyclist who dared block the path of their jeep or tractor, both rarely seen in Sardhana before then. It was this very attitude, I guess, which took Shah Mamu to a grisly death not too long after, Chand Mamu to the complete disintegration of property and family reputation, and Agha Mamu into an imaginary shell of his own making, where he dwelt to the end in extreme bitterness, his days of power and charisma a distant memory.

But in his salad days Agha Mamu who, I suspect, modelled himself on Clark Gable, upstaged his siblings completely. He was the third of (at a rough count) twenty children Naushaba Begum bore, of whom eleven survived, which means she must have done precious little but bear children for close to thirty years. Though there was almost a quarter-century of difference in age between him and the other two, it had more to do with the confidence quotient actually, as was visible one evening when Agha Mamu, who had arrived a few days later than the others, and Chand Mamu were seated side by side on modha chairs in the courtyard of Habib Manzil, with all us adoring children sitting around. Shah Mamu seldom appeared when Agha Mamu was holding forth as he was now, his arms expansively spread on the armrest; and never before had I seen Chand Mamu look so small, though he in fact possessed a remarkable personality himself. Ratna in fact ranks him among the most heart-stoppingly handsome men she has ever seen, but that evening this man who so far had lit up the gathering with his presence was almost unrecognizable, sitting with arms stuck meekly to his sides inside the armrests. This I suppose was my very first lesson in acting.

Before we'd know it, however, March would be upon us, and it would be time to return to school. Shirt and trouser cuffs were rearranged; toiletries, one new pair of shoes, and a few new clothes each were acquired, along with many instructions about looking after them and studying harder this year, 'as now you are in Class—.' Parting hugs from Ammi, prayers blown over our heads, a perfunctory peck from Baba and then the return journey overnight to Delhi, joining up with the 'Delhi party', meeting friends, swapping news, warm toast in the refreshment room if we were lucky, then upwards on to Bareli and thence to Kathgodam and Nainital. Back to the twin towers and the strap, the cold fried eggs at breakfast and Brother Burke's knuckles rapping on your unsuspecting head. BUT a wondrous new store of movies as well. Titles of movies to be shown through the year would be published in the school diary at beginning of term, and I salivated copiously reading the list. I wasn't particularly happy in that school, it was for the movies I wanted to return every year, and as I got older and grew away from both parents, I couldn't wait for vacations to end, because home was no longer the happy, carefree place I wished it could remain. I was no longer a child, I was told, and disapproval abounded. It became worse than school could possibly be. I suppose I could live with the disapproval of the teachers. I cared not a whit for them, and even after all these years I have to struggle a bit to suppress the aggrieved feeling that, in all my years there, not one teacher in that school ever made the slightest attempt to reach out to me. But I suppose that's what I was sent there for, to learn to live by myself. And I guess I did.

My class teacher in Classes 4 and 5, after the pretty Miss Brendish and the kindly Miss D'Silva, who wore rimless glasses like my mother, was Miss Winnie Perry. If you were to ask any junior student of fifties Sem about Miss Perry it's an even bet she still figures in his nightmares. I drove her to despair, she always said, but she never gave up on me. If I hadn't been so petrified of figures and of her I might have become the world's greatest mathematician, considering the time Ma Perry spent on me. She would gleefully play along with our whispered suspicions that she went home on a broomstick, and when in really severe mode she used the handle of a feather duster for chastisement.

In later life after having been roused to fury by something my own children did, I often, on calmer reflection, realized that it was my own insecurities and failings in something completely unrelated that had made me bully them thus, and I did it only because I could. When I've struck any of them or felt the urge to do so, my own frustrations have always been the cause. I sometimes wonder how many disappointments and failures poor Miss Perry or Brother Burke must have lived with to relish being so relentlessly cruel to the children in their care.

Shah Mamu had a dramatic face-off with Miss Perry one Sunday when he came to take us all 'out'. Going out of school on Sunday was a big thing but Miss Perry would always keep some student or the other 'in' probably because she couldn't bear to be alone, and on this and many another weekend I was the one chosen to get some maths drilled into my unwilling head. Shah Mamu the handsome dog's grand arrival obviously made an impact on the old maid but he was told to wait. After standing around politely for a while, not his style at all, he barged straight into the drawing room where the extra class was on, and brazenly demanded that she let me off. Miss Perry held her ground until something sounding suspiciously like profanity to her ears was said. She blanched and weakly threatened to send him to the Principal. My hair stood on end when I heard him snarl, 'What the damn Principal will do? He'll hang me?' And to my utter astonishment, instead of pulling his ears for his atrocious grammar and taking the 'skin off his back' with her feather duster after disabling him with one of her roundhouse forehands, or much worse, putting a hex on him and turning him to stone, she actually caved in and turned quite mild before letting me off the hook. Valiant valiant Shah Mamu! To Ma Perry's credit, she did not hold the incident against me, I guess she didn't need to, I gave her plenty of other reasons anyway and I didn't dare defy her. But one day in the grip of a fit of insanity, which I suspect was inspired by Shah Mamu's sparring session with Miss Perry, I started imitating Brother Burke's nasal drawl right under his nose. I leave it to your imagination, dear reader, to visualize what happened to me. A real sight for the gods would have been a run-in between Brother Burke and Shah Mamu.

Old Burke, after continuing to terrorize (and according to many, also teach) students rather well for many more years, went back to Ireland in the mid nineties, and finally mingled with his own earth. My prayer for him is that in the big projection room in the sky he has the most comfortable seat and an unending store of his favourite movies for all eternity. That, and I also hope he keeps getting rapped on the head with a hard knuckle every now and then when he least expects it.

As for Miss Perry, sometime in the mid nineties I learnt she was in a home for the aged in Lucknow. I wrote her a letter, I don't know why, and she replied saying she remembered me, but I doubt if she did. I heard later that she'd suffered a brutal death at the hands of an intruder. I don't suspect it was one of her students.

Cricket, my second, er . . .
third love

My grades continued to slip, my tonsils were removed, my pubic hair began to grow, a hundred 'naya paisa' replaced the sixteen annas in a rupee, kilometres replaced miles and the unsatiated curiosity about the opposite sex began its torment, causing me to sink deeper and deeper into myself. I still never got a chance to act on the stage, and the gulf between my parents and me began to widen. Through my time in Sem I was befriended by two people, Karan Chand Raj ('KC') Singh who was the prince, not that I would ever have believed it then, and is now the raja of an estate called Kashipur, and Satvinder ('Pearly') Dhingra. Both from privileged homes, they were kind and generous and didn't consider me inferior; both unselfish, undemanding friends who liked me for what I was and wanted to share their affection. I have had only fleeting contact with both over the succeeding years but can never forget how they made me feel.

Going home for the vacations was now drudgery worse than school. Most maternal uncles and aunts were long married, and the assemblages at Sardhana were for funerals rather than festivities. Habib Manzil was losing its grandeur, it looked kind of washed-up now. The old walls were starting to crumble and new walls were coming up with succeeding generations laying claim to their share of the houses and the lands. The divisions had begun. The antique Model-T Ford was sold and replaced by a tonga, which didn't last long, a horse being more trouble to maintain than a car. Ammunition had become prohibitively expensive, and blackbucks were disappearing from the face of the earth, so that was more or less the end of shikar as well. Expensive luxuries were now being done without. The gramophone was catching rust with neither the stock of records nor the stock of needles being replenished. The cousins were all growing up and getting on with their lives. Sardhana was becoming a bore. No one even saw ghosts there any more.

And Ajmer and vacations only meant Baba's gimlet eyes boring through me from over his reading glasses, questions on whether or not I'd given any thought to the future, me weakly justifying an even shabbier academic performance this year, and having to endure unending tuition classes, which he decided I needed. So apart from the Maulvi saheb who tried to teach us Arabic and Urdu, there was a procession of tutors on whom my poor misguided father spent another good portion of his salary, and who I hoped would be devoured by Zulu, our crossbred German shepherd, on their way in. (One almost was, but got away with ripped trousers and a sprained wrist, but no blood.) Holidays, in fact life, had become a monumental drag. The cricket field, the scene of so much gloriously sweaty laughter, lay abandoned. Now there was only the occasional tonga ride, the cricket commentary on the radio, and Zulu to play with and, of course, the Sunday morning English movie at Prabhat Talkies.

Back at Sem, Miss Perry was succeeded as class teacher by John Lefevre, a dapper, affable bachelor who had a rumbling baritone, rolled his cigarettes and always smelt of tobacco.

Certainly not intending to stay celibate like the Brothers, he'd often have lengthy consultations with various lady teachers who'd go giggling by while he was in our class. He'd also often, during class hours, put his head on his desk after admonishing us to 'do anything, but don't make a noise' and stay oblivious to us through the hour. He was kind and much loved. But though my association with him did not help me learn any more than Miss Perry's cruelty had, it did help my collection of cricket pictures.

Cricket was trying to force itself to the forefront of my awareness, and was grappling with movies for the honour. Apart from the literature stories and the odd poem worth memorizing, I found nothing of the slightest interest in any of the books I was made to read in class. Cricket was interesting. I was up on the details of every score of every Test match being played; there weren't one-hundredth the number of matches being played then as there are now. I played too and briefly dreamt of a career in cricket, but gave it up as no one ever told me whether or not I was any good, and I couldn't figure it out on my own. The last-straw thing happened when I was the third victim bowled round my legs in a hat-trick pulled by one Prabhat Kapil. I continue however to sustain a passion for the game, which at that time was aflame. I had a vast collection of pictures of cricketers past and present which, when I left school, I just left behind. Those pictures would be priceless today. Half my weekly pocket money of one rupee went religiously into buying *Sport & Pastime*, a fabulous magazine, now defunct, which I'd read from cover to cover, then cut up and stick the cricketers' pictures in my physics practicals notebook. What useful purpose I hoped that'd serve I don't know and didn't know then, but I did become known as the guy with the most cricket pictures.

I didn't linger long on the horns of the cricket-versus-movies dilemma. Cricketers were godlike creatures blessed with special gifts; besides, there were so few. There were many more actors, so I plumped for the easier alternative. Cricket is a heartless mistress and much tougher than acting. It's not as if I'd always watch a film instead of a cricket match but cricket, though it comes pretty close, didn't for me compare then, and does not now, with the magic of what appears on the screen, which is probably why it has become such a TV-friendly game. The actors in those exclusively American or British films we saw then didn't look like real people to me but this world looked safe. In cricket one mistake could be the difference between humiliation and glory. In the movies, everything always turned out all right. You could put your faith in a superhero and rest your own head on your pillow and sleep. This magical world didn't exist yet you could escape into it whenever you wished.

The few Hindi movies I saw as a child, however, didn't grab me. They seemed silly and have never stopped seeming so. The actors didn't seem so much unreal as fake. The back-projections looked like back-projections. I actually remember an actor wearing a wristwatch in some period costume drama. Everything in those movies seemed tatty and in poor taste; watching one I never felt convinced that this was actually happening. Sometimes decades later, at work on the sets of a Hindi movie or while listening to the script narration of one, this same thought has recurred, 'This cannot actually be happening!' Yet Hindi movies continue to enthral (and generate) billions every day all over the world. So I guess there is something the matter with my perception. Be that as it may, Hindi movies and their actors have never held much fascination for me; a role model in the Hindi film industry has been hard to find except perhaps for the eccentric Mr Raaj Kumar, and he not for his acting which was dreadful but for the way he safeguarded his interests, prolonged his career, and sent all Follywood on a flying fuck to the moon whenever he felt like it.

Nazrul Haque, a classmate, introduced me to cigarettes and found a willing pupil, a fascination for the smell of burning tobacco and the manner of people who smoked it being not uncommon among young boys. The remains of a cigarette were actually found by the dorm matron once in the pocket of one of my shirts going to the laundry. The punishment for smoking was expulsion and no questions asked. While I vigorously protested my innocence in the face of undeniable proof, it did seem for a while that my trunk would emerge shortly from the box room on its own. But on pondering the question, the matrons decided not to bring the matter to the Principal's notice, the common consensus among them being that I was too much of an idiot to pull off something like this. It was common knowledge that many senior boys smoked, and it was concluded that the cigarettes had been planted in my pocket; some senior was shifting evidence that might have damned him.

The suspicion that I was a complete idiot began to grow into a conviction, and I had not a clue what to do about it. In spite of my falling grades my father continued to remind me that I was 'basically an intelligent boy'. This belief must have made it even tougher for him to swallow my increasingly dismal performance. I think he did believe it, and wanted me to believe it too, but it was a little while before that happened, and in the most unexpected way. My utter disinterest in learning anything except cricket scores and the speeches in *Julius Caesar* had now reached the proportions of an ailment. Zaheer, the brains of the family, was deputed by Baba to coach me in maths, and he valiantly tried, sacrificing his own precious study hours trying to drill some mathematical sense into me. In vain, I'm afraid. My mind would not sit still long enough to assimilate the solution of one problem, and then it would be time to move on to the next! I'd pretend to understand, and I guess I didn't do a convincing enough job, because Zaheer would sigh and move on. Sometimes he'd grind his teeth. I could hear them go 'Grinnnd! Grriiind!! Grrriiiiinnnnnnnnd!!!'

I think I know what the ability to lie convincingly as a child is symptomatic of: children who were convincing liars become good actors, but to what I owe the complete inability to concentrate on anything that doesn't interest me I have no idea. It is a tendency I've always had. If a conversation doesn't interest me I can go so far away as to actually not hear what is being said. It has often been a boon too in later life while having to sit through the narration of a script one has given up on in the first five minutes. Anyway, academic rock-bottom was hit when in the final exams of Class 9 I fared abysmally and actually gave in my trigonometry paper empty, with an inscription that I hoped would amuse the examiner: 'If you know the answers, why ask me? And if you don't, how do you expect me to?' The old stiff obviously had no sense of humour and awarded me a zero for my wit. I averaged about 30 per cent, not enough to get me through. But when we went home, I told the parents I'd done all right, and the vacations that year started to go past as usual, with complete amnesia on my part about the exams—until the results arrived.

Baba went to work on his gleaming Hercules bicycle kept in tip-top condition always, not like the orderlies' rickety cycles on which we all learnt to ride. We'd hear the bell when he returned and there'd be a race to grab and park the cycle, because whoever got to it got to ride it round the house once, otherwise we were forbidden to touch it except maybe to clean it. That day I got to it first. When I saw Baba, steam seemed to be coming out of his ears, but then he often looked like that. He handed me the cycle without a word and entered the house. Completely unaware of what was coming, I merrily rode the bike around to the back of the house to find Baba, face black with rage, standing there like the wrath of God. He flung at me a folded piece of very official-looking paper which got me bang in the chest and, just like in the movies, fell right into my hand. I didn't need a second glance to recognize the report card; the words 'has failed the examination' jumped out and hit me between the eyes. I knew how I'd fared in the exams so it shouldn't have been a shock but it was. I couldn't hide my head in the sand any longer. However, instead of the remorse and regret that should have been flooding my heart, I began to have visions of all the movies that would be screened at Sem that year and that I'd now miss.

Preparations to admit me into a school in Ajmer began, the only hitch being that all schools in Ajmer were almost at the end of their own academic terms, with barely three months to go before final exams. Even though term-end was close, Baba managed to prevail upon the Principal of a Jesuit school called St Anselm's to admit me into Class 9 and to let me appear for the exams. In those days the term 'capitation fee' hadn't been coined but doing favours for schools was appreciated, and Baba was not without influence in Ajmer. It was a brilliant plan, designed to see that I lost only a few months, and not a whole year. But I managed to foil it as well. Even with the additional three months of attention, tuitions and the very same curriculum I'd had the year before, I failed again. Though the teachers at St Anselm's were angels compared to those at Sem, their kindness did no more for me than the Christian Brothers' cruelty had done. And as I write this, the disquieting thought creeps into my mind that, for younger actors who may be reading this, I am hardly an example worthy of emulation, and I begin to wonder why I am writing it at all. Is this a story worth telling?

No matter. I invoke the venerated music critic and cricket lover Neville Cardus who in his wonderful book titled simply *Autobiography* puckishly observes that no one was 'under any compulsion to read it and is under no compulsion to read further'. For me it's an exorcism of sorts, and it's for my children if they wish to understand me better. But whatever they do, I doubt if they can (rather, I pray that they don't) ever match the complete apathy I displayed towards just about everything in my life at this stage, but I daresay they have inherited some of my qualities.

Having received my second 'failed' report card for Class 9, I went for as long a bicycle ride as I could to avoid going home and breaking the news. I wasn't terribly distressed, didn't contemplate suicide or anything, I just rode and rode and rode, with a completely empty head, until I couldn't put off the inevitable any longer. But I had managed to delay it. Turning my cycle homeward at last, I frantically searched my mind for what lie I could possibly tell this time. It still gives me a twinge when I recall Baba's worried but hopeful face when I returned, a good three hours or so after I should have, and the way it crumpled when he got the news accompanied by my weak protestations about how the marks for the half-yearly exams which I hadn't appeared for at this school, naturally, had been included in our aggregates and that's why I had failed. He didn't say anything. Just quietly told me to go eat. I must confess that on this day I actually felt sorry for him.

Through the looking glass, sort of

And so I went into Class 9 at St Anselm's with a third set of classmates. But before I go into this, for me, totally momentous year, I must first go a little further into what my years in Sem did for me, and to talk of the only other friend I had there, apart from Pearly and KC—the mirror. No one ever passes a mirror without glancing into it. If there isn't one, there's always a windowpane or rear-view mirror or someone's dark glasses or a desktop or some reflecting surface to look at oneself in. In Sem, there were a number of rather large mirrors all over our locker rooms. On one occasion, tardy in dressing, I got locked in there for the duration of morning prep. I was delighted, I'd missed bloody prep and I was alone. I went around the locker room looking at myself in every mirror there. The most fun was looking into the mirrors in the senior section, which we weren't supposed to go anywhere near.

Like anyone else I really wanted to know what I looked like. Try as I might, however, and no matter how long or hard I looked, I couldn't get a proper picture. I couldn't see myself sideways, for example, and though I liked to believe I had a profile like John Barrymore's there my reflection was, a mousy-looking guy with a very small chin and a very big nose, unruly curly hair growing almost into his eyebrows, small, crinkled, frightened eyes. Not even any sign of a moustache. I'd try painting one on with pencil, and when that didn't work, I'd use my imagination. I'd try a heroic look, an angry look, a sorrowful look. I'd examine my smile. These sessions with the mirror would leave me terribly unsatisfied yet they never stopped. I could see I looked nothing like an actor should, and felt discriminated against by nature. Why did I have only Clark Gable's ears? Watching impossibly handsome film stars playing larger-than-life figures in the movies, I became convinced that these people were photographic tricks. How could anyone look so perfect, not a hair out of place all the time? Hell no, these people did not exist, it was futile dreaming of being one of them, and if they were real I wasn't anywhere near them physically. A foreboding of defeat was accompanied by a complete loss of interest in academics, and in life. The mirror ceased to be my friend for a while.

Then one day we were shown a film called *The Old Man and the Sea*. It had two central characters, a fisherman played by Spencer Tracy, and a large fish he catches and tries to bring home. The fact that it was a classic of literature was not something I knew or would have cared about at that time. But being introduced to this old man, who was a photographic trick of course, was a revelation. He looked so real, he almost smelt of the sea. The sunburnt face, the tattered clothes, the bare feet, the calloused hands. He looked like he had spent his life on this boat. And this was an actor?!! He looked like old Habib Shah at moments and he looked as real. The travails he endured in the movie looked real, the way he rowed his boat looked real, when he hauled in the fish it looked real. His strength and his suffering, even his sweat, looked real.

I now just had to know whether I at least had these qualities, or nothing at all. At the first opportunity, I re-established contact with my old friend and carefully examined my own face to see if twenty–thirty years from now I could maybe play a part like the Old Man. If it was going to take that long I was prepared to wait. I ended the session somewhat satisfied that I could. I had no problem seeing myself, hat at a rakish angle, fag in mouth, gun-belt dangling at my waist, strolling down a deserted street and languidly turning to knock down half a dozen bad guys with unerring aim, but evidently no one else could. So I tried visualizing myself as the Old Man walking home exhausted, oar in hand, dragging his nets behind him. A hockey stick served very well as the oar and my sports jersey as the nets. It was a not unconvincing effort, I have to say. I saw the same Mr Tracy later play some really heroic parts (*The Mountain*, *Bad Day at Black Rock*) and my joy was uncontained. 'Hey, this old guy's not really a fisherman, he does the pistol-packin' stuff as well.' That meant that maybe I could too. My dreamworld, now slowly enlarging itself, was becoming an almost tangible reality and beginning to engulf me. I retreated completely into it and was, as I realize now, in very real peril of getting lost.

But.

The fisherman was an actor! And he was real. When absolutely alone, and I guess this was where I unconsciously started to train myself, I began to will myself to believe I was actually trudging up a snowy cliff as I ascended the stairs to the dormitory, and I found that I could. I could believe, as I lay in my bed, that I was in a boat adrift in the sea. I believed I was searching for lost treasure and evading snipers' bullets while walking down the school corridor. I believed I was stranded in a desert as I stood alone on the First field with my towel wrapped around my head. I was the avenger and the thin green bamboo in my hand was a flashing blade. I was the war-weary veteran returning to his family, I was the shadowy killer, I was the clown, I was the wicked sorcerer, I was the wronged lover, the righteous hero, the infuriated father, the ruthless gangster . . . I was everything I wanted to be. This imaginary world, compared to which the real one was downright drudgery, was where I constantly dwelt.

Enjoying my own company most, even though I considered myself pretty stupid, may have cost me my supposed childhood when one should be happy and joyous and revelling in friendships, and learning, but it was the path I took, and I have not regretted it for an instant. I started then and have not stopped. This role-playing thing was great fun then and it has stayed great fun. The marvellous Stellan Skarsgard with whom I once acted, in an utterly unmemorable film, had remarked to me at the time, 'Isn't being an actor wonderful? You are paid to stay a child.' Chafing as I was to grow up, I actually didn't much enjoy being a child but have certainly enjoyed staying one as a grown-up!

The weekly letters home had become a chore, I had absolutely nothing to say to either of my parents. Nothing exciting ever happened to me. There were no achievements to report. No joys to share. No troubles to unburden myself of. I once tried writing a long letter to Baba about *The Old Man* but got a curt reply telling me to concentrate on my studies and that was what he wanted to hear about. He was 'not interested in stories of pictures which you write to me'. As for his letters to us, seldom more than two or three sentences long, they'd be typed on his office stationery, always ending with his signature in full and his name typed in brackets below it. The only paternal touch in those letters would be 'your mother sends her love to you' and the 'yours affectionately' at the end. None of us could write Urdu legibly or read it at more than a snail's pace, so communication with Ammi would be non-existent when we were away at Sem, or it was via Baba. Not good enough. She always complained that he never read out our letters properly to her. They'd visit us once a year, normally in June, and these meetings, though enjoyable to a degree because we could go out of the school with them, would quickly turn into sharp interrogations about my progress in studies. Displeasure would be expressed, I would be reminded of the enormous expense going into my education, threats to pull me out of this 'expensive' school would be issued and tears invariably followed.

Around this time, the suffocating relationship with Baba made me start detesting and fearing his company. Ammi was emotionally supportive, and I could vent things on her, but with Baba it came to a point where all I got was sternness and disapproval. Though he never ever struck any of us, I don't think I've ever been as terrified of anyone in my life. His desire to see us well educated consumed him, and he believed I was throwing away the opportunity to equip myself for life. The unanimous opinion of my teachers that I'd find it difficult to amount even to a small bag of beans made him begin to despair for me and, in turn, whatever I felt for him was replaced not by fear of his disapproval, which might have spurred me to do better, but by sheer undiluted terror of, and extreme hatred for, him. I don't think either of us ever recovered what we lost, and I do know that I was never ever at ease in his company again, nor he in mine.

I had finally escaped Ma Perry's clutches, but was still Burke's favourite punching bag. One evening during games hour I found myself partnering him in a game of badminton, which I was reasonably enthusiastic about and not at all bad at, but being on the same side of the court as this gargoyle reduced my game to novice level, and I couldn't do a thing right. We got creamed and a couple of hard knocks on the head was the reward for my pains. He once caught me reading

Billy Bunter during study hour and the mandatory knuckles on the head preceded an order to stand in a corner and memorize three pages of my history book in the remaining time. He was probably slavering at the prospect of knocking me around some more when I'd be unable to accomplish the task. But to his utter astonishment (and mine) I managed it even before the hour was over. My recitation done, the disbelief in his voice is a memory I greatly treasure: 'Ah caan nat oonderstandju, Teddy Bear,' addressing me by this appellation which I abhorred but could never escape in Sem, 'you cum laayst in yer claysss, yet you caan lurrn three pages so quicklyyyy!' I didn't remain in Sem long enough to be in Burke's class or to get my nose bloodied by him again, but he did manage at the sports trials to disqualify me, unjustly I still believe, in the hop-step-jump, the only athletic event I ever was any good at.

After reading *Treasure Island* and identifying with Long John Silver of course, I once mailed a 'black spot' to a classmate, grimly informing him that he 'had till ten tonight'. The spidery handwriting being identified as unmistakably mine, I was hauled into the Principal's office no less, and informed that writing anonymous letters was a grand crime for which I could go to jail. I fervently protested for two whole days, hoping for the kind of miracle that had happened before with the cigarettes, but on this occasion my guardian angel had nodded off and the stains had led straight to my doorstep. I was kept standing outside the Principal's office from morning till night, allowed only to go for meals, and then to bed with the injunction 'Come back here tomorrow morning, Shah' ringing in my ears. The third day was movie day and the thought of missing the movie made me crack. I confessed, believing I'd get away with a mere public flogging, and get to see the movie. But after I had received the mandatory 'six-up' in the study hall in front of all present, old Burke stepped into the act.

Deciding that I needed further correction, he made me sit behind the projector with my back to the screen through the movie. I heard the entire film but did not see a frame of it. A more perverse punishment I would not be able to devise even for old Burke. The film was called *The Charge of the Feather River*. It's one film I've never ever come across again; probably just as well.

Mr Shakespeare and
St Anselm ride to the rescue

The Cowardly Lion in *The Wizard of Oz*
Captain Hook in the animated *Peter Pan*
Spencer Tracy in *The Old Man and the Sea*
Jose Ferrer in *I Accuse!*
Rex Harrison in *My Fair Lady*
Peter O'Toole in *Becket*
Dustin Hoffmann in *The Graduate*
Geoffrey Kendal in *Shakespeare Wallah*

All these film performances, which I first saw between the ages of five and twenty-five, hold special significance for me. It may seem strangely pretentious to some that there's not a single Indian actor in that list. Let me explain. It's not as if there's never been an Indian actor I liked. I watched and loved almost every Dara Singh movie, and I found Shammi Kapoor, the 'starriest' star we've ever had, quite fascinating. The utter fearlessness, the astounding physical and emotional agility with which he performed is a quality he shared with Hindi cinema's certified nutcase Mr Kishore Kumar, but both are undervalued as actors because they seldom or never did films of any consequence. Doubtless both these gentlemen appear terribly excessive in today's context but then which

Indian actor of that era doesn't? With the possible exception of Mr Balraj Sahni and, in his middle phase when he allowed himself to be directed, Mr Dilip Kumar. These two gentlemen by virtue of their quiet intensity, their economy and precision of expression and their dignity and poise stood way above the crowd. For the rest, Dev Anand's performance in the transcendent *Guide* was a one-off. Mehmood, one of the most skilful actors I've ever seen, was not quite up there with Chaplin in terms of ability but much ahead in terms of self-love. Yakub was a great actor who got buried in the myths of the pompous 'dialogue delivery' of Mr Sohrab Modi, and the very calculated cool of Mr Motilal. One could question Mr Amitabh Bachchan's choice of projects though never his commitment to his job which was being a film star, and there is absolutely no denying that early in his career he delivered some of the most searing performances ever seen in Hindi cinema. And I fully endorse Satyadev Dubey's view that Mr Pran Sikand was 'the best bad actor in the world'.

And there were the luminous ladies: Waheeda Rehman and Nargis, still Hindi cinema's most modern actresses; the divinely gorgeous Madhubala, the statuesque Meena Kumari, the unbearably sexy and utterly unattainable Nutan, the off-centre Tanuja. There were the 'perky sex-bombs' Asha Parekh, Rajshree, Mumtaz, Kalpana; and of course the 'temptresses' Nadira, Shashikala, Bela Bose, Cuckoo, all décolletage and smoky eyes. I just love them all. And there was the one and only Helen. Delectable stars, every one of them, all worthy of lighting up any screen in the world.

But none of the above do I consider seminal inspiration in any way. The fact is I stumbled upon Hindi cinema somewhat later in life although the first film I ever saw, and I recall it vividly, was *Bahut Din Huwe*. This particular film probably because of two factors: a) It had a child hero, and b) Baba was Deputy Collector in Nainital then and the entire family had free access to any cinema at any time. Ammi never watched movies until I started acting in them, and Baba only occasionally watched English-language war films. Hindi cinema being anathema to him, we would get to watch only films of his choice, either in English, or Dilip Kumar starrers in Hindi, so I was probably taken for this movie by Akabi or her younger sister Nikhat, both Hindi film addicts who made full use of this government perk during their frequent visits to Nainital. I also recall seeing *Nagin* which might well be the cause of my abiding terror of snakes, and one of the first Hindi colour (by technicolor) films, *Sangeet Samrat Tansen*. It was after the Cowardly Lion and Captain Hook, however, that some living actors made an impression: Errol Flynn in *Robin Hood*, Richard Todd in *Rob Roy*, Stewart Granger in *Scaramouche*, Alan Ladd in *Shane*. Other movies I saw—*The Golden Blade*, *Tarzan and the She-Devil*, *The Bottom of the Bottle*, *Purple Plain*, *Trader Horn* and many others—now form only a vague mishmash of memories but along the way there were also *Insaniyat*, *Azaad* and *Uran Khatola*. For some reason the first actors' names that registered in my mind were Alan Ladd, Shelley Winters, Dev Anand and Johnny Walker.

Even though in Ajmer I was under Baba's spyglass, movies began exerting their inexorable pull. Starved of the weekly fare in Sem, my attention turned to what was available. The Sunday morning English movie was still allowed me but the Hindi movie posters I saw everywhere provoked a mad curiosity because I had seen so few. Genuine curiosity or craving that had to be stilled, I do not know, but my bicycle (as consolation I actually had my own one now) would often, instead of heading to school, turn in the direction of Prabhat or New Majestic Talkies almost of its own accord. Classes began to be skipped to catch the afternoon matinee; a friendship with the

Baba *(left)*, and a friend, in a rare flighty mood.

Ammi at her glorious best.

Shortly after Zameer *(extreme left)* rejoined the family, his discomfiture is evident.

Assembly of Ammi's side of the clan, Sardhana 1953.

Shah Mamu with his big cup, me *(centre)* with my tiny one. It is one of the few years Zameer *(left)* didn't win anything; I never won anything again in that school.

Agha Habib Shah with a leopard he
killed, and the tigers he spawned...

Khalid (Chand) and Babur (Shah)

Agha Mohiuddin

With Ma Perry.

With John Lefevre.

AT ST ANSELM'S

NCC camp, JR on my right.

Confident at last.

Moustache courtesy JR.

son of the Plaza Talkies owner and free movies thereafter was the fallout of my frequent visits to that theatre.

Playing the morning matinees would be B-movies or old classics. Some of the so-called classics were pure brain-damage but I got irretrievably hooked on Dara Singh and the kitsch he starred in, to practically bail out a then floundering Hindi film industry I later learnt. To call these films shabby would be high praise; they were often just a series of wrestling matches put together to form a sort of apologetic narrative, stolen in bits from ancient Douglas Fairbanks or more recent Steve Reeves starrers. The movies had difficult-to-believe titles like *Marvel Man*, *Fauladi Mukka*, *Tarzan and Delilah*, *Rustom-e-Rome*, *Trip to Moon*, and were, for most people I knew, difficult to digest but I managed each and every one that came my way, I have no idea why. I guess they served as case studies. And frankly they weren't that much worse than the so-called good Hindi films. While I couldn't have enough of Dara Singh, I also became aware of the unique qualities of Dilip Kumar's acting; I daresay neither of these gentlemen would be flattered if they knew! Balraj Sahni's earlier great performances (*Kabuliwala*, *Do Bigha Zameen*) I only watched much later; those days he always played the boring goody-goody elder-brother or upright-cop roles. The two-hanky family and social dramas I gave a wide berth to, but I saw everything else I could, including, astonishingly, dubbed versions of Fellini's *The Sweet Life*, a Brigitte Bardot starrer called *The Truth* and Clouzot's *Wages of Fear* in the Sunday morning shows at New Majestic.

What I missed out on was an 'extra-hot' movie showing one weekend. It was in fact a World War II drama made by Vittorio De Sica, titled *Two Women*, and probably because it starred the buxom Sophia Loren it had this reputation. I would give anything to know Mr De Sica's reaction if he were ever told that his dark harrowing film was being described as 'hotter than hot' on the billboards in a town of northern India, and that practically every lumpen guy there had turned up to see it.

Repeating Class 9 at St Anselm's with me was Girish Tandon. When the new term began, we had quickly bonded over humble pie, and almost as quickly discovered each had as much of a movie bug as the other. Combining our creative juices, we worked out a strategy for seeing as many Hindi films as possible. Ticket prices for the cheaper seats were well affordable then. Oblivious to my secret film watching, Baba would still innocently give permission, and ticket money, for the Sunday morning English matinee. It was the weekday afternoon/evening Hindi ones that were a problem to catch. A brainwave hit. In summer, classes gave over at one thirty so we invented cricket matches in school in the afternoons and took off, ostensibly to play them. What probably persuaded my parents to swallow this story was their knowledge of my obsession with the game. The two of us would dress up in full cricket gear, except bat and pads of course and cycle off to imaginary cricket. Strangely both my parents were quite uncurious about the outcome of these matches.

But *Two Women* with a 'Strictly for Adults' certificate was showing come Sunday morning. Absolutely not to be missed. No question of asking for permission either. Wouldn't get it. We decided there would be an all-important school match that day. The money for the tickets I helped myself to from Ammi's little box and hid in my English textbook until Sunday dawned. Looking faintly ridiculous in our cricket gear we met at New Majestic a good hour prior to show time, parked our bikes, and joined the end of a serpentine queue extending into the street, and seeming to consist of every ruffian in town. Ducking sweaty armpits and elbows in our faces we advanced at a tortuously slow pace towards the ticket window, each of us clutching our precious and by now pretty moist Re 1/50p in palms dripping with sweat. Would we make it to the ticket window before the movie began? Would there still be tickets?? Our whites were in end-of-match condition by the time it was our turn. Summoning up my deepest baritone, I thrust the money through the grill only for it to be instantly returned with a 'No! Pitcher not for you, only adult.' I stood there appalled at the injustice of it, stuttering, 'But . . . but I . . . I am adult!' not for the first time cursing my youth, but in a matter of moments we were shoved aside by the drooling mob which would now get to ogle Sophia Loren's mammaries. No cricket match was ever so ignominiously lost. The visits to these shrines however never stopped or decreased, but my regret at missing *Two Women* that day remained with me well after my teens and beyond.

I have a very keen memory of these movie theatres, my temples of learning, with their sometimes Victorian, sometimes art deco facades and almost identical baroque interiors. Flat glass cases full of movie stills, the winding staircases accompanied by very widely grooved wall panelling adorned with movie star photos. No Indian star ever featured. Inside, some had a contour curtain which rose to dramatic music and purple lights when the movie, after an interminable wait, was about to begin, and I could feed my distracted gaze upon something, apart from the round-bottomed cherubim blowing little trumpets amongst billowing streamers and bunches of grapes in bas-relief above the proscenium arch. Popcorn was unknown to us, but at the first hint of interval approaching, the tea and samosa vendors' cacophony would begin. Even recalling the names of these movie houses still makes my heartbeat rise to 48 frames per second: CAPITOL and LAXMI in Nainital, PRABHAT and NEW MAJESTIC in Ajmer, RIALTO in Mussoorie, PALACE in Meerut, and of course the old concert hall in Sem where it all began. All of them are now defunct except maybe the hall in Sem.

St Anselm's had a sort of concert hall too, though it was seldom used for dramatic activity. Apart from the classes that were often conducted in one section, inter-house debates and soporific lectures by visiting 'dignitaries' were all that ever happened there. The infrequent film screenings, mostly old mythologicals, didn't star Dara Singh so they were of no interest to me. The projection system was ancient even compared to Sem's and the sound was terrible. I began to go terribly snobbish about Sem until one day, as I was leaving school, a red open-topped Willys jeep driven by a white man with a highly recognizable face pulled up. The passengers in the jeep were two white ladies and a most interesting-looking Indian person. It took me a minute to identify the driver. He was Geoffrey Kendal. The others were his wife, Laura, daughter Felicity, and the interesting-looking Indian was Marcus Murch, for long a staple member of Mr Kendal's troupe Shakespeareana. I had witnessed them perform in St Joseph's often, they were a much anticipated annual feature there. Mr Kendal himself had always seemed to me to be on a par with the greatest actors I had seen on the screen, but like them he too was, I thought, an illusion unreachably distant and impossible to touch. Among my repertoire of acting fantasies was a pretty close imitation of this man who had already affected me profoundly in some mysterious way. I had no idea as I stood there gaping at this red-faced god as, cigarette-holder clenched in teeth, he alighted, how much his life (about which I was to discover later) would inspire me, and that memories of his attitude to his work if not the work itself would keep coming back.

Shakespeareana had been founded by Mr Kendal with the express purpose of 'spreading Shakespeare' as he himself put it to me many years later in the only private conversation I had with him. He had fallen in love with India when posted here to entertain troops during World War II. I assume it was then that he decided that competing commercially for acting jobs in England's provincial theatre was not his cup of tea, and he'd be far more content doing the work he loved and doing it for people who needed it: school and college students in Asia. Never doing a commercial performance, the troupe travelled extensively over the subcontinent and in fact over most of the continent, with no permanent base, without a home, ever willing to perform wherever they found an audience. Their austere approach to theatre was startling, and any one of them alone could fill the stage. The purity of their communication of the bard's writing is for me still unmatched; I have seldom heard actors make such sense of Shakespeare's words, and resultantly his plays. But Mr Kendal's true greatness I would realize very much later. At that time it was enough that this, in real life rather ordinary-looking man could onstage transform himself into anything. With no fuss at all he could be the manic-depressive Hamlet one minute, and love-stricken Malvolio the next. Almost before our eyes he'd change from a heroic Henry V into a malevolent Shylock, then in a blink to a tortured Brutus or Othello. His voice had the mellowness of old oak and his body was an instrument capable of any virtuosity. He looked huge and intimidating with as much ease as he managed to look timid and funny. And when required, he could just disappear. An actor-manager in the old sense of the word, he always played the central parts but conceded to his fellow actors the space they merited. Never once while watching him perform—and I watched him perform over a period of well-nigh forty years—did I feel that he was at all concerned with anything but serving and conveying the text. That, along with his astounding versatility, produced the sheer clarity and precision of the result. Mr Kendal always had the same effect on me as that mystery man dancing on that platform in another lifetime . . . I wanted very much to be up there with him.

But to return to the red jeep, lent to them by the legendary Principal of Mayo College Mr Gibson: its load also consisted of a pair of familiar-looking folding arches, a throne-like chair and a small stool—usually all the setting they ever used. Flinging my bicycle aside I sprinted up to the jeep, heart pounding in anticipation of a conversation with HIM. He didn't exactly seem delighted at my offer to help them unload, but before he could refuse, I was at it. Somewhat disappointed at how little stuff there was, I deposited it in the auditorium and hung around for as long as I was allowed to. There was no sign of a rehearsal about to begin and I was obviously overstaying my welcome. After a brusque 'That'll be all, thank you very much' and a brief handshake, I reluctantly departed. But I had shaken hands with this great actor. He was real too! I had actually touched him. I resolved that at the first opportunity I would pour my heart out, beg him to let me join his troupe and come away with him. The 'To bait fish withal . . .' speech he would doubtless ask for as audition had long been performance-ready anyway. He couldn't turn me down, he'd be getting another actor cheap and I would and could do any part he asked me to. Certain that I would knock him over, I commenced fantasizing about travelling and performing with Shakespeareana while my classmates were slogging over physics and maths. Poor benighted souls, my heart bled for them. There was of course the small matter of breaking it to the parents but surely Mr Kendal would take care of all that. Baba was partial to the English anyway. And now that there were only four in the troupe surely they could do with an extra hand.

When Shakespeareana visited Sem, it was an occasion. Usually ten to fifteen strong, they were the toast of the school. Some then youthful Indian aspirants who later moved on to greener pastures were also among them. Their very presence among us whether in the dining hall, on the playing field or onstage was invigorating. They were a very cool bunch of people all playing many parts, all having a grand time. The productions themselves were basic in design. The costumes were functional but the authenticity of the acting and the intonation of their voices—I reiterate I have never heard Shakespeare spoken better—made these straightforward uncomplicated presentations appear more splendid than anything I had seen on the stage till then or have seen since. The troupe over the years shrank in size, most of the members having taken what I can only hope were their own directions in life. But the Kendals' spirit and their conviction in the path they had chosen were strong as ever. In the mid eighties when there were just Geoffrey and Laura left, I witnessed what would prove to be their final performance in India, and not only had they not wearied of their mission, they were in a state of thanksgiving for having had the opportunity to lead their lives the way they had chosen to. Seldom have I encountered such contentment in people at the end of the road; the complete satisfaction of knowing you have done whatever you could with your life.

Watching them perform was to know what it is to be one

with the spoken word, and the verve and joy with which those two septuagenarians still approached their work gave me a final lesson in what it is to love and serve the theatre. I have continued to feel hugely indebted to the Kendals despite the fact that that day, after they had performed their 'Gems from Shakespeare' in St Anselm's, Mr Kendal, probably tired, sweaty, too preoccupied to deal with a star-struck young follower and in no mood to say or hear anything at all, was changing out of his costume when I managed to get into the green room. My carefully rehearsed speeches flew out of my head as I stood before this giant glowering down at me in his half-costume. He didn't say a word, just took the autograph book from my hand, signed it and continued undressing. I sneaked out with my back to the door, having received my life's first and last autograph. I did not hear of or see Mr Kendal again for another dozen or so years but this encounter was, I daresay, the one which really lit the spark, and made me resolve to take control of my life and actually DO something.

In St Anselm's, students had a choice of subjects they could opt for. One didn't, as in Sem, have to study everything. You could opt for arts or maths or bio. Sensing a heaven-sent opportunity to escape the maths monster, I thought I'd do the arts course. Studying only English lit and history and social studies seemed like a breeze. Plan was duly nipped in the bud by Baba who still nursed dreams of a 'respectable' profession for me, possibly medicine, and so biology was thrust down my unwilling throat. Well at least I'd escaped maths! All I retain of the biology I was taught are the words di-cotyledonous and Paramecium Caudatum, and I'm reasonably sure what they mean, but I make no further claim to any knowledge at all in either botany or zoology.

And then one day a play competition was announced in the school. Each class was supposed to produce a half-hour piece with the best ones to be staged on Annual Day. The students themselves were supposed to take the initiative in devising the show. I knew instantly what I thought our class should do, and since no one else displayed any enthusiasm about it my vote carried. With Kendal/Shylock fresh in my mind, a newly acquired friend J.R. Khan, and of course the ever-willing Girish T in tow, we ransacked the mouldy, long-unused costume cupboard and came away with a mean-looking dagger, a brown cassock, probably donated to the school by some Franciscan monk (the cassock, I mean, not the dagger), also what I thought would pass off as a 'lawyerly' gown, and some velvety, vaguely Venetian-looking pantaloons and jackets for Bassanio and Antonio; the idea being to do scenes from *The Merchant of Venice* with me as Shylock naturally, and, as Portia in man's garb, the best frog-dissector in class C.P.S. Shastri, now a psychiatrist in Chicago, not that his playing the role necessarily had anything to do with that. JR promised he could stick on me the best beard ever: he produced a bundle of crêpe hair and a tube of rubber solution to prove it, so I got rid of the 'hooked on to the ears' beard but retained the skullcap I had purchased from the Dargah bazaar. The voluminous copy of Shakespeare's *Collected Works* which had been gathering dust ever since Zaheer had received it as a 'Best Actor' trophy in Sem some years ago was retrieved and the sections to be performed marked out—all Shylock's juiciest speeches of course. My own performance had been ready for some time; all that remained was to get the others to learn their lines and take them through the paces.

Out of our motley group of four, the only one with 'experience of the stage', as I missed no opportunity to remind the others, was myself. So what I said went. And amazingly, for me, I seemed instinctively to know what I should do. The stage, I really did feel, was where I belonged. It was the only place apart from the cricket field where I felt happy in my skin. During this time, coincidentally, I also got called to a try-out for the school cricket team, and so cricket now became my alibi for going to rehearsals. The cramping inhibitions that had so beset me in Sem and the nervous twitches I'd always had began to erase themselves. The crushing feeling of bewildered incompetence about myself, the conviction that I was extremely stupid, diminished but didn't go away. It still hasn't fully. However, in this new school where the extent of my idiocy had not yet been noticed, I could operate with a degree of confidence I had not known before. In real life too, people began to listen and they sometimes approved. I had not known that before either.

The day arrived. I had a feeling we couldn't lose.

Among the top contenders were something called *The Ugly Duckling* and *The Referee*, both farces being done by Classes 10 and 11. In the former, a guy called Ashok Wahi delivered a pretty competent performance as the Queen, and the latter, a play about mistaken identity, had cricket captain Arvind Ahluwalia in a double role. We preceded these two with our *Merchant*. Being on that stage was like being submerged in warm rose water, I didn't want to ever get off. Our performance followed the juniors and seemed to be over in a flash. Everything had gone by in a sort of daze; I can't say I felt satiated or relieved or anything, I just felt it was all over too bloody soon. I wanted more, I could happily have stayed on that stage forever, and in a sense I have. Whether I'd done well or badly was of no consequence. As an imitation of Mr Kendal it wasn't too far off the mark, but the real revelation for me was the charge of energy I felt that day, and have continued to feel whenever I am onstage. I found myself doing things I hadn't planned and doing them with complete certainty and to the approval of the audience. It was as if another hand was guiding me. This feeling has stayed with me till today; and therefore, though I am grateful for compliments, I never take full responsibility for either my successes or failures but do try to make sure that the 'theatre god' does not turn his back on me. The heady euphoria of acceptance I felt then I can still recall and savour, despite the fact that we lost out for Annual Day to *The Referee*.

BUT next morning the Reverend Cedric Fernandes who had directed *The Referee* came to our classroom, took me aside saying, 'So . . . You're a very good actor eh!' I treasure the moment not only because the Rev. Cedric went on to be my first mentor but because for the first time in my life I was being told I was good at anything. Rev. Cedric had in his hand what looked like a few typed pages. He fiddled with them a little, this was obviously proving difficult for him, then, 'I want you to replace Ahluwalia on Annual Day,' he said and quickly handed me the pages. 'Can you stay after class to attend rehearsal?' What I didn't tell him was that I would have walked on fire and chewed broken glass to attend rehearsal. It never occurred to me to consult or commiserate with Ahluwalia, I felt no sympathy for him. He later went into the army I think, so he probably wasn't devastated about losing the part to a junior. My self-esteem took a gigantic leap upwards and it was days before it stopped soaring. Annual Day came and went, my parents didn't turn up. At the end, two special prizes were announced: Ashok Wahi 'Best Actress' and myself 'Best Actor'. We were handed an envelope each, which on being torn open turned out to be empty. Sure that there was some mistake I opened and examined it repeatedly; maybe I'd missed a trick somewhere, maybe the hundred buck note had gotten stuck to the side. No, it was well and truly empty, but even that did not dampen my spirits, and in the time it took me to cycle home and eat a cold solitary dinner, I had decided that acting was what I was born to do. No way was anything going to keep me from doing it for the rest of my life. Even the prospect of some day having to share this conviction with Baba didn't appear too daunting, given the strength of my belief. Life suddenly seemed worthwhile. I had trouble getting to sleep that night, and still do every night after a theatre performance.

Back to their roots

Life went on apace, new Dilip Kumar films now appeared only once every few years instead of annually, much-loved Jawaharlal Nehru died, youthful John Kennedy got shot and Cassius Clay became King of the World by destroying mean old Sonny Liston. All this while my stock in the school was growing. I began to be known as 'that actor'. People were actually taking the initiative to befriend me. I played a few cricket matches (actual ones) on the school team without doing anything spectacular. I started finding a leggy athlete from St Mary's very attractive, she began smiling at me and we exchanged letters. Word quickly spread 'Shah has a girlfriend yaar!' I had not so much as brushed her hand with the back of mine but I was well and truly on the way to acquiring the 'cat' status I had so long yearned for.

Debating was another field in which I found I could participate, and mostly bullshit my way through. My speeches, peppered with quotes from Shakespeare, were well memorized, thoroughly rehearsed and delivered with all the panache I had acquired at the feet of Mr Kendal. I invariably blustered my way to some prize or other but seldom did I know what I was talking about. Far from taking on the opponents over what they had said and providing a rebuttal I would just wittily, so I thought, mock 'the worthy gentlemen on the other side'. While it all obviously went down very well with the judges because it made them laugh, it was not debate, it was elocution. This served me extremely well at the school, and later college, level but I was finally caught out a few years later in a national level debate at Baroda where, representing Aligarh University, I came away empty-handed despite having had the audience eating out of my hand. Neither acting nor debating would I have discovered had I stayed on in Sem. What a fortuitous coming together of energies this was: in a school founded in the memory of an eleventh-century monk who opposed William Rufus in Britain, in a town blessed by a Sufi saint from Iran, I was shown the right path by an Indian Jesuit priest who later quit the order. Before the year was out, Rev. Cedric had also done *The Bishop's Candlesticks* in which I played the convict and a Christmas pageant where I was Pontius Pilate. I attempted coaxing him to try *Julius Caesar* next. He was reluctant.

Even my relationship with the parents was somewhat on an even keel. Ammi, in any case, was always unconditionally supportive. She regarded me with a kind of detached amusement, making no attempt to get into my head apart from occasionally enquiring what was going on inside it. She never criticized, never chastised, I think that deep down somewhere she instinctively understood. Baba thought I was applying myself better, when all that had happened was that I was at last doing that which made sense to me. The tutors kept coming and going and receiving some credit for their efforts though all I remember of them was one smelt of horses, another had huge muscles and one had his name tattooed on his forearm.

These were radio days. The Philips two-band Baba had bought in 1955 continued to serve him till his death, and on it he would listen to the news on the BBC or the Voice of America. He seemed to abhor music and wouldn't tolerate any of us, except Babar Mamu who he doted on and had practically adopted, tuning in to Radio Ceylon or Vividh Bharati. Cricket commentaries were permitted but within tolerable limits. So of course, the moment he pedalled off to work at 8.30 a.m. on the dot, wearing his hat (a sola topi for summers and a brown trilby for winters), I, already in school uniform and breakfasted, would wallow in film songs for the next half hour till it was time to go to school. Ammi never reacted to this infringement of the rules on my part, nor did she ever tell on me, maybe she secretly enjoyed the music too. Only once did I feel I was testing her patience when she caught me practising my dialogue in front of the mirror.

I began to feel that it might be possible to be a professional actor. In spite of the face I had, why not I reasoned. If I was good at it why should it be a lottery any more than going into the army or studying medicine would be a lottery? If my peers could decide what they were going to do, and many of them had and were readying themselves, what was there to prevent me from deciding what I wanted to do and prepare for it as well? The only hitch being I hadn't a clue what an actor does to prepare, and there was no one to seek guidance from. The only confidants, my brothers, were both bemused at the idea, but the elder Z did actively encourage me to dream the impossible dream and even showed me how Shylock should be played. Both were, however, sceptical about my chances. They had by this time embarked on the course of their future lives, and were well on the way to doing the family proud. The elder Z, among the toppers in his Senior Cambridge class, had been admitted to an Indian Institute of Technology. The younger Z, somewhat wilder, a prefect, athletics champ and all-round Cool-Cat in school, went into the National

Defence Academy and straightened himself out. As for me, having nowhere to go for the time being, I kept my dreams for the future to myself, trying to not aggravate the ulcer that later was to take Baba's life.

The only thing that interested me about life, I remember, was watching how people behaved. If I had been blessed with any 'gift' at all, it was an ear for the spoken word. I can still actually recall the grains in a voice I have heard fifty years ago. Oblivious to the strides I was taking in learning to be happy in my own skin, Baba would think up an alternative profession for me nearly every week. He and I both saw quite clearly by now that I hadn't the brains to study engineering or medicine, I wasn't gritty enough for the armed forces, nor well informed enough for the Administrative Service. That exhausted almost every possibility that then existed for a young man to plan his future around. In desperation Baba would then talk of the Foreign Service or law ('you are a good debater so . . .') then the police (Shah Mamu had recently become a cop), the tea gardens, then an agricultural college, a polytechnic institute. I suppose I shouldn't blame him that no kind of training in the arts ever occurred to him; I don't suppose he knew that such a thing existed. None of his ideas worked for me. I was set on what I wanted to do but the screws had begun to be tightened. Baba's tenure in Ajmer was coming to an end and I would be back in a hostel from Class 10. They would be moving to Sardhana to try to reclaim Baba's father's portion of the old house from the relatives who had squatted in it for ages and made it their own, never expecting us to need it. It was the only place Baba and Ammi could afford to now live in, and rather than settle in an alien town or in Ajmer which was beyond their means, they settled for the known devil.

The section of the house that was Baba's share was the centre portion of a haveli built by his grandfather Nawab Bahadur Shah. The old Nawab probably left no clear will when he passed, and the haveli was apportioned off to the various claimants, and divided even further by succeeding generations. Baba's father being one of the original claimants, it was accepted that his portion belonged to us, though Baba had so far shown no interest at all in it. It was in the charge of his cousin and the section of it that was not being used as a buffalo-shed was in ruins. There was a large section of the courtyard however, with two cavernous rooms on either side. The meeting to take back ownership was stirring stuff: emotional cards were played with great dexterity on both sides, a 'certain amount' was finally agreed upon, a wall was marked out, and began to be built. Another once grand haveli was being further partitioned.

The struggle to build and maintain that home in Sardhana cost both my parents heavily but they embarked on it with a zeal I never thought they had, grappling with family politics, greedy contractors, lazy workers, grasping relatives, even burglars who practically cleaned out Ammi's modest jewellery collection, but they slugged it out. Baba was to live most of his remaining life there, Ammi with one of the three of us for the rest of hers. No forebodings crossed their minds when they made the move. All they wanted was a place to rest their ageing bones, but their stay in Sardhana was by turns peaceful and turbulent, marked by a major falling-out between Babar and Khalid Mamu over (what else) property, a quarrel in which my parents naturally sided with the former, thus antagonizing the other. What exactly it was all about I have some idea, but do not wish to speculate upon it further. It forever soured relations between Khalid Mamu and us, and it hurt Ammi terribly that her brothers were at war with each other.

Everything was packed for the move, Baba typically giving

away all he didn't need or couldn't transport: a large dining table, an ancient Afghan rug, the two leopard skins. His complete detachment from non-essentials was the one thing that always affected me, no matter how bad the equation between us may at that time have been. He would give away stuff on impulse. He had practically gifted away the only car we ever had to Ammi's brother, sold his guns for a pittance to his own, gave away books, clothes, whatever money he could afford and once, to my great dismay, a beautiful antique pocket watch I'd had my eye on. He consistently refused the official car the Dargah kept offering him, choosing to cycle to work. He finally consented to be given what was then known as an auto cycle (a mo-ped) which he never used, and on which we were infrequently allowed to zip around. When it ran out of petrol, rare because it covered about a hundred miles to the gallon, you could even pedal the thing home.

The girl in the tent and the
miracle at St Paul's

My whiskers had by now sprouted fully, as had my libido; and in Class 10, now that Baba was not around any more, I grew a beard, something I had been dying to do. He had always disapproved of the idea, probably fearing it proclaimed a Muslim identity. Being able at last to see the 'adult' Gina Lollobrigida or Marilyn Monroe films did little to calm the raging need males of that age—or of any age—feel for female companionship. Those were the days before prudery became fashionable and much before the moral police had begun flexing their biceps in India. *Playboy* magazine could be found in bookstores, nestling between copies of the *Illustrated Weekly of India* and *Woman & Home*. While browsing in the only bookshop in town, Rampersad's, located under a giant tree and wedged between two shops, one of which belonged to Girish T's dad, I discovered a weird Scandinavian publication, *Health and Efficiency*, with a feast of pictures in it of nudists of all ages frolicking in their colonies. I couldn't have enough of it, fantasizing about naked women all the time but in the dark, so to say. I had no idea what one actually DID when in the act of sex. Though ignorant of masturbation, I knowingly bandied the term about when others did; it was assumed

69

everyone knew what was implied when 'five finger exercise' was discussed, which was often, and I would play along. The inevitable fallout (no pun) of this ceaseless stimulation was wet dreams, which despite being kind of delicious puzzled me no end and provoked Baba's wrath. I would ruin my health if I 'kept doing this' I was told. I had no idea what he meant.

My own beard, I realized, would look far better onstage than one of JR's stuck-on jobs. This time I wouldn't need the rubber solution and crêpe hair. Despite my energetic efforts to persuade Rev. Cedric to stage another play, he kept resisting. In an attempt to improve my mind or more probably to get me off his back, he suggested that I read *Macbeth* and *Hamlet*, 'because most people can't distinguish between the two'. I could, having seen Mr K as both. By the time I left his office I could see myself quite clearly in both parts, performing to hordes of delirious audiences. Without having read either play, I even mentally designed posters for both. When, a couple of weeks later, I tentatively suggested that we might try doing *Romeo and Juliet*, preferably in collaboration with the St Mary's girls, he came as close to swearing as he ever had, 'Have you even read the blessed thing? For that matter have you read the ones I asked you to?' Thus chastised, Zaheer's *Complete Works of W.S.* (which he, movingly, later presented to me when I joined theatre training) was hauled out and dusted off again and I manfully started plodding through *R&J*.

It was not my first attempt to read a Shakespeare play but as anyone who has tried to read him sitting comfortably in a chair will attest, it can't be done. It HAS to be recited or read visualizing it as it should look onstage. No mean task for one so green behind the ears. But with some persistence it began to reveal itself a little. I could sort of imagine it, just as I could sort of understand the language and the plot. What I had no problem visualizing, however, was that Romeo was not the part for me, Mercutio was my man. And attempting this play was absolutely out of the question anyway—too much hugging and kissing, and alluring though that prospect was I was no longer fool enough to not know that this dream scenario was just not going to materialize, at least not with the St Mary's girls. I followed up by attempting to read *The Merchant of Venice* in full but kept returning to Shylock's speeches and having memorized them all thoroughly, abandoned it. My reputation as a debater was also taking wing, representing the school at various (inter-school, district and state) levels with some distinction. Most memorable of all, however, was a visit for the state-level debate to Kishangarh, a town about 20 kilometres from Ajmer, but for reasons completely unconnected with debating.

We'd sometimes cycle all the way to Kishangarh for a picnic or just to loaf, and whenever we crossed the fringe of the town, our horny adolescent gazes would alight on some women of various ages sitting around not doing much, outside these half-dozen or so tents pitched in a field. These tents belonged to women referred to as 'nattnis', considered a coarser word than 'prostitute' but one which originally meant 'actress' in the folk theatre. 'Itinerant ladies of pleasure' would describe them better. Word was they were available really cheap. Despite being the object of much salivating fascination, none of us had ventured anywhere near them but this time we were staying in Kishangarh, there was no getting home before dark. Mir, a classmate, and I decided to visit the tents. Our combined wealth consisted of five rupees, an amount Mir assured me would suffice, 'Two rupees each' he confidently asserted. Girish was not with us, and JR refused to come along. This was long before HIV was discovered and named but he warned us we'd catch something. He sniffily assured us he knew.

At fifteen, all I knew of sex had been gleaned from books

written by Ted Mark: 'the sword entered the sheath and all heaven broke loose' kind of thing. At last I would uncover the mystery of the female anatomy, luxuriating on silken sheets, alabaster legs wrapped around me; I would be drinking from honey-lips by candlelight, the odour of roses and incense everywhere. On the way there I enquired with a great show of nonchalance what one was supposed to do after penetration. Mir nearly choked on his cigarette, 'Hold on as long as you can!' he snickered. I had no idea what he meant. I must be one of very few guys who had sex before learning to worship at the altar of Onan.

A couple of vicious-looking mongrels welcomed us as we made our approach. Two girls, not exactly young, were outside and a distinctly older one made an appearance shortly. Mir seemed adept at the bargaining, it was short and expert. Between the two younger girls, Mir and I both decided on the same one, then to avoid further delay left it to the girls. The fancy I'd felt turned out to be mutual and so the greasy four rupees having changed hands, I found myself alone with the woman who was to initiate me into manhood. My anxiety and impatience tried like hell to transform the smell of burnt rubber into the fragrances I had envisioned. I thought a little romance was in order. My favourite Shammi Kapoor fantasy routine involved hoisting a woman in my arms and sweeping her off her feet on to the bed, but when I attempted the manoeuvre it didn't quite work, she was heavier than I expected and had no time for tomfoolery, she had a job to do. As I blundered around in the vicinity of her breasts she slapped my hands aside, closed the ragged tent flap, hoisted her kameez, holding its hem under her chin as she undid the drawstring of her salwar and, issuing a terse monosyllabic instruction, plonked herself on the bed with her legs in the air, the salwar dangling from one ankle. I was aghast, but mad with desire as well. I don't know if the illusion about sex I'd had shattered then or I found thousands more. My trousers were at my ankles by the time I found my way to know orgasm for the first time, curtly guided by the lady in the tent who wouldn't let me kiss or touch her anywhere. At the end, as a very great concession, perhaps because she liked me so much, she finally allowed my hand to venture into the neckline of her dress for the briefest of moments, but in its groping, dislodged a button and so in strong colourful language the session was declared closed. When I emerged, somewhat dazed, Mir was still in his tent. The world hadn't changed but I felt different. And I felt great. I felt grown-up. This was like the whole experience of acting enclosed in a capsule.

Having tasted blood, so to say, the appetite started its demands, but making love to more women at that time did turn out to be somewhat more difficult than doing more plays. I tried to persuade the leggy athlete from St Mary's to come cycling with me to Foy Sagar, then a deserted lake with many 'So-and-So loves So-and-So's carved into the trees there, but she'd just giggle and would neither consent nor refuse. It was the age when a 'young man's fancy turns' very determinedly to thoughts of sex. And love and sex do not seem separate, as indeed they don't at any age. I was Duke Orsino, drunk on thoughts of being in love, and to help this indulgence along, fate decreed that I soon encounter another person worth falling in love with, a North-Eastern girl, daughter of one of Baba's starched-collar associates. I flipped for her because she was the first girl in my life to take the initiative in starting a conversation with me. I saw her once in my life, I later even forgot what she looked like, but devotedly believed that I had found the woman who was meant for me. The closest I got to her physically was getting her to write a message in my autograph book. Then we sent each other many letters; mine made her laugh, she always wrote. I asked for her photograph several times but she didn't oblige; I sent her mine but got no reaction. Later she said she hadn't received it. The moment I made a declaration of my ardour, she terminated the correspondence.

Schooldays were now numbered. I now only had to figure out whether potassium permanganate dissolves in water or not and how a poor chloroformed frog is opened up without cutting it to shreds. The thought of the approaching final exams was giving me insomnia but, as usual, without the accompaniment of that which I thrived on, I began to lose focus again. The formulae and the Latin classifications once again became meaningless jargon. Final exams rolled around, physics giving me special nightmares. The opening paper was to be chemistry, followed by physics. I mentally put my head upon the chopping block and closed my eyes. With some whispered prompting from the chem teacher who liked me and had once enquired from me in some despair, 'Why not you become actor?!' I managed not to disgrace myself in that subject. Exiting the exam hall I noticed feverish consultations in progress among the few knowing students, the 'bastards' as they were admiringly called. Turned out that in a nearby school, St Paul's, instead of that day's chemistry paper the next day's physics paper had been distributed by mistake. Discovering their blunder the teachers kept the students locked in the exam hall for the rest of that day and night, but the damage had been done, the contents of the paper leaked out anyway. I still marvel at and bless the resourcefulness of the guys who managed it. And on reading that questionnaire, the horror! The horror! Prof. Bannerji (of 'Prof. B's Guess Papers') at his most devilishly sadistic would not have been able to cook up the kind of knotty problems it

contained. I was not the only one who would have been floored.
There was a question on the Wimshurst machine (if I've got
the name right and a particle physicist I know assures me I
haven't), an object the size and shape of a knife-sharpener's
wheel with what looked like a number of cut-throat razors
attached to it in circular fashion. I had spotted the accursed
thing in the physics lab and had always left it well alone, as
evidently had the rest of the class. What it is used for I still
couldn't tell you but I managed that night to chew the cud and
ingest enough information to regurgitate it all on to the paper
the next day and scrape through by the skin of my whatsits.
The frog dissection in biology practicals was a disaster but
by getting some pretty complicated Latin spellings right I
managed to compensate in theory. The rest of it was a breeze:
Eng literature/composition and Hindi secured me the marks
I needed to get through with a second division (52 per cent)
as I discovered after a nerve-racking month and a half in
Sardhana before the results arrived. In those forty-five days I
prayed five times a day, making that 225 rounds of namaaz. I
even performed the 'muezzin' duties once in a while, preparing
myself to blame the god I believed in, in case he didn't come
through again this time. I had a sneaking suspicion I had used
up my quota of miracles.

  Meanwhile, in the weeks before the final exam I had finally
started to think about the future. Reading the fortnightly
Screen in a barbershop one day I saw an ad for something
called the *Filmfare*-United Producers' Talent Contest. I
promptly cut out and pocketed the attached application form,
wondering where I'd find the money for the 'three cabinet size
photographs; one front face, one profile and one full figure'
that needed to accompany the application. Those would
cost a fortune. The only possible saviour, Shah Mamu who
had a camera, was now a cop posted in Poonch. My pocket

money, ten meagre rupees a week, wouldn't suffice. I actually considered asking the divinely beautiful Mrs Capoor for the money, but shuddered at visualizing the meeting and the refusal and the trouble that would inevitably follow. There was nothing to do but watch the parade go by. Every story does not have a great twist or a happy resolution: that application stayed in my pocket, and the dreams in my head, as long as I was in school.

And then one day, final exams had just given over and I was savouring the bliss felt ONLY once in life, of being done with school, when in the very same barbershop I saw in a new edition of the same paper the results of the *Filmfare*-United Producers' Talent Contest. I examined the winner's face in the photograph very carefully, comparing it with my own in the barber's mirror. The man in the photograph already looked like a star: square-jawed with coiffed hair, perfect teeth, clear eyes and the confidence of having the world at his feet. I was glad I hadn't wasted my money, this guy beat me hands down in the looks department. But could he act? All the biggest guns of the industry had organized this contest and vouched for his potential so he was definitely no mug, I reasoned. I had to consciously check another strong attack of resentment at nature for not having given me a face like his. He was twenty-one years old and went by the name of Rajesh Khanna. And so that, as they say, was that.

The road less travelled

The euphoria of passing out of school didn't take long to dissipate. As reward, Baba had gifted me my first wristwatch though not before reminding me that my constant praying was responsible for my success. I chuckled inwardly at how very gullible this god I was dealing with was. I was also reminded that Zaheer was already at the IIT though emulating his example, to my enormous relief, was not even considered. The Foreign Service, the IAS, the tea gardens, even an agricultural college were considered. Appearing for the National Defence Academy, where the other Z was, was discussed and, not without reluctance, I sent in an application. Zameer's first homecoming from the NDA had been dazzling. With his height and good looks he had always cut an imposing figure anyway but that day, in cadet's uniform and newly grown handlebars when he alighted from a first-class compartment and the cop standing around saluted him, he looked as grand as Mr Kendal making an entrance onstage. For a few brief fantasy moments, I was already in the NDA myself and was coming home to make such an impression. But I had, while in school, attended NCC camp a few times and slept in tents with other cadets, whose favourite pastime late at night was to tie one end of a long string on to a sleeping guy's willy, then thread the string through the top of the tent to 'fly kites'. Kicked awake sore-backed on freezing winter mornings to put on starched uniforms and go parading, we then lined up with our enamel mugs and plates (same mug for ablutions and drinking) to get some slop to eat and drink, and then till lunchtime were drilled some more. This life was definitely NOT for me. But I dutifully filled out the forms for the NDA, imagining myself looking spiffy in army uniform, waxed moustache and all. Z shortly informed me that though as cadets they spent a goodish amount of time learning to ride and sail and box and handle weapons and cycled from class to class, there was to be no escape from maths, that carrying a gun and looking cool was not all there was to it. I knew the only reason I wanted to go to the NDA was to look good in uniform; that thrill wouldn't last a fortnight, and my endurance would give out even earlier I suspected. And then, Hell, I can wear all the uniforms I want to when I become an actor.

The prestigious St Stephen's in Delhi was where I fancied I'd go but they didn't bother to reply to my handwritten request for an application form; perhaps they couldn't decipher my handwriting, I sometimes can't myself. The only recourse was the institution in which two generations of my family had studied, the Aligarh Muslim University. Despite its imposing architecture and long history of noble intentions, this place has remained stuck in a time warp. Far from fulfilling its aims of helping create generation after generation of educated enlightened Muslims to contribute to the growth of the community and to integrate with the rest of the country, it has stayed a hotbed of communal conservatism if not downright fundamentalism. There still are strict codes of dress and protocol, though not necessarily of civility and ethical behaviour.

Besides, in Aligarh undergraduate classes were not co-ed so

I really did not want to go there. I once again tried persuading Baba to let me dump the sciences and do literature instead, but he was already warning me that as a doctor I would have to check my short fuse. So, consoling myself that I could probably make a great impact white-coated and stethoscoped, striding busily down a corridor issuing curt instructions to my assistants, I applied for the sciences only to be rejected for my poor percentage. I had been assured AMU rejected no one! At his wits' end, Baba took me back to Meerut with him and with a minimum of fuss, and the help of a first cousin, an influential lawyer there, I got into 'NAS' college, known as 'Nanak Chand' for some no doubt very good reason which I didn't have the time to uncover; my stay there did not last long. NAS had no hostel so Baba had me lodge with his paternal uncle Masoom Ali Shah who owned a sprawling bungalow in the cantonment. A retired Deputy Collector like my father, he was universally known as Dipti saab. When he died my father assumed the mantle of Dipti saab in Sardhana.

I was given an unused room near the porch for which, if I remember right, rent was charged. I was expected to clean it up and make it liveable. Ah bliss! My own place, a stone's throw from Palace Cinema. I had my freedom now, which I then went on to thoroughly misuse. Dada Dipti's bungalow and its grounds were huge enough to accommodate an army. There were three other families lodging in various sections of the mansion, and I spent some time with those of my age group, but none had the passion for cinema that I did, nor did any of them play cricket. The NAS college cricket team asked me to try out in the nets, but never having played at college level I blithely went in to bat without wearing a box, got hit where it mattered most and didn't make the greatest impression. I was to give cricket a very wide berth for many years after that, and not only because of this batting debacle.

NAS did nothing for me except for nearly getting my brains beaten out by half a dozen guys after a brawl with the resident 'dada' and that, cycling there every morning, I manfully eyed all the girls heading to Raghunath Girls' College nearby, and I spent all my pocket money, and a not insubstantial portion of the fees I was supposed to be depositing in the college, on movies at Palace Cinema. Palace, now standing abandoned, probably being fought over by various claimants, had, I discovered, been a swimming pool in the British days, which explained why the inside always felt clammy. Later converted into a cinema with the gradient of its floor remaining as it was, it served perfectly for various 'classes' of ticket-pricing, the shallowest part of the 'pool' being the balcony. Only American and British movies showed there, and every three days there was a change of bill. I gorged on each one. The movie virus had fully entered my bloodstream, was proliferating and raging through my system.

I don't know when the idea of going to Bombay first occurred to me but one day I remembered JR had a girlfriend in Bombay, SM, whose father was a character actor. My naivety said that anyone connected to films should be able to get me a job of some kind there, any job at all, I didn't mean to be picky right away. I started corresponding with her when I had the time to spare from drawing posters of imaginary films starring myself, and by and by confessed my dreams to her and asked if she thought I should come to Bombay. She was not dismissive of the idea, assured me her father 'would do his best' for me, and even offered to host me during my stay. Reeling at her generosity, I used up another biggish chunk of my college fees to book a berth for a month hence on the Dehradun Express which went direct from there to Bombay, picking up passengers in Meerut. My watch and bicycle I decided to sell along with my books and most of my warm clothes, which I wouldn't need—it was never cold in Bombay. The grand total, about five hundred rupees, would be more than enough to see me through the few days in Bombay before I would probably be rolling in it, dining fancy and signing autographs. I was heading to Bombay to stay in a REAL living actor's home and he was going to 'do his best' for me, I was going to be famous. What could possibly go wrong? I hadn't yet heard of Mr Murphy and his law.

They were at Bombay Central station to receive me, bless their souls: she, her brother and a cousin Yusuf with whom I later spent most of my time. I think I also expected a limousine to pull up and drive me to their, I imagined, palatial abode, I assumed all film actors lived luxurious lives. There was no limousine but there was tea and 'keema pao' in an Irani restaurant, my first taste of Bombay's gastronomical wonders, then into what I was informed was a 'local' train going to Bandra where I knew she stayed. In the taxi ride from Bandra station I rubbernecked till Mehboob Studios was completely out of sight; my dreams seemed to be materializing with a rapidity even I hadn't anticipated. We drove up gorgeous Mount Mary, I saw the Arabian Sea for the first time, and alighted in the porch of a not unimpressive bungalow, smaller than Masoom Villa but a bungalow! 'You'll be staying here,' I was informed. I was still searching for the words to voice my admiration for her house and my gratitude for letting me stay when a middle-aged lady, her aunt, emerged and was introduced as the owner. I couldn't believe my luck. If this was just the aunt's house, my imagination failed me as to what her own house must be like. Aunt ushered me in, not without many misgivings, as I learnt later, which would prove to be completely justified. Innocently imagining I was on a short visit, this good soul had been prevailed upon to host me for the 'week or two' that I was supposed to stay, never once suspecting that I had no intention of leaving. SM didn't bat an eyelid when I said as much to her, just suggested I take a stroll by the sea, which I did; and after having some difficulty deciding which bungalow on Mount Mary I should buy some day, I returned to find myself the subject of a stormy family conference.

News of my intentions, or lack of them, had been shared, and there were concerned looks all around. Her father, the actor gentleman, eyeballed me with authoritative curiosity and delivered his considered opinion that at sixteen I was not young enough to be a child actor and not old enough to play grown-up parts. I furiously quoted the film *Dosti*, a recent hit which had starred two boys my age; he mumbled something about 'lack of face' which I didn't quite catch. He promised to cast me as something in the film he was directing but that wouldn't be for some time; meanwhile I should go home and he would talk to my father when the time came. As far as he was concerned that ended the matter; but in a tone of arrogant entitlement, which still appalls me when I remember it, I made it clear I was staying. He lapsed into silence, sighing heavily. SM stayed inscrutable through this exchange and didn't let on one bit. To her everlasting credit I have to say that through this time, almost a month, she never once mentioned even obliquely the acute embarrassment I had caused her by imposing on her entire family, and burdening them with feeding and feeling responsible for me. She never once suggested it was time for me to hit the road, and of course it never occurred to me. In about a month, Aunt's patience was exhausted but I was still not asked to leave. A story about the house being demolished had to be invented and I was asked to please look for an alternative.

On Linking Road was an unemployed actors' hangout, Pamposh Restaurant, home to thousands of nascent dreams and as many dashed hopes. Successful stars were glimpsed whizzing past in their limousines while the not-so-successful ones preened on the sidewalk or 'measured out their lives' in cups of cutting chai. I was now actually hanging around with this crowd. My money had long run out but SM, even while turning increasingly preoccupied, kept supplying me with basic needs. The kindness of strangers sometimes got me the odd cup of tea in Pamposh. Meals were at her house, which was on Linking Road as well. When I went there for the first time I learnt why I hadn't been invited to stay. It was one room the six of them lived in with, those days, Cousin visiting as well. I would be given food on a little tray and would eat in the tiny porch outside their apartment, amidst now not-so-gentle reminders from her family that I should either move my ass to get work or go home. A ceremonious exit from the Mount Mary bungalow being imminent, Cousin had helped me find a place to sleep in, a large hall in Madanpura, the heart of the city, a fleapit by any standards. This hall in the daytime served as a cottage industry, manufacturing zari embroidery. For ten rupees a month each, about thirty of us there had been given pigeonholes to keep our things, and fixed spots to sleep in at night. By nine every morning we had to clear out whether or not we had anywhere else to go. I, of course, had: Bandra and Pamposh. Through the month and more that I lived in this Madanpura zari factory, I travelled ticketless on the local train at least twice every day and never once was I apprehended. Cousin had shown me a back route out of Bandra station and I discovered one at Bombay Central station on my own. There can be no further evidence of the fact that my guardian angel was on extra alert all this time.

I find it hard, to this day, to explain or even understand the peculiar apathy that overtook me then, and stayed with me for a long time after; apathy towards my future, towards my empty stomach, towards any chance of employment, towards my traumatized parents. My only attempts at initiative were as a result of SM and her family's goading. I was taken by one of her old man's hangers-on (in Bombay even small-time actors have hangers-on) to a beautifully situated restaurant called Bartorelli's with the sea on one side and the racecourse on the other, where he knew the manager. The plan was to try to get me a steward's job. I wondered if stewards got tips, and secretly wished for a waiter's job instead. Of course the manager was no longer the manager and so that plan came to naught and they were not in need of waiters at the moment. And getting a waiter's job wasn't by any means going to be the cinch I had imagined; you had to work your way up from washing dishes, were supposed not only to know the menu backwards but also the details of every item in it. But in Bartorelli's I saw a film star in close-up for the first time and when hanger-on said hello to him, I was impressed because he received an acknowledgement. I was of course very far from learning that you don't have to know film stars to say hello to them, and most of them invariably and automatically respond.

The other token attempt at moving my ass was brought on by Cousin who one day came at me waving a ragged newspaper ad stating 'Bellboys wanted at the Taj Mahal Hotel', the requirements were eighteen to twenty-five years of age, a high-school degree, good personality and knowledge of English. Salary Rs 200 per month. I thought I could fudge the age and, not having looked in a mirror at the pathetic apparition I had become, felt more than adequately equipped with the other two qualifications. A passport-size photo was to accompany the application. Cousin, bless him, produced the two rupees needed for this expensive operation and I painstakingly wrote out the application in longhand, attached the two photos, caught the train to Churchgate and walked to the Taj to get the employment I knew was mine. It was a sure thing, I mused, all one needed was the ability to carry luggage. I could do that, besides I was a high-school graduate, I spoke English and of course my personality was stunning. By the time I got to the magnificent front entrance, my knees began to give way and the gigantic doorman was distinctly unwelcoming. It was an eternity until I buttonholed someone milder looking, and was informed it was around through the back entrance to the personnel office that I was supposed to go. I submitted the application to a somewhat perplexed guy sitting at a desk and left, quite certain I wouldn't look at all silly in a pillbox cap and uniform, at least there was Jerry Lewis to think of. And then—a full stomach, fat tips from millionaires and, inevitably, being spotted by a really perceptive film-maker one day. I never learnt how good I'd be at this job either, because by the time they responded to my application, and something tells me they didn't, my sojourn in the city was coming to an end and so the Taj missed employing the best bellboy that money could buy.

When eventually I was compelled to go home, Ammi would often ask me whether I had missed her, whether I had ever thought of her. I would evade giving a straight answer, and dwelt only on my adventures, which by then had become 'the travails I endured'. The truth was that I hadn't missed home for a second, not once had I felt homeless or put upon, even the bus stop or park I sometimes slept in were comforting; not once was I awed by this city, never had I felt scared of it, or alone and anxious in it, it had turned out exactly as I'd expected. I had taken to it instantly. Not once did I wonder what would become of me, not once did I find myself thinking of my parents. That was a closed chapter I thought, I was done with them forever.

Hanging around one evening I was brought by Cousin into the presence of a flashily dressed gent whose attire and bearing announced 'Film industry' in no uncertain terms. He barely looked at me, and like the top-dog of Intelligence sending crack spies on a do-or-die mission, he singled out some dozen or so of us from those around and in an undertone instructed us to be at Nataraj Studio at seven thirty next morning. We were promised Rs 7.50 each for a day's work. The rate was actually Rs 15 daily but since we were not Union, the tout was swallowing half. In any case I was over the moon at the thought of seven rupees, and he said there might be more. It took me some thirty-five years of travelling through the film industry's intestines, so to say, to figure out what was actually happening then. Production on a film was nearing an end, there was patchwork to be completed, budget was probably strapped, extras were needed instantly and cheaply. The Extras' Union in Bombay is and always has been pretty strong-arm. It has the power to prevent or stall a shoot if non-Union members are being used, if dues are not paid, if its members are ill-treated, etc. This was obviously being done in an emergency and on the sly with non-Union members being used at much cheaper non-Union rates. But to me this was my big chance. I was going to act in a movie! With many adolescent dreams jostling for space in my head, and accompanied by Cousin, I got to Nataraj Studio, the place of rendezvous well before time. Nataraj, now defunct, then housed the office of every big movie mogul in town. I walked around looking at the nameplates—names and emblems I had seen only on the screen, my heart jiving joyously all the while. It was well known that every runaway to Bombay ended up going home defeated sooner or later, but I thought that not many must have succeeded in getting even as far as I had.

Arriving at the verdant shooting spot, I was astounded by the size of the movie camera, and by how many people were attending to it. We were lined up, the blinding reflectors adjusted and as the camera panned slowly past I caught sight of myself in the lens; that felt really good, I was inside the camera! There was a sharp reminder not to grin and NOT to look into the lens. I assumed my most sombre expression, it was a funeral scene after all, mustn't look happy. I did, however, manage to sneak a look into the lens every time the camera passed me, and I caught sight of myself every time. This shot did not make it to the final cut, and I would later tell anyone who cared to listen the oft-repeated strugglers' story of how the star had my scenes cut because I was so good. The film, *Aman*, did later get shown and it still survives, and I am present in a couple of shots, one actually with the leading man Rajendra Kumar (playing dead), a major star of that period. (One Lord Bertrand Russell also made his acting debut in this film though I didn't have any scenes with him.) Mr Kumar arrived for the shoot in a black Mercedes sedan well after we had been there more than an hour. The man in the flashy clothes seemed to be a particular favourite of his. Hugs were exchanged all around, much laughter rang out, many cigarettes were lit. Mr Kumar, after thoroughly checking his somewhat yellowish make-up, climbed on to the truck bed where a flower-covered bier awaited, the camera above him on the truck. The truck moved, the camera rolled and all of us paid mourners followed looking suitably stricken. I, quicker than the others and more desperate to appear on screen than any of them, managed to insinuate myself into the very first row and that was how I first appeared in a movie.

We were then given lunch and told we were not required

the next day but there might be something else soon. Cousin and I celebrated that evening by paying a visit to Falkland Road and had a woman each, which to my delight cost exactly as much as it had that first time in the tent. I wondered how come, surely everything cost more in Bombay? I began to feel maybe in Kishangarh we'd been ripped off.

After treating myself to two hard-boiled eggs at Bombay Central, I did my usual walk down Belassis Street, past Alexandra Cinema, left into Madanpura and home, counting the taxis lined in a serpentine row all the way, passing the time by checking if the doors were locked and locking them if they weren't. My good deed for the day performed, I lay on my mattress on the zari factory floor and slept contentedly that night. But with more than three of the seven rupees already gone and next month's rent to be paid, I began to keep an eye peeled at Pamposh for the saviour who had promised 'something in a day or two'.

Finally taking the family's now rather broad hints, I no longer ate at their house. I was fending for myself and not doing a great job of it. But flashily dressed gent reappeared and announced that we would be needed for another film; three days at the same rate. I felt loaded with money already. Twenty-two rupees fifty paise meant two whole months' rent and a couple of cigarette packs on the side! That I'd also need to eat didn't occur to me. The shooting was in Mohan Studios, yet another studio that has passed into the hands of time, and I was one of roughly two hundred attendees at a birthday party into which the leading man, the legendary Raj Kapoor ever the simpleton, stumbles with supposedly hilarious results. We were handed glasses of a Coca-Cola coloured liquid and instructed not to sip. Despite my best efforts, I didn't upstage anyone this time, and couldn't even spot myself when I saw the final film, *Sapnon ka Saudagar*, later. I considered paying up two months' rent in advance but dismissed the idea and the money was well spent on a couple of visits to Falkland Road and the cinema.

I still steadfastly refused to buy a ticket on the local, sneaking out of the side exits cost far less. At times, if I'd missed the last train, I'd just settle down at a bus stop near Pamposh. If roused and told to move on by a passing cop there was always the garden nearby where, along with some homeless types, regulars there, I would sleep undisturbed on the grass. A month's rent paid, the remaining Rs 12.50 disappeared as fast as a snowflake in hell. Flashily dressed gent was nowhere to be seen, nothing was happening and the empty stomach had begun its growling entreaties again. Even a cup of tea was getting tough to score. At Cousin's suggestion I sold the few clothes I didn't need at throwaway prices in Chor Bazaar. The wolf was truly at the door. Month-end was approaching and no sign of the US cavalry.

And then one day, when I was sitting on the pavement outside Pamposh, a long shiny grey limousine pulled up right in front of me. The rear door opened and a pair of well-pedicured female feet in glittering high-heeled sandals stepped out. I heard a voice ask, 'Is your name Naseer?' Nodding in assent and raising my incredulous gaze, I saw an immaculately dressed, vaguely familiar-looking lady towering over me. She curtly instructed me to get in the front, which in a stupor I did, and nearly froze as the blast of air conditioning hit my sweaty shirt. As the car drove off I was not at all sure this wasn't a dream, until the admonishments began and then I knew it was real. I recognized the lady now, I'd seen her picture in some magazine, she was Mrs Saeeda Khan, sister of the biggest star of the time, Mr Dilip Kumar, and now it began to make sense. Mr Kumar's eldest sister Sakina apa, a devotee of the Sufi saint whose shrine in Ajmer my father had administered, had often visited there, and on one occasion even stayed with us. Obviously it had taken the two months I had been in Bombay for Baba to finally overcome his natural reticence and contact her. The only clue to my whereabouts he had was the surname of the girl I had corresponded with. With that lead it wasn't tough, I suppose, for so resourceful a film family as Mr Kumar's to track me down. In the limousine I didn't even have the time to start imagining it was my own car before we were driving up Pali Hill, the residence of most film stars then, and a huge wooden gate was being flung open and we were entering Dilip Kumar's own bungalow!

I was taken upstairs into the presence of Sakina apa, who I had met before in Ajmer. She was a melancholy person, always remote and detached, but that day she was spitting fire, and the exhaustion and sense of failure I was keeping myself from feeling finally overtook me in a rush and made me dissolve into a flood of tears and apology. I won't go into all that was said that day; it has been and is being said even today to and by every young person who opts for acting as a career against the wishes of family. The upshot was I agreed to go home. The remains of my luggage were brought from Madanpura to Pali Hill, and I was lodged in the basement of the bungalow in a space obviously used at other times as a waiting room or a place for the domestics to rest. But I was being fed and even had access to a bathroom and to most of the house. I'd often wander into the drawing room where six or was it seven Filmfare trophies stood in a row on a shelf. I tried picking up one and found it so heavy I thought it was nailed down. I did manage to pick it up finally, held it in one hand, waved with the other and made a deeply moving acceptance speech.

At a remove from the main house was a cottage: the great

man's hideout, his thinking space, probably his working space as well, with two cosy interconnected rooms, a couch and mattresses on the floor, books stacked to the ceiling, paintings on the walls and a sitar. No one prevented me from going in there when I pleased. I was told not to go there when HE was around, but he never was, in fact he was seldom home at all, so I spent much of my time there. This was Dilip Kumar's private den I was spending hours in, poring over books on cinema! The only cinema literature I had been familiar with till then had been *Filmfare* and *Picturpost* and sometimes Hollywood's *Photoplay*. New names and faces now inundated my head: actors George Arliss, William S. Hart, Emil Jannings, John Gilbert; directors Michael Curtiz, F.W. Murnau, Georges Clouzot, Josef von Sternberg. Immensely depressed at the thought of perhaps never being able to see any of these works I, in one of my more Walter Mittyish—and dare I say clairvoyant—moments foresaw a day when one would be able to carry around a portable machine on which any film at all would be available to watch at any time. While I don't claim credit for inventing the video player, until that day came I had to wait, and I am still waiting for some, particularly the silent Westerns of Mr Hart, whose middle name, incidentally, was Shakespeare.

I spent the few remaining days before I was packed off in this paradise-like cottage, once even bumping into the man himself. Displaying absolutely no surprise or curiosity at finding me there and barely acknowledging my presence, he went about whatever he was doing. A couple of days later, spotting him alone in his garden, I tremulously approached him, hoping to ask if he would help me find work, but the words I would say had barely formed in my head when I realized he had already delivered a short lecture on why 'boys from good families should not join the film world' and dismissed me from his presence. Much much later, I acted with Mr Dilip Kumar in a film I hated, and could never bring myself to mention this meeting; in any case he probably had no memory of it.

Sakina apa then informed me that I had been booked on the Dehradun Express back to Meerut the next day. I would be given money enough to eat on my journey back and, taking no chances, I would be escorted all the way to my berth on the train. Things were coming full circle. It was only then that thoughts of how I would face my parents occurred. They were not comforting thoughts.

Prodigal

As the homeward-bound Dehradun Express was pulling out of Bombay Central I did consider alighting at the next stop and staying on but of course that would have been far too intrepid. The journey back was a blur. My imagination, usually very active, just refused to go the route it normally would imagining the homecoming; and now my long-term memory which is pretty acute also fails me. I just do not recall it. All I remember is reaching Meerut Cantt station around noon and, not wishing to be spotted returning in Sardhana, deciding to wait till night and hanging around at the station the rest of the day. With my last remaining rupee I got a ticket on the very last bus, the 9.30 p.m. to Sardhana. It got there in an hour and by the time I walked home with my luggage or what remained of it on my back, it was around 11 p.m., an ungodly hour for the parents. Ammi, however, was still awake, I heard her moving about in the kitchen muttering to herself. I was surprised at how comforted I felt hearing her voice again. I stationed myself under the kitchen window to prepare for the big moment, the knock on the door, the shameful homecoming. Thoughts of the mockery that awaited me at the hands of uncles, cousins, aunts made me hesitate repeatedly and before I could pluck up the courage to face the only two people who would not deride me, the lights went out and I knew I'd have to wait outside till morning.

I settled on my now considerably slimmer hold-all to pass the night. It was late February and the end-of-winter chill compelled me after a while to open it and cover myself in the only blanket I had left, the other two now warming some hustler in Chor Bazaar or bringing him a fat profit. Feeling not too uncomfortable, I dozed off and was awoken by 'Ayyy! What are you doing sleeping here?!!' For a moment I thought I was being hassled at the bus stop by a cop, and started gathering my things to move along, then remembered I was home and this was the one voice I hadn't missed at all— Baba's. They were both early risers and he had just risen and opened the door to find this bedraggled prodigal asleep on his bedroll on the doorstep. 'Get up! Go meet your mother!' he said, brushing aside my insincere apologetic mumbling. Ammi for the only time in her life abandoned her namaaz as I entered the bedroom. She held me in her arms with a fury I had never sensed in her, weeping and thanking the God who had brought me safely home. The smell of Ammi's clothes I can still recall and I wallowed in it for as long as I could. The first breakfast in over sixty days lodged in my stomach, and a much-needed haircut and bath having been administered, I was marched off to the mosque to gain further absolution by giving thanks for having been delivered from 'the path that had wrought (His) anger'. I instead entreated Him to ensure I would make it back to Bombay some day.

The mandatory visits to the grandparents followed, they both sort of made no mention of my adventure but the heroic mamus made it a special point to rub the humiliation in really deep. 'Laut ke buddhu ghar ko aaye!' went Chand Mamu, adding a translation in English in case I hadn't understood. Fine specimens of manhood that they were, it's not impossible they may at some point have entertained dreams similar to mine and were envious of my enterprise.

The beginning of the new academic year was not too far away and inevitably Aligarh began to figure once again in my life. Words like 'books', 'application forms', 'semesters', 'credits', which I thought I was through with forever, started cropping up all over again. Baba had by now, with a heavy heart, abandoned his 'my son, the doctor' dream and consented to let me try for the arts programme, into which I was duly admitted, but there were three more penitential months to go before term began. In these three months I did all I could (unsuccessfully) to quell Baba's disapproval. I'd wake early, get the kitchen fire going, put the kettle on, make the beds, help with breakfast, read the newspaper— mercifully there was nothing I had to study yet—and spend the rest of the day shooting the breeze with cousins or toting Baba's .22 rifle around and bagging the odd dove or green pigeon. All kinds of game had by then become pretty rare but when some unsuspecting cheetal or blue bull got bagged we all energetically took part in the skinning. I became pretty adept at skinning and cleaning.

With my rudimentary knowledge of the Arabic script I struggled through reading the Quran on my own without any help. When I completed this monumental task, to my surprise there were no fireworks and I wasn't carried shoulder high through Sardhana. Baba just grunted non-committally and Ammi smiled kindly and said, 'Better if you had a maulvi, beta.' That ended my study of the Quran but I was regular at namaaz and even at screaming out the azaan occasionally, as well as at sneaking off for a smoke in the afternoons when Baba and Ammi took a siesta.

In charge of the family mosque was a wizened, ebony-hued gent called 'Sufiji'. No one knew his name, or where he came from or when, but he seemed to have been there always. In retrospect, recalling his accent and complexion, I assume he was probably a refugee from East Bengal, but who knows, Sufiji took his secrets to the grave. Always dressed in a saffron robe, he had long, straggly hair, a grey pointed goatee, no growth on his cheeks, no teeth in his mouth and dancing eyes despite a bad squint in one. His laughter was just loud exhalations of breath and he laughed all the time. On my return from Bombay Sufiji was the only one to welcome me back with a smile. He said he knew I would return. Sufiji was a walking Ouija board, he claimed he had visitations all the time, and in the pre-namaaz gossip sessions whenever he casually let it drop that 'So-and-so [some long-dead ancestor] came to see me last night', we children were immediately excluded from the conversation. I don't know for a fact if these visions Sufiji had were geared towards attention grabbing or if he was pretending to pass on messages from the hereafter while actually being goaded to settle family politics, or if he was just stoned all the time.

When I discovered marijuana a few years later I knew I had smelt it before, around the Ajmer Dargah and around Sufiji. Whatever, the elegant little mosque from the late nineteenth century was kept clean by this mystery man. It sat tranquilly in the shadow of Jan Fishan Khan's mausoleum, nearby was the gate to Nawab Bahadur Shah's haveli. All around were verdant fields. Today the mosque stands in the middle of a teeming colony; in the lane leading to it you'd be hard put to swing a dead cat and there are unending rows of perfectly hideous cement houses and shops piled haphazardly on top of one another. It was after Sufiji passed that the itchy fingers of all those in the family with some claim to the lands around the mosque began to crawl towards their triggers.

Movies were totally missing from the agenda in Sardhana which had one mobile 'picture house', a tarpaulin-roofed tin shed which was not functional when it rained. The audience sat on the floor and the 'balcony' was two rows of benches at the back. There was a pause at every reel change. I would have loved to see the stuff they showed, mostly Z-grade stunt movies, but no member of the family could possibly be spotted there. Despite this restriction Chand Mamu, Zameer and I managed to sneak out one night and watch *Rustom-e-Baghdad*, a terrible Dara Singh film which I loved, and which probably put Zameer off Hindi movies for life. The only other person who shared my own now insatiable curiosity about Hindi movies was my cousin Mir Ahmed (Bobby), Agha Mamu's son, who had also always been a close pal. He and I had shared the odd smoke stolen from his dad's packet, and had broken many rules in tandem, until his recruitment into the NDA ended all his good cheer and peccadilloes—the result of a promise he made to his old man, a promise he has kept to this day.

It was Bobby who broke the news to me one day that Agha Mamu was contemplating buying a house in Mussoorie. The old man in his capacity as Superintendent of Police and later as DIG had resided in many palatial homes and was used to being waited upon hand and foot by a retinue which, since his wife's death in childbirth some years ago, had also included trusty old Akabi, who had reared Bobby and his sister Mohib. So the news that this grand old cat was planning a country-gentleman retirement did not surprise me in the least, he'd always been a splendid creature. What knocked the wind out of me was when I heard my parents discussing the possibility as well. I had no idea there was so much moolah lying around.

The house, it turned out, was going really cheap, practically at distress rates. 'Chaman Estate', consisting of twenty-four bungalows belonging to the Begum of Rampur, was being flogged for a pittance.

Somewhat like in a bad Hindi movie, the Begum had recently blown a considerable fortune unsuccessfully contesting parliamentary elections against her own son. Now finding herself somewhat strapped for cash, she had decided to dispose of these bungalows, probably lying forgotten for years. Though why anyone would want to build twenty-four bungalows all at once is another matter. DIG saab went for No. 24, the erstwhile 'Banquet Hall' , and Baba for No. 17, a 'smaller' but fully furnished house with five bedrooms, a parlour, a living room, an outhouse, and about half an acre of land around it. It cost twice his entire savings plus his provident fund, fixed deposits and all. The situation needed a hero and in stepped Agha Mamu, offering to buy half of No. 17 as well. After a few weeks of high anxiety the deal was settled with No. 17 being acquired for 35,000 rupees, half of which was paid by Baba, and we took possession of our own first real home.

Deciding which part of the house belonged to whom could have been the first bone of contention but Agha Mamu respectfully deferred first choice to Baba, the elder. The house came fully equipped with late-nineteenth-century teak and pine dressers, dining table, sideboards, sofas, chairs, coffee tables, all for some reason painted black. Dividing the furniture came next and that too passed without incident, with both deciding that the furniture should remain in whichever part of the house it already was—an agreement by which both dutifully abided, except that one exquisite roll-top writing desk from our part of the house mysteriously vanished and reappeared a few months later in Agha Mamu's bedroom. However no walls were built this time round, with both families having a free run of the entire place for a considerable time. It was years later, while an abortive sale of the house (proceeds to be split three ways) was in progress, that in a fit of nostalgia I decided to take all the furniture as my share. I brought it back to Bombay and had it stripped, and the exquisite grain in the wood then revealed itself. That furniture, by now surely about a century old, still serves us and has in fact survived a flooding.

Living in a house atop a hill with a view of distant mountains soon became a drag when shopping had to be fetched from the Mall, as I was the one normally deputed to do the carrying. It wasn't nearly as bad as having to do the same chore in Sardhana though, where, after word of my Bombay misadventure had spread, every time I ventured out, shopping basket in hand, it seemed as if every single person in that market dropped whatever he was doing to gape at this 'going-to-be-actor'. In Mussoorie it felt very very uncool trudging uphill pretending that the radish and turnip leaves sticking out of the basket weren't there. Not conducive to fantasizing at all and, besides, girls won't give you a second glance.

New friends we made there were Aslam Khan and his brother Akbar, a pair of colourful landowners in the area. Also of Afghan stock and domiciled in India as long as or longer than our family, apart from being Persian speaking, their paterfamilias and Baba hit it off instantly. Our maternal grandparents were ailing and soon to pass, Shah Mamu had quit the police and taken up farming in a place called Mahmudabad and Chand Mamu was at loggerheads with us, so none of them ever came to Mussoorie, but we accompanied the Khan brothers on many poaching trips into the hinterland. Game was really scarce by now and our normal bag would be a partridge or a wild hen or two. We'd often return not having even spotted anything, but flocking with their own kind is a tendency shikaris have.

It was at the start of one of these sessions that I was nearly the victim of a horrendous hunting accident caused by Agha Mamu of all people. Bobby and I were squatting at the back of the jeep, plastering the number plates with wet mud—a precaution taken in case we were chased by forest officials, of which there was a real possibility. I had already imagined the chase in cinematic detail, and was just getting up to wash my hands when I was knocked over backwards by a flash, an explosion and a whistling that went past my ear with the force of a small gale. Recovering my wits, I saw Agha Mamu standing in a shell-shocked state, the smell of gunpowder was everywhere and blue smoke curled out of the barrel of the 450.400 rifle he was holding. He who had subjected us to countless lectures on weapons etiquette had nearly blown my head off with a rifle that could lay out a blue bull. My thudding heart was stilled, however, by seeing the more than apologetic look in his sunken eyes. The danger to my life now past, I danced inwardly seeing him blanch and stutter in a timid voice I had never heard him use before, 'I . . . I . . . thought the safety catch was on . . .' No one dared ask him what he was doing fiddling with the trigger in the first place. Through the night, suddenly looking very old, he sat slumped silently in the front seat. Once again we didn't spot a thing. Nor did the exciting chase materialize.

Mussoorie had its share of drudgery, and it didn't end at vegetable shopping. Both the houses, in respective states of disrepair, needed considerable work. Doors had to be removed or installed, windowpanes replaced, sofas upholstered, roofs repaired. After the peaceful division came the discovery that all five bathrooms in the house were on one side, theirs; so washbasins and commodes were acquired and plumbing laid, stuff had to be carried back and forth, bricks and rubble cleared. Bobby, now a cadet at the NDA, and I were instructed to help in these tasks and were paid two rupees a day each. Since work continued for quite a few days we made a considerable killing. With my earnings I would head every evening to the Hakman's Hotel to play tombola, hoping for a windfall. I always ended up losing, which actually is a pattern that has repeated itself in my life many times over, whenever I have attempted to get something for nothing. It's almost as if nature is redressing the balance of having looked after the massive gamble that my life has turned out to be, and in which I have had moderate but highly satisfying winnings most of the time.

Bobby, though younger than me, was considered grown-up and responsible now and since *Sapnon ka Saudagar* was showing at the Rialto he and I could, without permission, go see it. It would be a while before *Aman* hit the screens and I HAD to know what I looked like up there. Despite sitting through the ghastly thing twice and keeping a virtual magnifying glass on my nose to spot myself, I had no luck. I was completely and absolutely missing from the film, not a trace anywhere at all. The leading man had done it to me again. I was 'if not disgruntled, certainly far from gruntled'. I don't know if I was relieved or embarrassed that my debut on screen had been delayed, but delayed it had been. Bobby patiently heard me out, clucking sympathetically at appropriate moments, and assuring me that my 'time too would come but wasn't that Hema Malini delicious?!' The one whose time did come with this film was the teenaged nymphet who went on to become and long remain the country's sweetheart. Some twenty-five years later, in one of those 'hard-hitting feminist' films, I was paired with this extremely dignified, utterly charming and still lovely-looking lady in a film where I seduce and abandon her. At our first meeting, I told her how our careers had begun almost together, and that I was in fact a film older. She'd probably heard similar stories several times, smiled indulgently and we then proceeded to enact a scene in which I untie the drawstring of her blouse and do sexy things to her back. She was married to Mr Dharmendra Deol, he of the formidable forearms, and it was with not very confident fingers that I did the needful.

The Aligarh University absurdists

The dreaded A word was cropping up all the time now, and in good time I found myself once more Aligarh-bound, having gained admission this time in the arts programme. Three of my paternal uncles lived in Aligarh, two others having gone to Pakistan at Partition and thence Westward. These gents, Baba's half-brothers, his own mother having died in childbirth, were all eccentric in varying degrees; two were confirmed bachelors and all three kind and affectionate. Unlike Baba, they were fond of talking, listening and laughing and were not at all averse to films or music on the radio. The house they lived in, a rambling place with spacious grounds, part-haveli part-bungalow, had been built by Baba's father. Baba had long ago relinquished his claim to it, so great harmony existed between the brothers. I never saw Baba look as happy anywhere else as he did with them. When he wasn't around I too felt free and uninhibited in this house, always receiving the attention I craved and being always 'on'. I would turn talkative, even gregarious, and needed very little persuasion to show off my Shakespeare. I had no idea why this personality hid itself behind a dark cloud whenever I went home and to this day I have not quite figured out which one is the real me, and after a point I stopped trying.

Anyway, accommodation secured in a five-seater room in Sir Syed Hall (Osmania Hostel, Room 64b), I had barely unpacked my things before being summoned for namaaz by the senior students. There is a mosque attached to every hostel in the university, so tardiness with prayers comes to be quickly noticed. I wondered if this would be the constant drill while I was here, and felt miffed at being compelled to pray when at the moment I had nothing to pray for.

Aligarh Muslim University already boasted a heavyweight history department, which later of course developed into the Institute for Advanced Studies, headed by the illustrious Professor Irfan Habib, son of the equally celebrated Professor Mohammad Habib. Intimidated by the prospect of memorizing dates, I wanted to duck history but the other alternative, economics, sounded nightmarish, as did Hindi. Geography I had always dreaded, and civics, social studies, psychology, linguistics were just words. I settled for what I thought was the simplest combination, English literature major with political science and history as subsidiary subjects. Theology study was compulsory for Muslim students. The 'semester' system had just been introduced in the university: one had a certain number of credits to clear in each subject by the end of six semesters, you didn't necessarily have to appear for the credit at the end of each, you could clear all the credits at the end all at once if you chose to do so. I chose to do so and of course it caught up with me in good time.

Though the 'ragging' was not half as vicious as it is known to be in some other institutions, there were some pretty arbitrary sartorial customs. For example, one could not go to the common washroom without a kurta or a shirt on; you could not go out of the hostel in only a kurta and trousers, it had to be a sherwani or 'pant-shirt'. With the sherwani, a cap was mandatory. 'Salaam-ale-kum' was the greeting everywhere.

Those who did not yell it out at the top of their voices and did not make a great show of attending namaaz were frowned upon, and quickly labelled 'communist'. Being one of the few English-speaking students there, I was immediately categorized as 'East India Company' along with the handful of foreign students there—Mauritian, Thai and Indonesian (all Muslim).

Shaw's *Arms and the Man* was in our literature syllabus, and having seen it performed more than once by Shakespeareana, I was off to la-la land on my dream-scooter right away. I managed to persuade the lecturer to distribute roles and let us read it aloud. Picking myself as 'the Man' of course, I decided upon three of my classmates for the other three male parts. An all-male cast reading was a bore and so the four of us set to work on the teacher to get some girls in with us and do a proper play-read. No question of putting it onstage, of course, as AMU has in its constitution a puzzling stricture prohibiting male and female students from appearing onstage together; not so puzzling of course once you've witnessed the reaction of the students there to an attractive female presence onstage. Only post-grad classes are actually co-ed, and intermingling of the sexes in public is rare and duly noted and much remarked upon. Luckily, in charge of proceedings was a feisty lady teacher who took the initiative and this fantasy actually materialized. I couldn't believe my ears when we were told that we would actually be going to the girls' college for a read-through.

The Abdullah Girls' College is, to male students in Aligarh, a mysterious erogenous zone they can venture nowhere near without a sibling studying there, and even then, no further than the front gate. To meet the sibling, or the one pretending to be, you must confront a formidably moustachioed gateman who takes the piece of paper on which your name is scribbled to the warden, who compares it with a list of permitted visitors supplied by the girl's parents. Only then is the girl allowed to coyly step out of a side entrance while the huge gates remain determinedly shut. To my knowledge no male undergrad had ever been privy to what lay beyond them. I took a while to decide what to wear, though my choices were limited to three or four sets of rather plain shirts and trousers. Deciding on something carefully careless, not wanting to seem too eager and adopting a casual swagger though my heart was jumping into my mouth, we entered that forbidden ground to be greeted by the same rather drab buildings as everywhere on the campus, except—they were all populated by the female sex. Trying to appear like the coolest creatures in the cosmos we strolled into one of the classrooms and met our co-actors—the girls. One more dream in my grasp, thought I. So far all the acting I'd done had been with bewigged or long-haired Sikh boys playing the female roles. Having the female characters played by actual females was aphrodisiacal in the extreme.

That first rehearsal was at least a few hours shorter than it should have been. I was playing the chocolate cream soldier and now actually speaking those lines I'd always felt I could deliver, and was doing it in front of a group that was appreciative. More important, I was able to perform more or less the way I did when alone. It wasn't particularly challenging, I'd done these lines so many times on my own anyway. The acclaim that came my way when we finally did a public reading went a long way towards making me somewhat known in the girls' college. I also briefly renewed my acquaintance with cricket, and learnt to play tennis on one of the half-dozen or so grass courts adjoining the swimming pool, the 'Meston swimming bath' as an ancient brass sign proclaims it to be. I daresay Mr Meston, whoever he was, would not have been amused by the shrine bearing his name now also carrying a curt handwritten sign, more recent, stating 'soap not allowed'.

The university had a 1200-seater auditorium with a huge mural by M.F. Husain, no less, on the facade. It was called Kennedy House because it had evidently been built with American funding. There was a cavernous stage, the largest I had ever seen, with a revolving mechanism; the machinery for that purpose catching rust since it had been deposited in a godown some ten years before and never installed. At the time of my last visit to Aligarh in 2007 it had still not been. There was and still is nothing on that stage—no backdrop, no proscenium, no wings, no sound system, no arrangements for lights. Performing there after well-nigh forty years I had the distinct feeling that the only thing that had changed, and that not for the better, was the audience.

AMU had a Riding Club as well. Horse riding being one of the sports Baba didn't disapprove of, I was enlisted as a member and equipped with the essentials: a pair of khaki breeches and a sola topi in which I looked faintly ridiculous walking down the road to the riding school since I had no bicycle of my own any longer, nor could I afford a pair of boots. I don't have the greatest legs in the world and in my breeches and Keds sneakers didn't exactly evoke Clint Eastwood, and imagining myself as the world's greatest tent-pegger living incognito didn't offer too many possibilities. So I carried the hat, imitations of Baba not being in my repertoire, and persevered with the riding for as long as was reasonable, getting to the cross-stirrup trot, at times actually feeling a few fleeting moments of bliss with the animal completely under control. But another play reading was in the offing, this time Goldsmith's *She Stoops to Conquer* and I was to be Tony Lumpkin, yet another character I had seen Mr Kendal play. Reading a play aloud was much more fun than getting sorebum trotting around in a circle on hot afternoons, and in any case the couple of female members in the club never showed. In rehearsal, now normally at one or other of the teachers' houses, there was always tea and cake and cucumber sandwiches and girls.

The feisty lady in the English department was Zahida Zaidi, known as 'lady in the car' because she drove around the campus, puffing furiously on a cigarette, in a white Standard Herald. She was, in Aligarh parlance, a very 'forward' person. Whisper abounded about her, and the gossip was far from kind. She was, of course, a 'communist' and worse. Zahida apa cared not a whit about such talk. Soon after presiding over the Goldsmith play, she did a reading of a play called *The Lesson* written by someone called Eugene Ionesco. I was not cast. Not only had I never heard of the play or the writer, I hadn't seen or read anything like it before. I found myself in complete empathy with the absurdity of the situation it was lampooning. The pupil's utter bewilderment at what she is being taught in maths or logic had always been my very own. I didn't understand the play but watching it enacted, the experience was almost tactile.

I was to be introduced soon after to more absurdism, Edward Albee's *Zoo Story* to begin with, a play which was to figure very importantly in my life some five years later. Ms Zaidi had got together a proper performance this time, not just a read of this play, and performed it in an open space, a lawn outside the Kennedy auditorium. The play went completely over my head, but the thought of performing in an actual space, not on a stage masquerading as that space, was invigorating. I was deeply envious of these actors and so duly went to meet the lady to ask to be considered for a part in the next one (for a few fleeting moments I had visions of being asked to now play the role of Jerry, the Father Cedric miracle repeating itself). Instead she gave me another Ionesco play called *The Chairs* which I read in utter bewilderment. I told her so, and stammeringly mentioned Mr WS but was rewarded with a hard look, a copy of *Waiting for Godot* to read and the mystifying observation that she would love to stage this one 'if there was another actor'.

Finding both plays equally incomprehensible I asked her to decide, and she promptly cast me to play the ninety-five-year-old man in a production of *The Chairs* to be staged along with a one-act farce by Anton Chekhov, *A Proposal*. The restriction about female students acting onstage was neatly sidestepped by casting two female research scholars who, strictly speaking, were not students. I was nineteen at the time. I wonder if Zahida apa believed I was capable of comprehending so scarily dense a piece of writing as *The Chairs* but I knew for sure I was not. Knowing how to create the impression that I understood it, however, was another matter and on that score I had little doubt. After all I had barely understood what King Lear and Shylock were saying when I had masqueraded as them, hadn't I? All one had to do was learn the lines and not bump into the furniture, but in *The Chairs* there were about fifty chairs onstage to not bump into. For the most part I succeeded, at least in managing to manoeuvre between them; and the audience in Kennedy Hall, consisting mostly of the teaching staff and a not inconsiderable number of Abdullah College girls, sat through our efforts.

The Chairs and *A Proposal* had been performed thrice when one of the ladies in it, engaged to be married, announced that she would no longer be available. Simultaneously the actor in *A Proposal* decided he'd had enough and pulled out as well. Without blinking an eyelid Zahida apa decided to play the old woman herself and asked me if I would mind also playing the suitor in *A Proposal* in case we had more performances. I didn't need any persuasion at all and we did actually have two more shows in which I played both parts back to back. Pure Heaven. Zahida apa's perceptiveness and intellectual

capacity notwithstanding, her acting prowess and actor-
handling ability was limited, but she proved to be a benefactor
in many ways. Apart of course from the tremendous high of
being onstage and wowing so many people, and the immense
gratification of being trusted and treated with some regard
instead of condescension, she introduced me to literature I
might not otherwise have read, I learnt how to drive in her
Standard Herald and I met Purveen Morad who would figure
emotionally in my life in a huge way.

The woman with the
sun in her hair

Purveen was thirty-four years old and a final year MBBS student specializing in ophthalmology when we met. She was well known in the university, as much for her free-thinking as for having been around a long time. She'd first done a BSc then a postgrad in education and now having completed the fifth year of her medical studies was in intern training. Not a serial degree-gatherer, she had enrolled in these classes in order to prolong her stay in India. A Pakistani national, she had stayed in Karachi with her father (estranged from her mother) since the age of five, and had now come to live in Aligarh with her mother, a much-loved teacher in the university. Experiencing maternal attention for the first time and liking the life there she took advantage of her student visa to extend her stay, doing one course after another. Not on the greatest of terms with her father, she had absolutely no wish to return to him but the bell had begun to toll, her medical studies were coming to an end now and there weren't too many other courses she could pursue.

She had been an object of some fascination for me from the time I first set eyes on her which, incidentally, had been at Tasveer Mahal movie house, while I was hanging around staring at the posters as I often did. She was obviously awaiting someone and seemed bothered. I do not know what it was about her that drew my attention; she wasn't particularly good-looking but I liked the way she was dressed, she was visibly much older than me (by fourteen years in fact) and at that moment far from cheerful, but I found her quite fascinating. I think it was the way her hair shone in the sun. I would have loved to make her acquaintance, but in Aligarh you don't just go up to a female and talk to her. When she came into a rehearsal of *The Chairs* one day, we hit it off right away though we were never actually introduced. She turned out to have two extremely attractive half-sisters. The elder one, Surekha, was a graduate of the National School of Drama (A school for drama??? Those words were music to my ears.) and was now married and settled in Delhi; the younger, Phulmani, was a postgraduate student of literature in Aligarh.

Purveen and I became friends very quickly. She encouraged me to dream and convinced me I was moving in the right direction, boosting my confidence by speaking of my being a good actor, not as a compliment any more but as a fact. She always said I had no option but to make good, mine was not the 'personality type to fail'. She even tried to make me think; she spoke perceptively about the meaning of *The Chairs* and tried to explain it to me a couple of times, then realizing I was doing well enough not bothering my head with all that, she let me be and became through the period of rehearsal a most wonderfully supportive audience, besides taking charge of the costumes and sound effects. On show days we had a make-up man, and we got ready in an actual dressing room with huge mirrors, with which I thoroughly enjoyed renewing my friendship. These mirrors had light bulbs all around them and their blinding brightness reminded me of the stage. Those bulbs felt reassuring—almost as if they were preparing me to go on again. I couldn't keep my eyes off myself, something she'd remark on, wondering if I was trying to hypnotize myself, as she'd sit there watching my make-up being done. Whether I was hypnotizing myself or not, it has since become a habit which I find also to be an extremely enjoyable way of concentrating before a stage performance. She smoked and laughed a great deal, her eyes crinkled in a lovely way when she smiled, she seemed to enjoy my company, would seek me out to spend time with me and I needed no encouragement at all to comply. Before long we were seeing each other every evening, my visits to the Uncles' home ceased, being with her was much more fun.

Aligarhians are notorious for minding other people's business and there was furiously whispered gossip generated by the sight of the two of us holding hands in public or seeing movies together. I was oblivious to it all. I had found someone to love and look up to and I was being loved in return at last, that was all that mattered. She participated backstage in every play I did in Aligarh after that, and once even acted (disastrously) with me in Tagore's *Chitra* directed by Dr Munibur Rahman, a professor in the Islamic Studies department. Dr Rahman's son Asif introduced me to Jasdev Singh Rehncy, an East African Sikh. With both of them, who now live outside India, I forged a lifelong friendship.

The plays Zahida apa wished to stage were invariably woman-centric, and so naturally she was unable to produce anything at all, but meanwhile, having shifted hostels from SS to VM Hall, I found in Dr Rahman, the drama-loving provost there, another wing to nestle under. His wife Elizabeth (Zeba apa to all) was Swiss-born and the two had met in Oxford, married and lived a blissful twenty-five-odd years in Aligarh. She was immediately recognizable driving her black Fiat; he equally so, cycling around contemplatively, lanky legs almost at right angles to his body, frizzy hair curling out from both sides of his head. When I met him he asked me what I read and receiving no answer other than 'P.G. Wodehouse' he sort of chuckled, cleared his throat, reached into his desk and producing a copy of Luigi Pirandello's *Right You Are if You Think You Are* told me to read that. A week later he handed me a copy of the *Dialogues of Plato*. Never once did he later enquire whether or not I had read the two books, nor did he ask for them back, but he did in my final year put me onstage as Socrates in a series of selections from the latter, calling it *Apology and Crito*. These were the most obtuse passages I have ever spoken onstage, but memorizing the dialogue, an activity involving many pleasurable hours with Purveen giving me my cues, was not a strain. Absolutely without self-doubt as I was at the time, the job was quickly done. Asif, also cast in the play as Crito, proved to be as terribly uncomfortable onstage in this one as he was in his dad's later production of Shaw's *How He Lied to Her Husband*, events about which he now has complete amnesia. Zahida apa meanwhile had decided not to do a play for a while but her attempts to educate me continued. I accompanied her to Delhi on a couple of occasions to watch plays done by the National School of Drama. I couldn't believe that there were people who actually shared my dream and were pushing me to grab at it. It all seemed to be coming together at last. Not getting into any other university but this one, having chosen literature and not science, the shift to VM Hall, all now began to seem as if the universe had indeed conspired.

Watching the NSD productions blew me away as much as anything else had. Here was first-class theatre work, with the kind of polish and technical excellence that existed in Indian theatre solely in that institution, then under the supervision of Ebrahim Alkazi, the director. The thought of being in this place seemed impossibly perfect and I wondered if there was a catch. Could it really be true that if I got in I'd be acting in several plays at one time and THAT'S ALL I would be doing? It seemed unreal, but I had met the students there; they were striplings like me, not star-sons or from privileged classes or from other countries, and probably with the same dreams I had. It did indeed turn out that if I was chosen for the acting course, acting was in fact mostly what I would be doing, apart from occasionally trying to learn how to draw a ground plan of the stage and fixing a barn door on a light and, wonder of wonders, I would be paid a monthly stipend of 200 rupees.

By now I was practically living in Purveen's mother's home. I seldom went to the hostel. Probably satisfied somewhat with my decent performance in the first two years there, Baba had ceased his surprise visits to my hostel room. For the first time I felt part of a family, something I'd never felt before, least of all in my parents' home. I felt wanted and appreciated and loved. The experience of being in a home with more than one woman in it was novel for me and they all actively encouraged me to pursue my dreams. Had it not been for the belief they had in me, I would perhaps not have taken the first step towards doing so: applying for admission to the NSD. But not before another event of staggering import had taken place in my life, one that astounded the entire university community and left my parents in deep depression for quite a while.

My feelings for Purveen were reaching obsessive proportions now and it had become normal for us to meet every evening— if I hadn't stayed over, that is. I had had fleeting contact with female attentions before but had never actually been on intimate terms with a woman. She was known to have had boyfriends before me and to have been pretty uninhibited about them, though of course the topic was never discussed between us. We both had our paternal progenitors to unload about. She would tell me about a traumatic childhood in Karachi where she'd been spirited away against her mother's wishes and kept for almost fifteen years, and I would continuously dump on her about my father's lack of sympathy for my dreams, his harsh judgemental nature and his inflexible temperament.

Fascinated by her energy and constant good cheer, her vast learning and varied life experience, her interest in almost everything, her skill with her hands, her compassion towards life and the attentions she bestowed on me, I began to feel a deep gratitude for her friendship and an overwhelming love for her. Here at last was someone in whose life I mattered. Someone who belonged to me, someone to whom I belonged. I could at that time see nothing beyond living my life with her always; that she made me happy was all I knew. Whether I had the capacity to make and keep her happy is something that hadn't occurred to me but, hell, I was nineteen at the time, my own happiness was all that mattered.

We soon became an 'item', in Aligarh parlance. Wherever she was present it was taken for granted I would be too. JR had been admitted into the university the previous year, and he and my Aligarh cousins, who all their lives had been thoroughly marinated in that town's vicious gossip about single women, tried to warn me about the pitfalls of this liaison and that proved to be the end, more or less, of my relationship with all of them. JR in any case had been suspicious of the reasons for my jaunt to Bombay and resented it deeply but never mentioned it. He later visited me when I was at the drama school in Delhi but the only thing he seemed interested in was whether or not I had screwed all the girls in my class and he kept referring contemptuously to my work as 'Bhandela-giri'. I decided to have nothing further to do with him.

Zahida apa, in a fit of generosity she was to later regret, once lent me her car so that Purveen and I could go to Delhi to watch the NSD production of Bertolt Brecht's (a somewhat familiar name for me by then) *Caucasian Chalk Circle* directed by the East German Karl Weber. The production was breathtaking and I knew that there was definitely nothing else I felt like doing now but coming to the NSD. I had no idea what kind of career prospects there would be, and despite having heard bleak stories of how all the graduates of that place ended up 'going back to where they came from' and how the two most celebrated NSD alumni, the husband–wife team of Om and Sudha Shivpuri, were just about 'eking out an existence' on radio and a bit of TV, I was not at all discouraged. A lead role in a radio play got one a payment of 50 rupees and of course I would be the lead! Four or five jobs a month should see me through, and now there was TV as well. This was 1969, there was only one TV channel then in black-and-white, the Doordarshan channel, which showed mind-numbing stuff most of the time but on which plays were also sometimes telecast.

Watching *Chalk Circle* it struck me that when I did come to this place I would have to be content initially with being one of the crowd or the guard or the messenger, and simultaneously felt convinced that I would be perfectly content to do anything in such a production. Just the thought of being part of the team creating this stupendous effect would be achievement enough for the moment. Purveen, of course, was of the opinion that I would and should get a better deal than that.

Playing the drunken judge Azdak, the absolute winner in the play, was one Shashikant Nikte whose impeccable comic timing, lithe graceful carriage and resonant voice made a big impression. He sang beautifully, something I have never even come close to doing, and I greatly envied this actor and the opportunity he was getting to display his wares, and I had a feeling which has returned every time while watching truly great acting—the feeling that 'I wouldn't have been able to do this'. Purveen didn't think so and insisted that 'this is the role I want to see you play'. My head full of how I would play Azdak, we were driving back to Aligarh after dark and had just gone past a railway crossing when two things happened simultaneously. I suddenly remembered that I had neglected to appear for my theology exams for the last two years. Not having attended any of the classes, my knowledge of the subject was hardly sharp and so I had been putting these off, taking advantage of the 'semester system' that permitted you to collect your credits at any time in the three years. 'Why bother my head now, I'll clear them all at the end,' was my reasoning. Well, the end was nigh, and before I got anywhere near to playing Azdak, I had three sets of theology exams to clear in the approaching finals. The second thing that happened was that I rammed the nose of Zahida apa's precious Standard Herald into the back of a truck parked on the side of the road. Luckily it was a glancing collision and the car suffered no major damage except to a headlight which then kept directing its beam into the fields adjoining the road as I drove back alone. Alone, because Purveen refused to sit any longer in a car I was driving. Brushing away my entreaties, she hitched a ride in the very truck into which I had collided. I followed as close behind as I could. It was the most useful driving lesson I have ever had.

One morning, answering the door at Purveen's I saw two gents whose white bush shirts, khaki trousers and brown shoes instantly announced their identity. 'CID,' said the one in front. 'Miss Morad lives here?' Purveen went even higher in my estimation. What an interesting life she leads, thought I, and had a quick vision of myself in mackintosh and felt hat, smoke curling from my cigarette, flashing my identity card at a terrified wrongdoer. Turned out that they hadn't come to dispatch her or me on a guns-and-gals mission, they had come to check if she was still in India and to remind her that her visa was due to expire soon. Those were days of frosty relations and mutual suspicion between the neighbours. The Bangladesh conflict was beginning to fester and the explosion was round the corner. Pakistanis visiting India had to register themselves and report weekly to a police station, and in some cases they were even kept under surveillance through their stay. I have no idea if she too was, but she had stayed on long enough to warrant notice. A lengthy meeting with the two gents followed, from which I was excluded, and when they had left, both Purveen and her mother were silent for a longish while. A couple of days later I was taken into confidence. She was on the verge of overstaying in India and the penalty for that would be deportation and a ban from ever visiting again. She had to return to Pakistan within the month. There was no way for her to stay on but to seek Indian citizenship which, considering the existing situation, would be far from expeditious. There was one way, however, by which she could stay and that was to marry an Indian citizen. To me there didn't appear to be any hitch at all. Here I was, a bona fide Indian citizen, madly in love with her; all I had to do was wait for my big break and I'd be marrying her anyway, sooner or later.

I think there is nothing more about that episode that I need go into except that we were married on the 1st of November 1969 with no one except her mother and Asif's mother Mrs Zeba Rahman as witnesses. My poor parents, completely oblivious to these developments and perhaps finally beginning to feel some easing of their anxieties—for to all appearances I was showing signs of straightening myself out—were now to be hit by another thunderbolt.

We had resolved to keep the marriage completely secret but should have known better. Within a couple of days it was common knowledge throughout the university. Aligarh is not far from Meerut and people go back and forth so the news quickly got there as well. I have no idea who broke it to my parents, nor how they reacted; and I have felt too ashamed of myself to even try and imagine it. But their heartbeats must have gone faint in disbelief. This surely was beyond even Baba's paranoid imaginings about me. I received a stunned letter from him telling me I was 'a gullible fool'. Ammi too wrote in Urdu, asking why I'd kept it from them. 'If you'd told us would we have refused?' she asked rhetorically. Baba informed me he'd had quite enough and my life was my own to live now, the way I pleased. Poor soul never knew that that was exactly what I'd been doing all along. I guess it's an indication of how far from them I'd travelled that all I did was mock their response.

In a misguided attempt, a couple of months later, to repair what was now becoming an impassable breach, I suggested to Purveen that she accompany me to Sardhana on Eid to meet them. She had travelled to Delhi on other occasions but now the anxiety of meeting them probably caused her to protest about being restricted from travelling to places for which she didn't have a visa. She was adamant that leaving Aligarh even for a day was risky. It took a couple of hours of persuasion before she finally consented, lying supine in the back of a cousin's car in case the CID was hiding in the bushes all the way there. I had miscalculated the time the drive would take, and hadn't factored in her opposition to my hare-brained scheme so we made it to Sardhana a good four hours later than I had planned, around ten thirty, dead of night for that one-jeep town. In my enthusiasm to persuade her to come I had painted a picture of hordes of carousing relatives awaiting the new bahu. My parents, I assured her, would be delighted, in fact would be the first to welcome her. I may even have promised a brass band and an all-night revel, I don't recall. Whatever she was expecting, it certainly wasn't what we got.

We arrived to the sound of deep silence; both Baba and Ammi had eaten and were struggling to stay awake. The greetings were edgy, almost curt. Neither the two of us nor the two of them knew quite how to handle this. Some food and strained conversation between Baba and Purveen followed, Ammi and I stayed silent. We informed them we'd be leaving before daylight, they didn't insist we stay. Ammi presented Purveen a necklace and a pair of earrings, kissed the top of her head and went to bed. Baba, never loquacious at the best of times, sat squirming for a while then also retired. At five in the morning we departed without saying goodbye, and got back to Aligarh before the CID could notice we were gone. Both the Zs, neither of them married yet, later came to visit us in Aligarh bringing gifts, and presumably went away baffled. Some decades having passed between then and now, I think I can understand why.

Some weeks before the wedding I had already shifted out of the hostel and was now ensconced at 2 Diggi Road with Purveen and her mother. Everything was going swimmingly, and then one day Purveen, who not too long ago had had to educate me on the menstrual cycle, informed me there would be no more 'chums'—she was expecting a baby. This possibility hadn't even occurred to me. At that age I had no fondness whatsoever for children, no fondness in fact for anything but myself. The enormity of bringing new life into the world escaped me entirely, and I don't suppose any amount of contrition later could compensate for my utterly insensitive treatment of the child when she was born, and when all she needed from me was to be hugged and comforted.

Meanwhile, I was admitted to the National School of Drama as a first-year student, and left for Delhi at the end of my final year at Aligarh. Moving into its unique common-for-both-sexes hostel was unbelievably liberating after Aligarh, as was living in a big city again though Delhi seemed positively tame after Bombay, the mother-in-law of all Indian cities. The scholarship stipend we received after fees and hostel charges were deducted saw me quite comfortably through the month. I didn't have to ask Baba for money—in any case the tap had been shut off a while ago—but better still, I didn't need to ask his permission any more. This feeling of independence was heady. What slipped my mind was that a child was on its way and that I was not equipped either financially or emotionally to handle the situation that would ensue. I had been in Delhi a little over a month, and one Monday morning I discovered a telegram a day old, stating that Purveen's 'confinement has begun'. Having taken a few seconds to decipher the message, I caught the first bus to Aligarh. It was around noon by the time I got there. Early that morning, some hours before I arrived, Heeba had already been born.

Heeba, gift of God

The bus fare from Delhi to Aligarh was about seven rupees, and the rickshaw fare from the bus stop to the hospital Purveen was in was half a rupee, eight annas. I alighted right in front of her room as her mother emerged with the news that 'it's a girl, at about six in the morning'. Evidently a successive telegram had already been sent informing me of this. Until that moment, I didn't realize how fervently I had wished it would be a boy. I am far enough removed from the day now to confess to the sense of crushing disappointment that seized me at that moment and didn't let go for a long time. 'A daughter!' My adolescent virility had convinced me that true men had sons. My friends would mock and sure enough, led by JR, later did. A daughter? How would I deal with this?? In my head I had already been arm-wrestling with my imaginary son and teaching him about guns and cricket—when I had a moment to spare from myself to think of his impending arrival, that is. A daughter demolished all those dreams. The rickshaw puller, overhearing the conversation, smilingly tucked away the rupee note I had given him, presuming he was to keep the change on this joyous day. I insisted on my eight annas back and a most inauspicious argument over the sad little amount I should have let him keep in the first place followed before I had even seen my child.

The reality of it hit me when I first saw Heeba (Purveen had decided on the name if it were a girl; a boy's name I hadn't thought of, funnily). She was a tiny apparition asleep in a crib covered by a mosquito net. I didn't have the nerve to touch her. When she later awoke and I heard her voice for the first time something stirred in me, but I had never held a baby before. In fact I didn't like them, they were noisy and messy; it was a challenge holding her in my arms. And later when she was being fed and I was being ignored I, like all immature fathers, experienced the most intense jealousy which only men ever feel, jealousy of their own child.

Through the period of her pregnancy, Purveen had turned really moody, and my utter incomprehension of the miracle occurring within her and total oblivion to what was expected of me didn't help. Many serious arguments, which I always got the worst of, were the result. Priapic twenty-one-year-old that I was, hopelessly self-absorbed, incapable of contributing in any way at all to making her feel good about herself, I found the bar on sex not easy to handle either. My attentions had already begun to wander and were beginning to zero in on R, a rather good-looking second-year student who as a whore in the NSD production of *Three-Penny Opera* had earlier caught my fancy, and now the two of us began spending a little more time together than was absolutely necessary.

My entering the drama school had coincided with the final month of the pregnancy, always a difficult one, and for Purveen now in her mid thirties, not the best time to bear a child. As for me, without a clue of the responsibilities it entailed, the trouble that's part of the whole deal, and then the indescribable joy it brings, I had no time to spare for the life I was helping bring into the world; only my own gratification took priority, nothing else mattered. I took no part in the building of the baby crib Purveen was fashioning out of an old basket and some sawn-off bamboos—a beautiful piece of work finally, in which Heeba spent her first few months. I did occasionally steal some roses from the university garden and bring them to Purveen in my cycle basket. That pleased her, but apart from that I played the part of the obnoxious adolescent to perfection. The role of father was way beyond my ken. After a dressing-down from Mother-in-law I started helping with the dishes but that was as far as it went. I slowly began to resent this child who was coming between me and the only woman who had ever given me any attention; and when the baby finally arrived, the neglect I displayed still shames me deeply all these decades later.

Four days after her birth Heeba was brought home, but in the interim I had had to rush back to the school to attend classes—being absent from class was rewarded with a further deduction from one's scholarship and I could scarce afford that. The following Saturday I returned to Aligarh to accompany mother and baby home in a rickshaw. It was a bumpy ride and I held Heeba in my arms. Mercifully no one I knew spotted us and we made it home without mortification. Heeba was laid in her crib, and I caught the next bus back to Delhi.

I wrote home about Heeba and not so astonishingly Baba immediately made his way to Aligarh to see her. A few days later I got a deliriously happy letter from him saying that he had just seen 'that lovely little thing, I have named her Attia'. His desire for a girl in the family was to find more sublimation than he had hoped for; Heeba was to be followed by four more girls in both my brothers' families. I informed Purveen of Baba's choice of name but he didn't exactly figure in the list of her favourite people and the name Heeba stuck. Heeba was the first of Baba's (now) ten grandchildren and when both the Zs later had their daughters, he ecstatically dubbed them all with archaic double-barrelled appellations which, to the girls' massive relief, were never employed. Heeba's arrival actually caused Baba and me to be civil to each other for a while, but now the gulf with Purveen had widened.

Her whole life now revolved around Heeba and she and I had precious little to say to each other any more and even less to share. The stimulation of being on the cusp of a life of professional acting ensured that I didn't miss her at all, and she seemed to lose whatever interest she had had in my obsession. The physical distance too began to grow. I was no longer this amusing little chap for her; I was now cast in a role which seemed like a hugely unpleasant chore and which I was ill-equipped to play: father of a child. It filled me with unease and inadequacy. The weekly visits to Aligarh became monthly visits and the stay there successively shorter. Now it was all milk bottles and diapers and suckling and cleaning and burping the baby, I couldn't be bothered with any of it. While I had absolutely no interest in baby care, Purveen was consumed by it—she had to be, this was something she had waited a long time for. My indifference to Heeba can only be explained, though not condoned, by the fact that I myself was then an insecure, ill-adjusted twenty-one-year-old with absolutely no conception of what it took to rear a newborn, and I completely shirked my share of the duties, while idiotically attempting at the same time to assert my rights as a husband. The only way of dealing with a wife, in the world according to the Shahs, was with firmness and authority. Not unaware that I was thoroughly incapable of either, I retreated into a resentful shell. It hurt to know I was no longer the most important thing in Purveen's life. There was no telephone in Aligarh and her replies to my letters got more infrequent and finally ceased altogether, as then did my visits there.

In Alkazi I had at last found an inspiring teacher—one who liked and appreciated me and didn't make me feel like a fool, one who was interested in helping improve my mind, and pushed hard to make me realize the potential he perceived in me. Purveen's family had already had that positive influence marginally, but now I was under the wing of someone who could show me the way; he tried to teach us art appreciation, introduced us to classical music, to the myriad Indian theatrical forms, to serious cinema; he goaded us to read, to wake up early, to work on our instruments. I learnt that Eugene Ionesco and Anton Chekhov were not the only great playwrights apart from Shaw and Shakespeare. Reading things I could actually understand was a tremendous high. The fascination and admiration I'd had for Purveen got transferred many times magnified to Ebrahim Alkazi.

I have no idea in what sort of light I will appear if I say that for an unconscionably long time I felt nothing whatsoever for the child Heeba, but it is necessary that I confess it. She didn't figure at all, it was almost as if she didn't even exist. When I did visit her in Aligarh she'd look at me as at a stranger, she seldom came near me and neither of us was comfortable when she did.

School of drama, tragedy and heartbreak

In the opening class on modern Indian drama the kindly Mr Nemichand Jain, professor of that subject, after his introductory talk enquired from us about the number of Hindi plays each student had read. Most rattled off a number of names I hadn't ever heard before and everyone had read at least a couple if not more of what seemed to be very well-known works of Indian playwrights in Hindi. Everyone, that is, except me. I hadn't heard of any of these plays and the only extra-curricular Hindi I had ever read was film magazines or Must Ram's porn. An astonished Jain saab had to ask me thrice over whether I was absolutely sure I 'hadn't read a single Hindi play ever??' I assured him that such was indeed the case. Thereafter he always treated me as somewhat special and perhaps somewhat challenged.

The very first play I acted in at NSD, a children's play *The Little Blue Horse*, gained me a mention in the only review of it that appeared, and that made my head swivel a little further. I was then cast as Brabantio in *Othello*, Mathew the gangster in *Three-Penny Opera*, and to my astonishment as Barot, the court poet, in a production of a folk play *Jasma Odan*, a singing role!

This last was probably Alkazi's attempt to get me to train my singing voice, a venture in which he failed completely. Despite the singing instructor's relentless coaxing I just could not hit the notes. Being told to shut up any time I tried singing at home and being laughed out of every trial for the musicals in Sem had come home to roost. I was convinced I could never sing, and no amount of encouragement now was any help.

I had no realization then that my voice was a thing under my control if I bothered to listen to it, and all I had to do was recognize the habits I had accumulated along the way, and THEN work my butt off to rid myself of them. But I faltered at the first step. Far from being able to free my voice, I just could not tell a false note from a pure one, and it was maddening to constantly be told 'No! No! Try again' when I had no clue what I should be trying for. Fortunately for me, most of the other singers were only marginally better and so I didn't suffer too much in comparison. And after all, Rex Harrison had 'speechified' all his songs in *My Fair Lady*, hadn't he? That performance for me had been one of seminal influence. I decided to do the same and found my escape route through sheer laziness: I spoke the songs to rhythm, even receiving moderate praise for my diction. But sing I did not. The writer and director of *Jasma Odan*, the dynamic Shanta Gandhi, then no longer with the school and thus having no hand in my landing the part, after watching a performance of the play was aghast at why I had been cast. I did not blame her. As if having to sing in one play was not bad enough, fate had yet another trick up its sleeve.

A month-long winter tour to Bombay, Poona, Hyderabad and Bangalore was announced. All three productions would be travelling, and it was whispered that accompanying them would be a revival of *Caucasian Chalk Circle* with the role of Azdak up for grabs as Shashikant Nikte, the original Azdak, had left. Something like a premonition began to gather. I no longer visited Aligarh any more and even though it was unheard of for a first-year student to be cast in a lead role, I had a feeling that this time the impossible would happen, as Purveen had predicted it would. I wished equally fervently that she would come to see me in it. Relations with her were now practically non-existent and she did not reply to my letter telling her that the role was practically mine, though that was far from being true. There were not a few aspirants in line and at least one gent with a very strong claim, a third-year acting student who was not unsuitable. What went in my favour was that he was likely to leave after his course was done and I would be around for another two years; besides he couldn't sing any better than me and Azdak had not one but two solo numbers.

Alkazi saab, the ferociously dedicated 'padrone' of the theatre, liked to personally set an example, asking no less of himself than he asked of anyone. Blessed with impeccable taste, and acutely aware of his place in history, he bestowed a sense of aesthetics and sophistication and, more important, organization and discipline on Indian theatre. His productions were examples of what 'finish' in theatre design actually meant. A designer by training and by temperament, widely travelled and formidably well read, Alkazi's compelling theatre presentations had, in the context of Indian theatre then, no equal.

I had to wrench myself away from being around this dazzling personification of charisma and the other-worldly bliss of living, eating, sleeping theatre in order to pay to Heeba's existence the attention it needed. Thoughts of my infant daughter were non-existent in my mind. A total disconnect with my life in Aligarh had happened, it all seemed like another time altogether. As my fascination with city life and theatre work grew, my connection with what I suppose were my roots began to shrivel. One of the things left behind was my relationship with Purveen. My relationship with Heeba had ossified before it began.

I got the Azdak part. My sessions with the singing instructor started anew, bearing as little fruit as before. Luckily for me the songs in Brecht's plays are dramatic set pieces where the clear rendition of the words is of prime importance. Brecht himself even demanded a somewhat 'unmusical' quality from his singers; so that listeners are not lulled by the melody but pay heed to the content. Alkazi made the mistake of explaining this to me one day during rehearsal and of course I thought in that case I'm doing it right, and abandoned any further attempt to sing well. Laziness again hindered me, I was unable to rectify a shortcoming that only grew with time. And to top it all off: on our Bombay leg (my first revisit to the city I somehow knew I would spend my life in), all the plays performed to jam-packed houses. *Chalk Circle* was specially commended and I got a mention in the *Times of India*.

The morning after the show I was woken by Rajendra Jaspal, a classmate and close friend by now, showing me the review. We shared a great big laugh and a celebratory joint first thing in the morning. Jaspal was a small-town guy like me though older by a couple of years. He didn't speak English too well, was somewhat embarrassed about his lower-middle-class upbringing and the fact that he'd worked in a bank before coming to the drama school. With a marvellous singing voice he was as good an actor as I was and yet had to be content with playing the chorus while I, the star of the show, got to strut my off-key stuff. We seemed to have a lot in common apart from the feverish desire to succeed. Because of my English and my general air I guess he took me to be from a very well-to-do family and often stated that he wished to be like me. I admired his talents and he admired mine; we always got cast as buddies and became inseparable in real life as well, to the extent that we began to be referred to as one person: 'Jaspal/Shah'. We did everything together, we seemed to have similar tastes, and our careers at the school followed similar trajectories, until *Chalk Circle*, that is. It escaped me completely that he may have aspired to the part as well. I just felt that getting it was my prerogative and he had seemed genuinely to share my happiness. I was incapable of reading between the lines then, and I had not a clue of the involvedness of the relationship that was forming and of the tragic (for him and nearly for me) consequences that would follow in a few years.

After triumphant turns in the first two cities, we began a show of *Jasma Odan* in Hyderabad with the forty-five-strong cast prancing on to the stage in celebration at the beginning of the play, only to be faced by row upon row of empty seats. There were, literally, fewer people in the auditorium than there were onstage. Some sponsor somewhere had messed up along the line and Hyderabad was a blip in an otherwise totally intoxicating, nay inebriating, tour for me. Even though I struggled with a strained voice (never once attempting to give up smoking though) my performance received favourable attention everywhere we went. R and I also broke off and patched up several times but became extremely close in the course of the tour, and despite her strong disapproval, I discovered the magic of marijuana.

Purveen never ever saw me play Azdak even though we performed the play several times in Delhi after the tour. I made a few feeble attempts to get through to Heeba, going to Aligarh and trying to spend time with her but we would both be tongue-tied on meeting. She was now two, walking and talking but had nothing to say to me and probably didn't want to go anywhere with me. I think she must have been somewhat confused as to who I was and how she should behave with me. I was in a similar predicament. I didn't know how to deal with children, I didn't even know how she would respond if I tried to hug or hold her, and the reception from Purveen was always so unfailingly hostile that I finally decided to cease performing this onerous duty and in fact didn't see Heeba again for another twelve years.

In my first year at NSD I was involved in more plays than I had done in my life thus far and I had got my picture in the papers for the first time. The prospect of doing this always just seemed too good to be true, until with the year-end exams done and Jaspal/Shah having secured first and second place respectively, Alkazi announced to both of us that he expected us to study direction instead of acting, saying that intelligent students like us would be more suited to study direction. What he was probably trying to do was shelter us from the abysmally inept acting teachers, and take us under his wing. We both initially resisted but couldn't hold out; when Alkazi set out to persuade he succeeded. He was obsessive about many things, mainly order and cleanliness, about not neglecting the smallest detail, even seeing to the maintenance of the toilets, not infrequently doing a clean-up himself. Costumes not respectfully folded and kept in their proper place after a show would bring the wrath of God down on the transgressor. Everything he said was said with complete conviction, he seemed to have the right take on everything, he always made sense. We both agreed to enter the second year as students of direction and took one more step towards confusing our identities with each other. In the two-month summer break neither of us went home. Getting permission to stay on in the hostel we both acted in a production of three one-act pieces, attempted by a couple of (then) enterprising young men, Rajendra Gupta and Devendra Ankur. The production was staged in a theatre in as professional a way as we could manage. Alkazi saw it and pronounced himself 'pleased, but not with the noisy backstage'.

Sometime during the vacations I received a letter from R ending our relationship; something she tried to do repeatedly in the two years we knew each other; maybe she sensed we were wrongly matched, but I was just too smitten to see it. I went off to Aligarh for a few days to be with Asif and Jasdev. Asif's parents had migrated to the US and he was due to follow as soon as his medical studies were done, Jasdev was to join his family in London after his commerce course. Luckily for me, these events were still a couple of years away and I had the solace of their friendship for a little longer. They both goaded me to visit Heeba but I didn't. It was impossible for me to face my own inadequacies.

Meanwhile the report cards for our first-year exam had been sent home, mine resulting in yet another furious tirade from Baba. Unable to find anything to berate me about now that I was no longer wasting his money, he had probably been stewing for a while, and then like manna from heaven my report card arrived. Disregarding totally my tremendous achievement of for the first time in my life not being among the last few but the top two, he decided to pick upon a bit of criticism by Alkazi regarding my diction and habit of speaking nasally. How did I 'hope to become an actor with such hopelessly bad speech' though Alkazi had made no such observation. I ignored the letter, but set about correcting my habit of gabbling my dialogue and speaking through my nose.

In my second year at NSD an uneasy feeling that I hadn't really learnt anything new about acting began to gnaw at me. I was fascinated by the theatre history we were taught; and reading new plays, even if they were completely incomprehensible, was stimulating, as was watching Alkazi breathe life into a comatose scene. But as far as learning acting went, the classes made absolutely no sense. It was the curse that has always beset the training of actors: only the failures come back to teach, and most have failed because quite simply they didn't know their job. And in any case most student actors are only too happy to listen for hours to esotericisms spouted by acting teachers and are obsessed only with getting employment, not with understanding the mechanics of their work, which in any case the mountebanks who teach are not equipped to help them with. Thus the completely erroneous belief that 'some can act and others can't' continues to hold sway. Students of acting in most places, instead of being made aware of their work as a craft, are pushed to recall past incidents and manipulate themselves to laugh or cry or rage, all resulting in great cathartic releases of emotion but giving the actor nothing except a momentary high of wallowing in memories. The actor is asked simply to recall, there is no guidance on how to sift these experiences and use them while working; no breakdown of the process of expressing. The notion that great acting 'just happens' is encouraged; the purpose of an actor's job and his place in the scheme of things seems nebulous to everyone; meaningless words like 'talent', 'inspiration', 'involvement' are tossed about and most actors feel their job is done by merely mouthing these, bowing to the stage when someone is watching, sitting nervously alone before performing, and learning how to spell Stanislavsky.

Alkazi himself was a designer and had little patience with actors. He never bothered with the dynamics behind the action, for him it was all composition. His vast knowledge of painting, sculpture, music, literature and theatre had so honed his instincts that he knew the effect a particular composition could create. It was up to the actors to find their own truth, if they could, within that composition; it was never spelt out for them. He himself had been an actor once, had in fact played Hamlet and Tartuffe and Lucky (somewhat showily I suspect!) but his reputation rested chiefly on his impeccable productions in which the opening lights coming up on an elaborate empty setting could garner applause, but in which the acting was somewhat soulless, never less than competent but far from inspiring.

Vacations over, R returned and our relationship gradually resumed, not before she had one day mocked me mercilessly for hanging around some guy perusing an eveninger in which my picture had appeared, hoping I would be recognized. Gupta and Ankur's little effort had not exactly made a killing but had been liked and had come out with a small profit, a rare enough event in experimental theatre then. My share of the proceeds, about 30 rupees, my first earning from theatre, made me feel like a professional at last.

But to bring me back to earth was a notification from Aligarh University instructing me to appear for my three theology papers, failing which my degree would be withheld. The notification had been forwarded to me by Baba without a word, he had so far been under the impression I had sailed through my exams. Either he was displaying enormous self-control or he was just exhausted. Followed a week of deep study of Sunni theology, of which I cannot claim to remember much, in classes at the university; and then the three examination papers in quick succession, bang bang bang.

Then it was on with the second year at drama school. I was not too perturbed at never landing the leading parts in the new productions but I reasoned that was just a matter of time. Despite enjoying the classes in direction, I never seriously considered the possibility of becoming a director. Dreaming of being one was far less enticing than dreaming of being an actor. Playing even a walk-on was fun, but being an apprentice in direction meant running around fixing sets and arranging costumes and getting vertigo clambering into the catwalk to adjust lights, making ground plans and drawing out actors' moves on them so they could be replicated exactly.

Purveen, I knew by now, had gone to London. Before leaving she had in fact come to meet me in Delhi. I was aghast and extremely suspicious at seeing her appear in the hostel one morning. She gave me a hug, handed me a flower and expressed regret about not responding to my overtures so far; she then started tidying up my room, all the while gently berating me for being tardy. I could not believe this, not just her turning up out of the blue and behaving as if nothing had happened but the way she looked. Her open hair had strings of flowers in it, there were beads around her neck and wrists. Her eyes seemed unfocused and so did her mind: this was not the person I knew. She kept saying we should get back together, give it another try—a conversation I did not know how to handle. In desperation I rang up her sister Surekha and begged her to take her off my hands, which she did, much to my relief, but only after extracting a promise that I would eat at her house that night. She lived in a large bungalow in a high-end New Delhi colony and the food there was really good. Those days one spent quite some time dreaming about food and an invitation to a home-meal could not possibly be passed up. That night, though, I had to abandon the dinner halfway because I could not cope with Purveen's by now increasingly hysterical insistence on repairing the breach between us. Shortly after that, I assume, she left for London with Heeba and another child she had since had.

Babar (Shah) Mamu too had gotten married around the same time as I did and had a son almost the exact age as Heeba. After quitting the CRP he tried for a short service commission in the army but was turned down because he had wangled a recommendation from a superior officer. Shah Mamu never fails to astonish me even as a memory. The man was a mere sub-inspector in the CRP yet he hobnobbed with the commandants, was pals with Ajmer's most influential families and dated all the prettiest girls. What he found difficult to do, presumably, was find some direction in his life. In the course of sowing his wild oats, it was whispered in the family, he had done things too terrible to mention. Blessed with almost superhuman strength and a very short fuse, he seemed always to be daring the world to take him on and at least twice have I seen him single-handedly get the better of more than one guy. As a student at Aligarh University he hijacked the vice-chancellor's car just to horse around in and was expelled. Subsequently he loafed for a few years then got partially adopted by Baba who helped him get his first job as a malaria inspector in Kishangarh a few miles from Ajmer; and later a sub-inspector's post in the CRP in which he lasted a few years, got fed up and returned to Sardhana with the intention of claiming his share of the land and living off it. The plan amounted to naught because Chand (Khalid) Mamu, a few years older than him, and the one who had tended the land all along, felt aggrieved at having to give up to the wastrel brother a substantial portion of the land he had so long toiled on. With two such aggressive hotheads involved, things didn't take long to go on the boil. Baba and Ammi, compelled to take sides in this ugly affair, were naturally sympathetic to Babar.

When threats began to be hurled and the danger of violence became real, the two were persuaded by the eldest sibling, Agha Mamu, the final authority in all matters, to sort things out amicably. We were too young to be included in these matters so only conjecture can serve. The upshot, however, was that Babar was given, in lieu of what he was claiming in Sardhana, a mango orchard and some fields in Mahmudabad to manage. The catch was he wouldn't own it—he would only manage it and collect half the produce annually, the other half going to the owner. Who the owner was is not very clear, but the land evidently once belonged to the Raja of Mahmudabad and had been appropriated by the government under the Land Ceiling Act and the stopping of privy purses. Babar Mamu and his wife, a doctor, and their infant son Akbar moved to Mahmudabad and for a while it did seem as if the prodigal had finally come home. He had been there about two years when one day I received a hurriedly scribbled postcard from Baba containing the message: 'Your mother and I are leaving for Mahmudabad today, we have heard that Babar has been shot dead.'

When I went to Sardhana to condole with Ammi and my grandmother (Grandpa had died a year or so ago) I learnt that he had not in fact been shot, far ghastlier than that. He had been hacked to death by an unidentified group of people. The only eyewitness had also been killed. Evidently one day at dusk Babar was informed that someone's cattle were grazing in his fields. The plan obviously was to get him incensed and alone when it was growing dark. He fell for it, sallying forth accompanied by a friend, his .22 rifle slung over his shoulder, probably intending, as was his wont, to mete out an almighty thrashing to whoever was responsible. Though I wasn't anywhere near, I can imagine the things that must have been said. Presumably before he knew what was happening, he was surrounded, and the axes and scythes and spears and lathis did their job. His corpse was found three days later in a canal, some distance from the spot where he was attacked, meaning one of two things: either he tried to run and only got that far, or his dead body was thrown in. I prefer to believe the second; the heart refuses to accept he would run away from a good fight even though fatally injured. Running away, in his book, would have been worse than death. The murder is still shrouded in all sorts of dark tales and an impenetrable haze of contradictory versions.

I decided to spend the vacations after my second year with Ammi and Baba in Mussoorie. The two of them were devastated. Babar Mamu's widow had, very wisely, severed all connections with the Sardhana family, and returned to Sitapur where she belonged, to set up practice there. Ammi was the only one in the family she ever stayed in touch with thereafter. Baba the stoic remained dry-eyed; and Ammi too, though always visibly affected by a death, showed amazing resilience. Very soon I was the one in need of consolation every time Babar Mamu was remembered. Ammi, to whom he meant very much more than he did to me, came to terms with it much easier than I did. I have to say that it haunts me still, I just cannot get the macabre way he died out of my head, and my imagination fails me when I try to visualize how it must have happened.

During these vacations Baba made me almost regret having come home—when it wasn't my scuffed shoes or tattered jeans or beard or unkempt long hair that got his goat, it was my tardiness at rising in the morning that would set off the sarcasm about whether it was 'necessary for artists not to bathe'. And of course THE eternal 60 million dollar question: had I thought about the future? What was I planning to do after the course was over? I had not the foggiest idea what I was going to do but I assured him he had an exceptionally talented son who could not be stopped. I also tried asking him whether, regardless of what I did later, it was not of any

importance at all that I was now doing something I really loved.
His eyes would glaze over and he would say nothing. He never
enquired about what I was learning at the school; possibly he
feared it was nothing at all, or it didn't interest him, or more
possibly it would have been quite beyond his understanding. I
don't think he was too well-read and had definitely not even a
fleeting acquaintance with dramatic literature; I tried talking
to him about absurd drama, Shakespeare, Chekhov but I don't
think it grabbed him.

While I was in Mussoorie we received the news that Baba's
older sister, the only one ever, incidentally, capable of telling
him off and who was particularly dear to him (his other
seven siblings were half-brothers/sisters), had passed away in
Meerut. She had been under treatment for cancer for a year.
Baba and Ammi left immediately for the funeral, I stayed
behind because I felt like hanging around in Mussoorie for a
few more days by myself. When I got to Meerut, Baba looked
visibly haggard. It's the only time I've ever seen him unshaven.
He didn't say much but just as I was readying to go off to
Delhi that night, he asked me to stay.

If I had to wipe out all memories of my father and keep
only one, this is the one I would keep. He actually wanted
me to stay on another day, he actually wanted my company!
He had never sounded anything but authoritative in all my
conversations with him, but this was a side of him I had not
known before, or had completely forgotten. He was almost
plaintive, well aware that I might refuse; and instead of the
authority which came naturally to him, there was the tone of
a father who had begun to feel he wanted to spend the little
time he had left, or as much of it as he could, with his son. This
feeling was new, I was never the son he had wanted to spend
time with, but that day I stayed on and for once in my life I
was able to talk to him about my dreams. He listened but his

universe was too far removed from mine. His only concern was what would become of me.

The other thing worthy of note that happened in my second year at NSD was R's announcement that she would be going to the US next semester to do a postgrad course in drama at Smith College.

We returned from vacation for our final year, to be informed that auditions would be on for the next production, a Kabuki paly in Hindi, *Ibaragi*, to be directed by an expert from Japan. My awareness of this classical form was as immature as that of a twenty-two-year-old drama student can be expected to be. We had never actually seen a Kabuki play but had been shown films of some performances. It would be a stretch to perform like that, I knew, particularly with the vocal acrobatics required, but I felt more than confident that the big part in it would be mine. Even though I then had frequent laryngeal trouble, and had to often perform with a voice that was no more than a ghostly whisper, I was cocky to the core that if anyone could pull this off it had to be me. It did not occur to me that there were other actors too, not as showy as myself, who had been far more diligent in practising their craft than I had been. Arriving at the school for the first read-through, we were told that only the students of acting would be cast. We, the students of direction, were to only observe and assist in the production. I was gutted and so was Jaspal, who had naturally assumed that with his vocal abilities, he would be a shoo-in. And who should get cast in the main part but Om Puri, also a classmate, who had very quietly persevered in self-improvement through the time he had been at NSD.

When the play was performed Om, for once cast as a flamboyant warrior, was a revelation. I was stuck doing production duties for this play I would have killed to act in, and could only watch him in wonder and envy. Despite intensely coveting the role, it was difficult not to be thrilled at the level of performance he had achieved. Something told me I could NOT have done what he did. Om had always been a model, if somewhat stodgy, student and human being: completely virtuous, genuinely considerate, deeply compassionate, industrious, punctual, attentive, thoughtful; but had so far received attention because of his sweet temperament rather than for his acting. Now he had delivered a knockout performance, and I could see there was no magic formula responsible. He was so astoundingly good because, quite simply, he had gone for broke and expended every ounce of his energy in preparation. Om continued to inspire me for a very long time. Even though I initially found his sincerity amusing and quite unnecessary—at complete variance with my own attitude—I finally began to see its virtues, and had to admit to myself that none of my own performances in the school productions could begin to approach Om's achievement in *Ibaragi*.

Next morning Jaspal/Shah were in Alkazi's office, insisting on a transfer to the acting course. We couldn't bear to not be acting in any more plays, and that is what now seemed likely, with direction students normally assisting with the lighting and backstage jobs. We wanted to act, at least I did and I suppose Jaspal did as well. I find it hard to remember who was the mover behind all these decisions we took in tandem and who the follower. Alkazi was reluctant to let us go, reiterating time and again that we would benefit more by doing the course in direction. And he was right: we would have learnt more but, hell, we didn't want to learn, we wanted to act. As a last-resort kind of thing to assure me I had a future as a director, he gave me a classroom assignment to direct Acts One and

Two of *A Doll's House*, with Om acting in it, and even though I acquitted myself reasonably well as director, with Jaspal as stage manager (it was incidentally the first of two more later unsuccessful attempts at directing Om), it did not deter me from resuming my pleas to rejoin the acting course, a request Alkazi finally had to grant.

The penny drops in super slo-mo

One evening, in Delhi, with nothing better to do, I wandered into Regal Cinema and watched a movie called *Piya ka Ghar*, a family drama—a genre I abhorred, and the actors in it were hardly my favourites, but seeing it proved fateful. Playing all the important parts in the movie were, I realized, at least five graduates in acting from the Film and TV Institute of India (FTII), Pune. I had visited the place during our tour in the first year and seen some student films with students acting in them. These films with titles like (and I exaggerate a bit but only a bit) *Apocalypsis-cum-Genesis*, *And unto the Cosmic Void*, *Madhyasurya ya Mrigtrishna*, *Tribheeshan ka Teevra Maadhyam* were pure punishment to sit through, but at FTII, acting students got to act in front of a camera! I would get to see myself on screen, finally find out what I actually looked like, it seemed like a thrilling place to be in. It was a time when a large number of graduates had gained immediate employment in the industry, the fallout of a couple of them having fortuitously attained stardom overnight, and FTII had become a factory for manufacturing stars. A list of its acting graduates, both male and female, from the mid sixties to the mid seventies, who enjoyed a quick but short-lived stardom would be as long as both my arms. Almost all of them also disappeared just as soon into the mist. Not looking that far ahead, however, I could see that FTII was the place to go to. Granted, I wouldn't end up prancing around trees and beating up bad guys but there seemed to be plenty of other acting employment I could land in films if I only had the FTII passport. I could play the cop who turns up in the last reel, 'Koi apni jagah se nahin hilega!' I could be the doctor who emerges and says, 'Maine injection de diya hai,' I could be the villain's henchman, 'Mal aa gaya hai Boss!' I could be the honest union leader who catches a bullet in Reel One. All I needed was one perceptive film-maker who would give me the opportunity. By the time I exited the movie theatre my mind was firmly made up. The first thing I did was go to Jaspal and confide my plan, asking him whether he thought it was a good idea, and whether he was game to go along. He seemed to see the sense in it.

One of my last performances at NSD was the lead in a production by Srilata Swaminathan, of a play called *Marjeeva* (living dead). It didn't excite me terribly but in NSD we were powerless to turn down any part we were asked to do. When we started moving the action, Srilata instead of instructing the actors asked us all to move as we felt we should and when we felt we should. I interpreted this trust of the actors' choices and regard for their abilities as sloppiness on her part and kept insisting on being given a ground plan of the moves; I was incapable of performing without one and, lazy devil that I was, could not be bothered coming up with anything on my own. Add to that my natural boorishness and arrogance and the fact that at that stage I understood nothing of what an actor is supposed to do but still managed to put on an all-knowing attitude, and you've got one noxious mix. With saintly patience Srilata kept telling me that I could move when and where I pleased and I kept insisting she tell me when and where I should move. The situation became an

Newlyweds Purveen and I.

With Heeba at 14.

Quite a few unsurprising similarities!

My parents at 17 Chaman
Estate, Mussoorie.

IITian Zaheer in his
graduation gown.

Capt. Zameer
in his army uniform.

And undergraduate Naseer in his
first proper beard.

Jaspal and I at NSD,
'a time of innocence, a time of confidences'.

Om Puri and I at NSD,
first year, flat broke;

somewhat better
days;

and really
prosperous!

GREAT PERFORMANCES

These performances from the 1970s for me touched perfection and
demonstrated the level it is possible for an actor onstage to achieve.
I still consider them the greatest theatre performances
I have ever seen anywhere in the world.

Photograph by Bal Paranjpe, courtesy Dr Agashe

Mohan Agashe in *Ghasiram Kotwal*

Photograph by Saroj Parulkar, courtesy Dr Agashe

Chandrakant Kale in *Begum Barve*

Courtesy Popular Prakashan, Mumbai

Shriram Lagoo in *Adhe Adhure*

Om Puri in the Kabuki play *Ibaragi*

Courtesy Natrang Pratishthan Nemi Chandra Jain Collection

Courtesy Arun Kakde, Aavishkar, Mumbai

Sudha Shivpuri in
Billi Chali Pehen Ke Joota

Sulabha Deshpande in
Shantata! Court Chaalu Aahe

Courtesy Vijaya Mehta

Courtesy Salima Raza

Bhakti Barve in
Ajab Nyaya Vartulacha

Salima Raza in
Azar Ka Khwab

In Mrozek's *Out at Sea*, with Jaspal, directed by Kirti Jain *(above left)*;
and *The Lesson*, with Jyoti Deshpande *(above centre)*.
Surekha Sikri seems to mirror director Srilata Swaminathan's despair
at my behaviour during a rehearsal of *Marjeeva (above right)*.

In *Danton's Death*, B. Jayshree and Rajesh Vivek watch with compassion
as I flounder in a part I was pathetically ill-equipped to play.

Mr Geoffrey Kendal as Shylock, c. late 1950s.

A private moment with Geoffrey and Laura Kendal on the sets of *Junoon*.

This moment took twenty years to arrive and was over in a flash.

impasse and ultimately about a fortnight before the play was to open, she threw in the towel and resignedly worked out my moves for me because I refused to do so myself. I had not only contributed nothing, I had mistrusted the faith she had in me, and messed up an opportunity to explore this quite novel and what should have been really exciting approach to acting. It was quite a few years before what Srilata was trying to do sank into my brain but then I could only apologize to her for my earlier stupidity. I cringe inwardly even now when I recall this episode and often wonder what I would do if I were ever to encounter an actor with the attitude I had. To my great relief none has showed up yet.

Jaspal/Shah, now certain that they wanted to go to FTII, once again were at Alkazi's door to unload. Why we felt the need to do this I don't know, but after hearing us out he blew a gasket saying I was betraying the faith he had in me. He called me a traitor to the cause of theatre and accused me of misleading others. I think he could have given Jaspal more credit than that. Alkazi for all his greatness could be unbelievably churlish at times; this was one of those times. Net result was that he barely stayed on speaking terms with either of us for the remainder of our stay. What it was that so hurt and offended him, I can still not figure out. I wonder if it ever occurred to him later that among his students in Bombay I was one of the few who actually continued to work in the theatre.

On completing their courses at NSD the students who returned to their native places would promptly attempt tatty replicas of Alkazi with themselves in the leading parts, some joined the Song and Drama division, an undertaking of the Information and Broadcasting Ministry; some got teaching jobs in schools and some got employment in radio or on TV, then in its infancy in India, and some were absorbed by the school's Repertory Company and paid 500 rupees a month. Staying on in the Rep and being paid for it was naturally considered the most secure temporary recourse for students. It was another matter altogether that most of them would hang on there for years if not decades. None of these alternatives appealed to me in the least and I thought I'd chart my own course. Alkazi in any case had made no bones about the fact that neither of us was getting into the Rep (one of the reasons given was our open use of marijuana) and on the other hand disapproved of us seeking an alternative for ourselves. 'So what am I supposed to do?' I countered. 'Sacrifice for the theatre' was his oratorical response. For once he didn't seem to be talking sense. I saw my dreams of playing Tughlaq or Danton vanish in the haze. No matter, I told myself; only a matter of time before a film of *Tughlaq* would be made and guess who would be starring in it.

R had adjusted to the US by now and her letters dwelt less on how much she missed me and so forth, they were about the excitement and stimulation she was experiencing. She persuaded me to also apply for a course in America so we could be together, something I reluctantly agreed to (even sitting for a bloody TOEFL and GRE exam) and to my relief was rejected. I was certain I had no future in America and she didn't think my going to the Film Institute was a good idea. I wouldn't get in, she predicted, 'You're not good-looking enough to be in movies.'

Jaspal/Shah went ahead with their plans, spending 25 or so rupees each getting photographs taken (close-up, three-quarter face and full figure). When the precious pictures came out I shuddered inwardly at the thought that maybe R was right after all, but recalling what Edward G. Robinson and José Ferrer, for example, looked like I felt a lot better. I decided there and then that there was no fear in going for the audition looking as I did. I mean real-looking actors like Messrs Robinson and Ferrer must have started somewhere and must surely at that time have been mocked about their looks. Since I bore absolutely no resemblance to Shammi Kapoor there was no point trying to look like him. There wasn't in fact a single actor in the world I resembled except, I feared, Anthony Quayle or the *Mad* magazine mascot Alfred E. Neuman. And anyway, why the hell should I try looking like anybody? These apparitions were not going to come to my rescue and get me work. I had to make do with what I was and if this was how I looked then this was how I looked. I would be myself and the damn film industry would have to put up with it. I hadn't a clue what was expected of film-acting aspirants, but if it was to be the preening-like-a-peacock act then I knew my chances were slim. I used to be good at that when I was in college but no longer. Now there was no alternative but to depend on what I was, I just had to convert my perceived weaknesses into my strengths.

I borrowed the colossal sum of 400 rupees from Jasdev Singh Rehncy to finance my trip to Bombay for the audition, an amount I have still not returned. I had also in the remaining months played a few small roles in *Tughlaq*, been hopelessly miscast as Danton and then played the Professor in an excellent student production of Ionesco's *The Lesson*. I had by this time been converted to Om's approach and way of working, or rather I was compelled to adopt both, considering the nature of the role in *The Lesson*. Without burning the midnight oil I could see that this time I wouldn't be able to even memorize the lines, there were so many. So for the first time in my life I found myself waking early without being compelled to and doing what was expected of me. The results that this kind of application produced were not long in coming. Most exhilarating of all, for the first time I felt

I was in complete control of what I was doing onstage. The warm praise I received for this performance, particularly from Alkazi, was therefore not entirely undeserved even though my 'betrayal' had still not been forgiven.

The entrance tests to FTII consisted of an audition and a screen test. Heading the acting department then was Professor Raushan Taneja who fortuitously, someone slightly acquainted with him informed me, had seen and liked my performance in *Chalk Circle* at Pune two years earlier. Also on the selection board were Ms Jaya Bhaduri, an FTII graduate who had shot to stardom with her first film, and Om Shivpuri, then the most celebrated NSD alumnus. Mr Shivpuri later informed me that but for him I wouldn't have got in. Evidently the big question mark that arose was why a student who had already done one acting course in theatre wanted to do another in cinema. Wouldn't I be depriving someone else of a chance? Mr Shivpuri, after turning out excellent theatre work in Delhi for more than a decade with his company Dishantar, had himself recently abandoned the theatre for more lucrative prospects in films, and I wouldn't be surprised if he did vociferously argue my case as he claimed he had. Possibly it was a combination of that and the hangover of *Chalk Circle* on Mr Taneja, with Ms Bhaduri presumably in a neutral corner, that got me in. Jaspal had gained admission as well. He had auditioned in Delhi whereas I travelled to Bombay for the same. We, or rather I, had calculated that the odds were stacked against two NSD students being chosen from the same centre. Through the kindness of a friend's sister in Bombay I got a roof over my head for the month I was there, then I moved base to Pune to stay with yet another friend's uncle until the Institute reopened and I could move into the hostel.

Admission fees plus two months' hostel rent and tuition charges had to be paid before anything could move. A grand total of 600 rupees which neither of the Zs could afford was required pronto. I shot off a telegram to Baba who, despite his reservations about my doing yet another course in acting, came through. 'You will study this bloody acting for five years?!' he had incredulously enquired, 'Might as well have become a doctor!' But a money order from the old man for the required amount arrived quicker than I had hoped. For the two years I was there, however, it was the two Zs who helped me keep body and soul together by sending me 100 rupees each month without fail. Considering they were both married now and themselves each earning something in the region of 600 rupees a month, this was magnanimity of the highest order.

Jaspal and I were allotted a room together and went through identical ordeals of the rather vicious and stupid custom of 'ragging' which I had encountered only in its mildest form in AMU. My beard, grown to disguise a weak chin, was long and straggly by now, as was Jaspal's, and we both looked anything but potential Hindi film actors. The two of us with maybe three pairs of jeans and two pairs of shoes between us (I had a suit as well, which I had worn twice at the siblings' weddings) were ragamuffins compared to the peacocks who usually populated the acting course and we were the cause of much mirth and not a few deeply cutting observations by the seniors, all in good spirit, of course, ha! ha! 'You are acting students???!!!' 'Have you seen your faces in the mirror?' 'What roles will you get?' 'Come on, show some acting!' etc. ad nauseam.

My confidence was not at an all-time high those days, and this sorry state was not helped by our screen tests being shown to the entire student body in the Main theatre. My burning desire to see what I really looked like was fulfilled at last—I had known I didn't look like Sean Connery but this was no Spencer Tracy either, not even Jerry Lewis. I looked like a frightened rabbit badly in need of a shave and a meal; all I could see was teeth. I was not the least bit reassured, sitting amid the trumpeting laughter and booing that greeted each of us on screen. On meeting my classmates, either well-hung, strapping hunks or adolescent girls out of school, most of them heavily Hindi-film-influenced flakes, I could see very clearly that Jaspal and I didn't fit into this place but I was determined not to let that faze me, or at least not to let it show. I kept to myself, and stumbled upon that part of me which revels in being alone. I was also desperately unhappy. R's last letter had sounded the death knell of our relationship. She wrote of her great need for a friend, someone to share things with; how she hated the terrible winter, 'the snow like a widow's garment'. There was also frequent mention of someone (male) who she seemed to be spending much time with. I needed no help in deciphering the writing on the wall.

The tumid conviction when I entered NSD that I knew it all and was going there to finally start plying my trade had deflated completely towards the end of my stay. My first attempt at working hard had yielded results, I began to suspect there was something more to this acting business than I knew, but hadn't a clue what it was, nor where or how to learn it. The stint at drama school gave me immense self-confidence in strutting the stage but had not really taught me the nuts and bolts of the job, and I could see it was high time I tried coming to grips with those. I was watchable onstage but had not the faintest idea why. Each performance went by like a blur—over before I knew it, and always too soon. I always felt I'd done wonderfully each time and those who were dissatisfied didn't know what they were talking about.

Now, the nagging suspicion that I had been kidding myself was fuelled by watching Om's steady growth from being a modest insecure wallflower into an actor and person of considerable assurance. I, though, was exactly the same arrogant loudmouth I had been when I joined NSD, had found nothing new, had learnt nothing in three years; the thought would hit me like one of Delhi's hot winds that in these three years I had grown only in my conceit. I hadn't gotten any better than I had been three years ago. Om without a doubt had, but I being incapable of that kind of genuine humility had instead frittered away the time, falling in and out of love with various women and thinking that was all there was to make life complete. The thought that my time there had been a total waste had to be swallowed. My adolescent boast that 'I would show the bloody world' began gradually to transform itself into a resolve to become worthy of the arrogance nature seemed to have bestowed on me in such abundance. If I wanted to survive as an actor I had to bring more than just competence and cleverness to the table and I suspected I didn't have very much more than those. It was time to learn my job.

The Film and TV Institute of India, Pune was the last place I expected it to happen though, I just needed the 'passport that would ensure entry into the film world'. No less a person than Mr K.A. Abbas, when I had gone knocking at his door, had assured me that that was exactly what the FTII acting course was.

Professor Taneja walked into class on the first day and launched into his daily ritual of changing from dark glasses to clear ones, briefly drumming two forefingers on the table edge, clearing his throat and going 'Mmmmm' for a second as if testing out his voice, and having found it working beginning to speak. That day he barely got to 'Er . . . I need someone to . . .' before I was on the floor itching to display my magnificence to the rest of the class, ready to do anything he might ask—laugh, cry, mouth magnificent dialogue, get angry, get dejected, make funny faces, stand on my head, roll on the floor; whatever he came up with I could do it. What to my astonishment he did ask me to do was go out of the door and come in again 'just that, nothing more' he added, pre-empting the 'why, what for' questions. Ah! He wants me to think about it myself, I thought. No problem. In the few seconds before entering I furiously thought about how I could make this entry interesting, assuming that was the purpose. Summoning up the pathetically scant tricks I had from my bag, I 'made an entry', deliberately tripping over the doorstep and berating an imaginary person who I had not in fact imagined at all. Barely had I begun when I heard 'Stop! Shah, you're not right for this one, sit down. Someone else please.' Completely mortified, and clueless as to what I'd done wrong, I took my seat while Vikram Mehrotra, a handsome hunk who was not really interested in acting, and who in fact later never worked as an actor, but generously provided me many a breakfast while at the Institute, took my place on the floor and executed Taneja saab's instructions to perfection. He came in through the door and stood in the middle of the floor not knowing what to do—precisely what was needed to make the point.

Prof T then, taking Vikram's watch from him, told him to repeat the action exactly, only 'this time you are coming in to get your watch', and there was a discernible sense of purpose when Vikram entered this time, no awkwardness or self-consciousness at all; he knew exactly what he had to do—look for his watch, which the Prof had concealed in a drawer. Far from performing 'exactly the same action' he was this time actually looking for his watch; he was actually thinking, and looking in places it should reasonably be. BINGO! It made sense to me instantly why I was not right for this exercise. Incapable as an actor of responding to immediate stimulus, I had always needed a map, so to say, and was lost without one.

Here one was expected to wing it, to respond on the spur, so to say; something, which despite dear Srilata's exhortations during *Marjeeva*, I had not realized was an essential requirement for an actor's work. The meaning of the word 'improvise' began to make sense. After all when in life one threads a needle one doesn't have a ground plan, so why should one be needed when handling an imaginary needle and thread? So far all I had understood of 'improvisation' was two actors each trying to say cleverer things than the other, with the wittier of the two being considered to have 'improvised well'. It was always just an improvisation of put-downs, each actor trying to outdo the other, paying no heed to creating a situation or a relationship. To make matters worse, we had often in NSD been asked, in improvisation class, to imagine ourselves as characters, the portrayal of which would strain the resources of Mr Daniel Day-Lewis himself. Without even possessing the acting chops to respond convincingly to an imaginary cup of tea, we were asked to believe in complex imaginary situations like being a roadside dweller, a beggar, a thief, or discovering a spouse's infidelity, being struck by paralysis, warning a crowd about a fire, and so forth. 'Stay true to the character' was a constant admonition without any guidance at all towards understanding even the physical characteristics we were asked to represent. We were just told to believe we were these people, we were expected to 'fully understand' and represent the character's behaviour without even being given a context. The Stanislavskian phrases 'super-objective' and 'emotional memory' and 'psychological gesture' were flung around quite a bit without anyone ever explaining them or illustrating what they meant and they were invariably misunderstood.

Now, for a change we were being told to 'throw characterization out of the window' and perform each action as ourselves, the attempt being to help us understand our own behaviour and reflexes. More importantly, it began to become clear that when you enter a scene, you are coming from somewhere to somewhere else and unless you know where and why in both cases all you will manage is to attempt a 'great entry', the very narcissistic trap I had fallen into and made a habit of. Along the way since then I have managed to extricate myself from this pit of self-absorption. We had been taught at NSD how to stand effectively onstage, how to be bang on cue, how to handle costumes, how to catch the light, how to project the voice; how, in short, to make a good picture. We were made to learn the Five Ws (who, why, what, where, when) by rote like the two-times-two table, but no one had been able to emphasize the importance of applying them, much less bothering to explain how they were to be applied.

What in FTII we were instead being asked to do had the elements of organically incorporating the Five Ws: 'plan nothing but the intention behind the action'. I had never heard these words at NSD. Prof T went further that day and said, while looking pointedly at me, 'Some of you have a lot to unlearn.' The words 'entry', 'exit', 'props', 'costumes', 'settings', etc. were to be expelled from our vocabulary. Whatever we would perform was to be unplanned (not unthought about though) and, most significantly, as ourselves not as an imaginary character. I was tempted to ask right away what I should do when playing someone different from myself, but desisted from jumping the gun. What had been said so far had made enormous sense and a weak ray of light was peeping through the cracks. I figured I would get some answers in good time.

Mr Taneja himself, after studying under Lee Strasberg at the Actors' Studio in New York, had returned to India to take over the acting department when the Institute was founded. He was in every way the absolute antithesis of Alkazi: somewhat rotund, with a head of unruly curly hair, cheerful, unfailingly patient and fully inclined to overlook minor disciplinary infractions. Adored as he was by both the current students and the successful ones who often made the pilgrimage to Pune to pay obeisance, I have no idea how seriously he took himself but having your feet touched on a regular basis by the country's biggest stars must have some effect on a man's psyche. Taneja saab seemed to take it all with many grains of salt. He seemed distant initially but with time I grew to love him deeply and feel tremendous gratitude for his concern and for opening my mind to what it is possible to learn as an actor.

Watching movies in languages other than Hindi or English, from countries other than England or the US explained to me why I found most of the acting in Indian movies so unbearably false. Compared to the level of understanding of life and of their work those Italian, Polish, Czech, Japanese writers and actors seemed to have, our writing and performing were infantile. The kind of acting I was now witnessing was, I realized, what I had always been after. I had no interest any longer in mastering the craft of running around trees or playing larger-than-life characters. I knew that was not my métier anyway, this kind of acting was.

I began to grapple with figuring out how actors in these mostly European movies could be so watchable and so real at the same time, and found my thoughts veering perilously close to 'only that which is real is watchable' which is (not so) obviously untrue, but which took a while to distil into a coherent realization. Laurence Olivier and Toshiro Mifune, for example, are both highly watchable but hardly 'real'. I thought I could figure out how these two giants did what they did; but how Dustin Hoffman, who I had then seen only in

The Graduate, or Per Oscarsson, a little-known but truly great Swedish actor, or Jean-Louis Trintignant, the Frenchman, who were also obviously 'acting' could, while doing it, appear so completely without artifice boggled my mind. These actors did not seem to be pretending, they seemed to be the characters they were playing, their poise was so utterly appropriate. HOW DID THEY DO IT?? I knew for certain that this was what I wanted to make myself capable of and I had a hunch that what we were being taught at FTII was a baby step towards that. And I had expected to be taught how to lip-synch to mediocre songs! My excitement, to coin a phrase, knew no bounds. I was going to enjoy learning at last, that was quite enough to dispel the not inconsiderable grief of R's desertion.

This elusive word 'method' was beginning to reveal itself at last. All the psychotropia available at reasonable prices then also provided a much-needed refuge from reality, pushing me further into the tunnel of beginning to learn what it is an actor actually does when he acts. This was a thought that, incidentally, had long bothered me; why actors could never be articulate about their work, why they almost always resorted to specious befuddlements: 'acting is nothing but farting about in disguises', 'no job for a grown-up', 'just the art of keeping a large group of people from coughing'. Or pseudo-mysticisms: 'I try to find my centre', 'I lose myself in the part', 'I become the character and everything just follows', while (actually not) describing what they do and how they do it. This reluctance to pass on anything but tricks of the trade means that the only thing in the possession of such actors is tricks of the trade. If acting is indeed a craft like a carpenter's, why do most actors find it impossible to explain how in their work, the wood so to say is sawed into the required shapes and the pieces put together to create. AND more important is the purpose of it all simply to play different roles, to grab eyeballs, to display your wares? 'Look at me! Look at me! Look at me!' as Sir Laurence reportedly described it once. In that case to what end? The answer is so glaringly simple that most actors do not confront it ever. But trying to figure out what an actor's role in the scheme of things really is, and trying to understand the dynamics that go into creating a moment of acting truth has been a long, often dark, sometimes blindingly illuminating, sometimes hopeless sojourn, but I am still in the tunnel and it is my spot. This is where I live. The light at the end of the tunnel is reassuring though, and in the past many torches have been lit along the way.

The term 'method' is an Americanism and probably coined in the US by, and as a result of, some of Stanislavsky's most notable pupils staying on to teach in that country after the historic early-twentieth-century Moscow Art Theatre tour. Stanislavsky himself, it is recorded somewhere, was not an overly gifted actor and therefore it is assumed he felt the need to create or discover for himself a system which did not rely upon cleverness in improvising or an innate ability to entertain, or in 'seizing the moment'. He wished to uncover a system not dependent on something as indefinable and unpredictable as a 'good day' or 'inborn talent'; a way of approaching acting that was based on accurate human behaviour; a system that would work regardless of audience reaction or of how the actor was feeling that day, one that would point the actor in the right direction, which would be more or less foolproof, a system which could actually be defined and practised.

In a reaction against the kind of shallow theatricality that was the norm in those days, Stanislavsky emphasized what he called 'psychological truth' by which he meant accuracy of behaviour, and finding the route to that behaviour by an empathy with the character's situation and an understanding of his relation to everything around. It was a fortunate accident for everyone that coinciding with, and complementing, Stanislavsky's research were the efforts of the playwright Anton Chekhov, who too helped break the mould of the 'larger than life' characters peopling the stage then and created dramatic works about the aspirations of the less privileged, the common people. The first conscious practitioners of the Stanislavsky system in cinema were probably American actors, or at least they were the ones with the highest profile, and thus became the best known for it. It also became an excuse for many incompetent actors to justify their shoddy work, and the accusations of the 'bum scratching, nose picking style of acting', as it was referred to by many detractors soon after, were not entirely misplaced. The psychologically driven style of acting personified by the early Brando very soon degenerated into as codified a manner of expressing as the older, staid, oratorical style. For evidence of the two vastly differing schools of acting, both then at their zenith, one has only to watch Messrs Brando and Gielgud in the same frame in Joseph Mankiewicz's film *Julius Caesar*.

Film, only a director's medium?

The December vacation began and at FTII there was no question of hanging around in the hostel—the celebrated tradition of students staying on as long as they like, often much after completing their courses, started some years later. Jaspal/Shah managed tickets to Delhi, and since I had no desire to meet the folks and was dying to meet up with and show off to old pals at NSD, we stayed on there as guests of Om Puri who in turn was rooming up with a friend (male) he had made in the interim. Bhanu Bharti who had directed the 'award winning' production of *The Lesson* in our final year was readying a production of *Hamlet* in Hindi with Om playing the title role, and asked me if I would play Claudius. I was on the verge of saying yes when another ex-classmate asked me to act in his production of a new Hindi play called *Tilchatta* (the cockroach) by the writer of *Marjeeva*. Even though it was more bizarre and less comprehensible than that one, I said yes. Being produced by the Repertory Company, there were to be ten performances so I asked for a payment of 100 rupees a performance, I was promised 50. I immediately accepted. It was not uncommon for the Repertory to pay actors employed from outside, but apparently when Alkazi later heard of my demand, he was livid. But it was too late, I had made my packet.

Everything else about *Tilchatta*, however, sucked in spades. Apart from being an incompetent production, the script was easily one of the most demented pieces of dramatic writing I have ever had the bad fortune to engage with. Equating humans with cockroaches and presenting a dysfunctional marital situation through predictable tableaux, utterly ludicrous character interaction and the kind of moribund dialogue the writer must have heard in his nightmares, it was pure brain-damage. I have only on one other occasion (in a disastrous production of *Cyrano* at the National Theatre in London some twenty years later) been involved in a play where when it was show time I felt like fleeing, when it was on I hated every second, and when it was over I wanted to cut my throat as soon as possible. My wife Ratna, then still in school, came to see *Tilchatta* she told me, and still remembers it, but we were at that time very far from knowing each other. Anyway, this production, for whatever it was worth, saw me through the next month and even subsidized my journey back to Pune.

The instructors in acting at FTII were ex-students who were kept on the payroll through the goodness of Prof T's heart. These poor bumbling travesties of acting teachers could scarce comprehend what they had been taught, perish the thought of passing anything on. What they did manage to pass off as teaching, while trying very hard and unsuccessfully to assume Taneja's saab's air of wisdom, was a small imitation of his jargon. My second stint with yogic excercises, the first having been with an ex-typist-turned-yoga instructor at NSD, proved as disastrous as the first and I became convinced that practising yoga was as useless for me as the 'playback' class. I foolishly avoided both these classes through my stay at these respective institutes, not even appearing for my playback exam and getting through because by the time I was due to leave, Taneja saab seemed to have lost all interest in the Institute.

Jaspal/Shah, both unwashed, always together, both bearded, both perennially stoned, both from the theatre, both unlikely candidates for the Hindi film world, not so strangely in FTII too were treated as the same person right from the start, probably being perceived yet again as one, or at least as identical. I suppose both of us somehow believed it too and kind of enjoyed it. How vastly different we actually were from each other would become apparent over the next two years.

Ram Gopal Bajaj, an elder from NSD who had befriended us both and who had been extremely supportive and encouraging even when I hadn't deserved it, first pointed it out to me when during our next short break from FTII, rather than going home, both of us spent the time at Chandigarh where Bajju bhai as he was known was heading the University Theatre department. In the month we stayed there Bajju bhai directed us in *Ajaatghar*, a two-hander written by Rameshwar Prem, and it was the cause of many heated arguments. Bajju bhai, being strictly old school, emphasized the importance of diction and clarity while emoting, and we were determined to thoroughly indulge in our rudimentary understanding of the 'method'. The play was performed, not without success, in Chandigarh and later in Delhi.

During *Ajaatghar* Bajju bhai expressed to me his concerns about Jaspal. We were not at all the same kind of person, he felt, and he was not at all sure this friendship would last; in fact he confessed it might be dangerous for me, I should try and go my way and let him go his. I was convinced he was talking nonsense then but in the light of what happened three years later, I have to believe that either Bajju bhai was clairvoyant or he had an incisive understanding of people. It was in the second year at FTII that the separation of personalities, and perceptions, began to take place. I moved into a single room, a perk for having stood first in the class here. A distance began to develop though we still smoked together all the time; and instead of eating, frequently endangered our health and our sanity with huge doses of Dexedrine to trip and then Mandrax to sleep. I should have detected the first sign of trouble when Jaspal said to me with just the hint of a grimace, 'Arre! WE came first yaar!' but I took it to be an affirmation of undying friendship.

So taken was I with what I was learning at FTII that I had prevailed upon Om, who was then in the NSD Rep, to come there as well, which he had; and after undergoing the humiliating rituals that are every newcomer's lot to endure, had settled down not very happily. He was dissatisfied and seemed uninterested in what had so greatly excited me. Not so strange, considering that Prof T's participation in the department was now minimal and the students were now completely at the mercy of the instructors. Om's second year, in fact, coincided with the strike and cessation of all work for practically the entire second half of that term.

The students of direction were entrusted with making, in their first year, a silent 5-minute film as an exercise in continuity, and then a 10-minute film with dialogue; in their second year a mise en scène and an ad film; and in their final year a song, a documentary and a 40-minute feature known as the 'diploma' film. Though acting students, and invariably the same ones, were mostly cast in these exercises, it was the diploma films which were naturally considered most important by all students as a show-reel to get work in the industry, and acting students were not necessarily cast in those. And that is where all the trouble started.

It was being whispered that the acting course was to close down and Prof T was involved in setting up an institute of his own in Bombay, so he was seldom present through our closing few months, also managing to be diplomatically absent when we the students of acting were with extreme fervour pressing our demands to be included in the student diploma films— an event that forced the Institute into temporary limbo and hastened the closure of the acting course.

It is not unlikely that my blood pressure will begin to climb when I recount the incidents which led among other things to a hunger strike, which completed the isolation of the student actors, made the chasm between them and those of other courses unbridgeable, created lasting animosities, and a heartburn that hasn't yet subsided. Arguments on integrity or lack of it were traded, all actors were bunched together into one generic group, a group that was in some way 'special' but not special enough to warrant inclusion in student projects. Whereas a cameraman or editor or recordist could not be recruited from outside the student body, the student directors were permitted free rein in their choice of actors— they could cast anyone they liked, acting student or not. There were actually students of acting who went through their two years without once facing a camera. When we made the first noises of dissatisfaction about this, the not even half-truthful justification about the age limitation of the acting students (most between eighteen and twenty-five) was trotted out to justify the student directors ignoring the acting department as material for their films. I encountered not for the only time the vanity of film-makers who refuse to acknowledge actors as an essential component of film-making and regard them only as a necessary evil to be put up with.

Preparations for making that year's diploma films had begun and teams were being assembled. Some actors, myself included, received more than one offer, while some didn't get any at all. Those who didn't had also been through the two-year course and we were all equally untested, so it was not a matter of confirmed capability. This judgemental behaviour of the direction students—ignoring actors whose prerogative it was to be included in the diploma films—was quite insufferable, as was the fact that outside actors were often cast for absolutely no reason but the flimsy 'my conception' and 'perfect casting' argument. That many of the worthies who as students were resolute on demanding complete freedom in casting the characters as they had 'conceived' them, and refused to 'be dictated to by bloody actors' later went on to willingly genuflect to the star system in the real tinsel world as far as casting goes, is another story.

Without mincing words, but deleting the expletives that rise like bile every time I recall all this, we student actors thought there was something mighty rotten with this situation. It stank. Apart from the fact of student actors missing out on what should have been an assured part of their training not being perceived as an injustice, it just didn't seem to sit well with anyone that we actors were asking to be considered as essential participants in the making of the films, on par with the technicians. We had to concede that none of us could be cast as a child, and as for playing older than one's age, well we all knew it has never been done in the history of acting! Despite giving in to these two conditions, our stand that apart from these cases only acting students were to be considered for leading parts in diploma films was considered to be 'limiting the film-makers' vision'.

The students of acting by and large, it must be said, had over the years not exactly endeared themselves to their colleagues in

other courses, had shown scant interest in anything to do with
the film-making process, had seldom or never stepped into
an editing room, had in fact isolated themselves during their
student days; and to make matters worse, many undeserving
ones had landed up at least for a short while on top of the heap
when it came to breaking through in the big bad movie world.
Not so surprising then that this aggravated the resentment
felt by students of other courses who, despite slogging away
and being good at their work, did not reap half the rewards
even an indifferent actor could if his luck was in. Flaunting
their newfound wealth and celebrity, or for those who hadn't
found either, flaunting the attitude of being somehow entitled
to both became the nature of the FTII students of acting;
all were marking time before the big band started to play for
them. All of them seemed well prepared for a life of fame as
if that were an end in itself, and learnt all the wrong things
along the way.

It was largely this not erroneous perception of the acting
course students that got us no sympathy whatever during
our agitation. A number of students from the other courses
who privately claimed to agree with us did not hold the fort
when it came to the crunch; and the crunch came very quickly.
The actors went on a hunger strike demanding that their
conditions be met and the battle lines were instantly drawn,
'Actors vs the Rest'. We were outnumbered, outmanoeuvred,
bushwhacked and slaughtered. We had no one on our side—
not the establishment, not the staff, not the other students,
not the press, which though not quite as rapacious as today,
happily jumped into the act to report that we were 'holding
the institute to ransom' by 'making unreasonable demands';
we had 'misbehaved' with a hotshot government official, one
Mr Jamal Kidwai, then Secretary in the I&B ministry who,
lighting his pipe, imperiously waved us away when we went to

explain our stand to him, so we gheraoed him but still couldn't get his ear; we had been 'rude to veteran film makers', actually only to Mr Hrishikesh Mukherji who tried explaining to us in words of two syllables why in movies the director is so much more important than the actor and was told by us to cut the baby talk. Apart from a token attempt to reach out to us made by Mr Mrinal Sen we found no one willing to even listen to our point of view. Girish Karnad, then the director, evidently still considers the strike to have happened 'for the silliest of reasons'. We were branded complete villains in the whole affair, thoroughly reviled, threatened with expulsion and even arrest. The police was brought in to keep the peace when arguments started getting out of hand on the third day. Girish, harassed beyond endurance, was on the verge of signing a scrap of paper conceding what we wanted. He never actually did but with our hunger and our demands reaching fever pitch he engaged with us and assured us justice would be done. He promised to personally make sure no acting student was left out of the diploma films. We ended our agitation, not suspecting it was all a ploy to facilitate Mr I&B's sneak exit from the back gate. The Institute was immediately declared closed and we were all asked to go home until further notice.

Through this episode Jaspal/Shah had played identical roles together: representing the actors, making the statements, taking the lead in the agitation, deciding courses of action. Now we began to differ. I saw no point in continuing a fight I could see we were losing, he wanted to 'fight to the death for our cause'. I was not sure what use we would be to any cause, dead.

Zoo story

Jaspal/Shah together scraped up enough to buy second-class unreserved tickets on the train to Delhi. If we'd had reserved seats or even if we'd had no tickets at all it would have mattered not a whit and we would still have been treated for the next twenty-two hours or so to the most memorable train journey of our lives. That day in 1974 coincided with the Indian Railways declaring a massive nationwide strike. This train was the very last one heading to Delhi for at least a few days. We had long since run through all our friends' hospitality quotients in Bombay, and the hostel in the Institute was out of bounds for us—nowhere to go, we just had to be on that train. That turned out to be so for a few thousand others as well. Our tickets in our pockets, we arrived well in time, so we thought; one look at the train already in position wiped the smug look off our faces for the next two days. There were people jammed in the doorways, half-leaning out of windows, clambering on to the roof, suspended between compartments, hanging on to every conceivable hand or foot-hold. Navigating through the sea of people and getting to the train seemed impossible. The coolie who, in return for the 10 rupees we handed him earlier, had promised us a berth had been swallowed in the mob. Using whatever strength we had and every manner of persuasion, we managed to get to the compartment door and when the heaving mass of humanity moved a few inches further in we got on board; a few others tried clambering in after us but there was no more room to move until some really observant soul discovered the toilet unoccupied. Half a dozen passengers accommodated themselves in it and a few more squeezed aboard. Through that journey every single one of us there, no exaggeration, stayed on the same spot. So did those with berths, incidentally, because each berth was housing at least a half-dozen, if not more occupants. After a while, magically, all of us on the floor managed to sit where we stood and even managed a wink or so of sleep. The very intrepid ones even managed to alight at various stations to relieve themselves. I could not risk losing my precious space, stayed put, and my bladder and alimentary canal held out somehow. In any case we had no money to eat or drink and nothing in our stomachs to digest or emit.

No one was enterprising enough to come checking tickets on the journey and the tide of humanity that arrived at New Delhi was too large to monitor and swept out of the station unmolested. I felt just a nibble of regret over losing good money on those damn tickets. Then straight to the old NSD hostel for a free meal, to meet up with old pals and clean up— this last took some doing. Bajju bhai, known for his unstinting generosity to everyone, was temporarily on velvet with one of his pipe dreams, a Hindi poetry-recording project to be financed by a small-time industrialist, set to take off shortly, a novel idea for India but way ahead of its time. Despite some pretty heavy-duty recording machines and vinyl-disc cutting equipment being imported, it ultimately came to naught. For the duration of the dream though, Bajju bhai was provided with a car and driver and was lodged in a furnished bungalow, which was open house to all, on Malcha Marg, one of Delhi's high-end neighbourhoods.

A lonely dreamer who had turned widower a couple of years ago, with an infant son and an immense store of affection and large-heartedness, he took us in to stay and I managed to bite his ear for the bus fare to Meerut where my parents, having come down from the Mussoorie winter, were staying in Dada Dipti's bungalow 'Masoom Villa'; the very same place from which I had fled to Bombay. Whether being there had reminded Baba of that misadventure or he believed what the papers had said about us acting students, I was received with a stormy look and the curt enquiry about whether I now intended to drive my teachers mad. 'How dare you challenge them? You think you know better?!' I felt like a moron, having come there hoping for comfort and understanding. Though I hadn't the energy to explain the whole Gordian-knot situation to him, I unenthusiastically tried and suddenly I just didn't care; he wouldn't understand anyway, he had made up his mind. 'Arrogance', 'stupidity', 'insubordination' were some of the terms he hit me with. I didn't 'know what I was doing', I had 'gone mad smoking that damn charas', what right did I have thinking I was 'superior to everyone' when I had in fact always been 'a stupid ass'. Was I 'trying to be a bloody communist going on strike'? He knew less than nothing about what had led to the agitation but he had not waited to pass judgement. The strain of the past three weeks, the unsympathetic situation at the Institute, the hungry stomach, empty pockets, having to eat crow after having been flag-bearer for a cause we believed in, all combined to make me snap. Ammi, just bringing in something to eat, found me on my way out and witnessed for the only time in her life one of her children yelling back at their father. I told him I knew he could not tolerate my presence, well I had news for him—the feeling was mutual, I had never cared for him just as he had never cared for me and I knew he just wanted an excuse to lose me. I told him he was done with me forever. As I went on frothing at the mouth, he stayed silent but hurt and fear appeared in his eyes. I picked up my bag to go but he did not move. Had it not been for Ammi's intervention at that moment I would probably never have gone anywhere near him again. So convinced was I that he deserved to be told all this that I was oblivious to how deep a wound I was inflicting. Ammi managed to hush us both up and made me stay for another two days, but in those two days he and I saw each other as little as possible and Ammi was practically an emissary.

I was dying to unburden myself and put their minds at rest about the clarity and integrity of my intentions but conversation would just not take off. When I was leaving, he typically stuffed a 100 rupee note into my hand with a gruff admonition to behave myself and not smoke too much. Ammi hugged me warmly and told me to 'try and understand him'. I left feeling drained, my heart weighing a ton. I had been too optimistic in hoping to be able to get through to Baba, but I had desperately wished that we might just find some contact if I talked to him seriously and feelingly about my work. I now knew for sure I was to find no meeting point with him, and that we had absolutely nothing in common, not even a desire to be friends.

It was made clear to the acting students that their conditions would not be met, and the Institute would not reopen until we gave in. When we finally received the blanket 'no' to our demand that only acting students be cast in the diploma films and that every student of acting get an equal opportunity, we decided that in that case none of us would appear in any diploma film. Not only was this stand accepted with an alacrity that surprised and hurt us but it also caused a falling-out among the acting students—some of whom were feeling that this ado over nothing much was endangering their one chance to display their wares. As a sop, the Institute offered to make films specially designed for the acting course students; films in which all actors would be accommodated. What still stings after all these years is that it occurred to no one to grant actors the same right accorded to any other member of the unit—the right to be considered an integral part of the whole, something that should be true of any team, particularly a unit in a film school where pulling together and contributing is supposed to be encouraged and where you are supposed to be taught to make do with what you are given, be it a particular camera or a particular actor. There was never any acknowledgement of actors being anything but a 'headache to be put up with', and the talk was always about 'appeasing the actors' or 'accommodating them', never about the necessity of 'working with them'.

The strike ended in disarray, 'acting course films' were promised to each of us and the Institute was to reopen in a month. We retreated and went our respective ways, but not before Jaspal had subjected me to a passionate and almost violent harangue on how I was a sell-out and a double-crosser and had betrayed the entire class, even though the decisions were taken in consultation with all present, some conveniently not being present of course.

The muddy taste that all this left in my mouth didn't last long, Ahmed Muneer from Bangladesh, a recent entrant to NSD, was to direct Albee's *Zoo Story* for a theatre festival at the American Cultural Centre, and asked me if I would like to play Jerry in it. In the audience, apart from the glitterati of the city, were to be the celebrated critic and writer Mr Jerome

Lawrence who was visiting. Muneer had an experiment in mind, which after my brief taste of applying the method at FTII, I enthusiastically endorsed. The idea was that since the two characters in the play have never met, the two actors playing them should not meet before the performance either, ergo we were to rehearse separately and meet only as the characters onstage. Thoroughly half-baked though this notion was, both the other actor Ravi Baswani, a long-time friend, and I found it worth pursuing. Muneer rehearsed with the two of us separately and had had a design on hand for a while.

I entered without apprehension into this play of which I had understood not a word in college but which on reading now, funnily all seemed to make complete sense. In the light of having to carry the burden of the uncertainty of my life, not to talk of the sense of failure and rejection I was in those days carting around as well, it is no wonder that Jerry's despair at the failure of human contact, the impossibility of getting across, his paradoxical need for and shunning of human company and his anger at God 'who turned his back on the whole thing some time ago' found such a resonance in my own frustrations. I sank all twenty-eight teeth into the role with relish, it began to consume me and it seemed to be controlling me. For the month that we prepared, I tried to make the words my own by saying them repeatedly. I would speak them all the time regardless of where I happened to be—walking down the street, travelling in DTC buses, eating at dhabas; I would corner strangers in a park, trying to engage them in what I was saying but succeeded mostly in frightening them away. Through this month, financed by Muneer, who was on a Colombo Plan scholarship and always flush, we did LSD rather more frequently than we should have; the last trip featuring a vivid state that felt as if my mind was a plank of wood being split lengthwise, then a tactile hallucination which scared the shit right out of me and gave me (later, on reflection) an insight into why people believe they have seen or felt the presence of the supernatural, and drove me to what was probably the limit of my sanity.

The mistake we made was to drop the stuff before the sun had set. By the time it started to take effect, the sunlight had turned orange and every colour began to practically glow and turn almost fluorescent. The psychedelic beauty of all this escaped me totally because I began to worry about having no more sun for the next twelve hours. Unable to cope with the growing dark, and after unwittingly transmitting a couple of visual hallucinations to a bemused Vikram Mehrotra, who was on nothing at all, we descended from the terrace where we had been. My head aflame with colours that don't exist and buzzing with the most mind-bending, never-before-thought-of ideas, all destined to disappear with the sunrise, I was descending the stairs when another brilliant idea, one I could put into action right away hit me. I would visit the lady with whom I had recently ended the liaison we'd shared for a year or so (I suppose I should mention that I had hardly been faithful to R in her absence). The lysergic acid diethylamide I had ingested that day kicked off some dusty memory and in the throes of its ecstatic enlightenment, the urge to repair this relationship suddenly began to seem like the right thing to do.

I knew she wouldn't particularly want to see me again but I was determined she would, tonight—maybe I was just curious about what sex on LSD would be like. I was stepping through the door that led to the road when a hand stopped me dead in my tracks. I couldn't see the hand but felt it quite clearly right bang in my solar plexus where the ribs join, and there was no mistaking the shape and the touch of that hand—it was hers. So utterly tangible was the feeling that it completely immobilized me, I couldn't move. The message came through loud and clear. It was her telling me not to come. Retracing my steps and recovering whatever was left of my addled wits, I went back into Muneer's room and launched into a dozen different renditions of 'The Story of Jerry and the Dog', hallucinated some more looking at a poster of Hendrix, then read the screenplay of the weird *El Topo* which made no sense whatsoever even in that state, nor incidentally did the film, on a sober viewing many years later. We then walked to India Gate to look at the sunrise, with Jerry's words bouncing around in my head all the time and often bursting out of my mouth; I just couldn't have enough of them.

Before the performance, Muneer thought I should not even have seen the theatre or the set. Ravi would be ready and seated onstage at show time, I was to wait at the NSD hostel, five minutes away, and Muneer would accompany me to the theatre and straight to the wing onstage from where I was to enter. The idea was that I should be completely unfamiliar with the space as well. Whether or not he had taken equal pains to ensure that Ravi (whose character visits the spot frequently) was thoroughly familiar with the space, I do not know. But all went according to plan, I entered on time and the performance went without a hitch except it was a little more chaotic than it would have been had we rehearsed together.

A few seconds after stepping onstage I knew that this esoteric call Muneer had made was not going to pay off in any way. If we had indeed gone all the way down that route then it should also have been an actor I had never seen before. The great experiment didn't yield any earth-stopping results but so solid was my conviction that at last I had found a mouthpiece to express myself through—these were the things I myself wanted to say—that I had worked harder on this performance than I had ever done on anything before. And boy, had it turned out to be fun. The mordant humour and

Jerry's seemingly disconnected bits of banter cutting closer and closer to the bone as the action progresses was a joyride. The play in any case has genuine tour-de-force possibilities for the actor playing Jerry and given the unstoppable intensity of Albee's language in delivering his nihilistic message, and the fact that I found myself in complete empathy with the character, the performance actually worked. My earlier flair for showing off had not been fully tempered but had taken a few knocks and so 'brash' would not now be apt to describe my attitude.

Feeling self-congratulatory after a performance was not new to me, I was usually very pleased with myself regardless of how I'd done, but for the first time since *The Lesson* I knew that this performance hadn't happened by chance or because of 'my natural talent'; it had happened because I'd worked like a demon on it, I had been in control of what I was doing, it had not gone by like a blur. I kind of knew now what was good and what was not good about it and kind of knew why. The heady thought occurred that I may be making progress at last, I may at last be learning how to act. Over the next few years I performed the same play several times and was gradually able to tone down the 'emotional muscularity' as Bajju bhai had called it, of the first performance, and was able to find the 'great weariness' the writer asks for. Also present at the first performance, apart from Mr Lawrence, to my surprise and delight were Alkazi and Girish Karnad, both of whom complimented me effusively. I wallowed in this euphoria for a few days before heading back to Pune. The Institute had reopened.

Two pleasant surprises awaited me on arrival in Pune with a third bigger one on its way. The first was that the Guru Dutt

scholarship I had been awarded at the end of the first year had
finally come through and I was suddenly rolling in money as
the previous year's backlog also, 200 rupees a month for the
last eighteen months, had been added to my hastily opened
bank account; and further, I would receive 200 rupees a month
for the remainder of my stay at FTII. The second surprise was
a letter from R informing me that her course had given over
and she, abandoning plans of looking for employment in the
US, was returning and would probably come to Bombay for
that purpose. I wondered what kind of work she would get;
she was good at neither acting nor directing. She was very
good-looking but I couldn't really see her acting in Hindi
films, still less see her being an assistant director—she was
way too opinionated for that, and I knew she was incapable of
roughing it out the way I was going to have to. She sounded
somewhat downcast, but said she would visit me in Pune. My
heart sang at the possibility. I sent off three letters right away,
two to both Zs thanking them for their generosity and faith
in me and telling them that now the skies had opened I was
no longer on the dole. The third letter was to R.

The Institute administration was now no longer bothering
to negotiate with the acting course; in any case we had been
trounced. Work resumed and the status quo was restored; the
directors were free to cast who they pleased and some actors
began giving in to the lure of the offer of a film or two and
blithely reneged on our agreement to not act in any diploma
films at all. As consolation, the actors not cast in diploma
films were told they'd each be given 1000 feet of raw stock
which any four of them could pool together to shoot and
edit into a 20-minute short and they could get anyone at all,
including non-students, to direct it. Despite the fact that it

would be practically impossible to find willing and capable film-makers for our needs, most actors promptly accepted this arrangement but to me it was the death knell of any chance of a rapprochement with the students of direction, with whom we were supposed to share training, work and growth; and it certainly was the final nail in the coffin of isolation into which the acting students were to be henceforth confined, away from the rest of the student body.

Surprise Number 3 was a summons to Girish's office whence I proceeded with some trepidation, to be informed by him that he had been sufficiently moved by my performance in *Zoo Story* to mention it to Shyam Benegal who right then was casting for his second film to be shot the next month. I daresay he also warned Shyam that casting me would be at his own peril; I was trouble, unreasonable, opinionated, hot-headed, and a dope-smoker, something verified by others later, all of whom I imagine also verified that I was no chump as far as acting went. Anyway, the upshot of it was that I was to go to Bombay to meet him as soon as I could.

I got a seat on an early-morning bus to Bombay the next day and arrived at Shyam Benegal's Pedder Road residence much earlier than he or his wife Nira had expected me to. She was on the balcony reading a newspaper when I showed up and I encountered Nira's legendary 'frosty glare' for the first time. It took a while for me to see beyond that facade before which better men than me have wilted, and to recognize the tremendous warmth and affection she is capable of. But that morning, boy, did the frosty glare do its bit. Seeing a bedraggled stranger enter her home at this hour, she swept resignedly out of the room and it occurred to me that this must be tough to deal with, and that this must happen to film people all the time. Trying to keep my voice from shaking and my knees from knocking I mumbled an apology, which was ignored. To my great relief I was left alone until my breathing returned to normal.

In a minute or two I sensed that I was being watched and turned to see Mr Benegal himself, freshly bathed and dressed, smiling down at me from his bedroom doorway. His smile I later learned was as famous as Nira's ice-lady look. His relaxed demeanour, his gentle baritone, his firm warm handshake immediately put me at ease. He asked me a few things about myself, all the while looking closely at me and glancing without disapproval at my custom-made (from Aligarh) cowboy boots and corduroy denim jacket. The character he was considering me for, he told me, was that of a dhoti-kurta wearing young brother of an Andhra village landlord, quite different from the way I looked. I had recently rid myself of my beard or else I may not have got the part—my face with a beard looks drastically different from my face without it. He assured me that I seemed right for the part age-wise, besides Girish thought highly of me and he felt more or less certain about me. I asked if I would need to do a screen test or if he wanted to see some acting but he waved all that away and as the conversation progressed it began to feel like a sure thing. He narrated the script in brief and my part in some detail: a rather simple-minded younger sibling to three tyrannical village landlords. The character, though married, gets badly smitten by a village schoolmaster's wife who his brothers then kidnap to do him a favour.

Among the other actors were Girish himself playing the schoolmaster, the central part; and Shabana Azmi, whose performance in *Ankur* I had greatly admired, playing the female lead. Then there were to be Amrish Puri and Mohan Agashe, both of whom I had seen on the stage several times, and amongst all these tigers I had so far beheld from much below, my part was in fact the second lead! My euphoria hit

the ceiling when Shyam told me I should come back the next
week to sign the contract. Things had gone so fast my head
was reeling. As I left his house I was tempted to pinch myself,
I knew I was really awake but if I was dreaming then, hell, I'd
rather stay asleep, this was too good a dream. Even though
there had been no mention of money yet, it was a given that
apart from getting the job I would be paid real money to do
it. I didn't dare dwell on how much but there were sure to be
quite a few zeroes in the sum. I kept telling myself something
would happen to fuck it up, he would probably find someone
better-looking to do the part, and I began steeling myself for
the disappointment to hit me but for the moment I had been
told the part was mine. I returned to Pune astride a cloud.

If I could have hired a rickshaw fitted with a loudspeaker I
would have driven into the Institute blaring forth the news. I
thanked Girish warmly but he only advised me against talking
about it yet to anyone at all, 'Many a slip . . .' I asked if my
taking two months off for the shoot if I was chosen would be
all right, he with a nudge and a wink assured me he would be
taking the two months off as well. Ignoring Girish's advice, I
dashed off a letter giving the joyous news to R and practically
making plans to live with her when she came to Bombay; I
would actually be earning good money from now on. Her
reply was unenthusiastic; in any case she was never a dreamer.
Hard as nails in her pragmatism she could probably visualize
the kind of poky life I would actually end up living in Bombay
better than I could and she didn't fancy it.

I was self-righteously furious that she planned to look
for work in the hospitality business and not in the theatre.
'There's no future in the theatre,' quoth she. After having
lived on theatre scholarships for five years, having taken
up a place and received a stipend which another aspiring
enthusiast wishing to contribute to theatre could have put

to better use, she was now ready to throw it all away, wanting to be a damn lobby-manager or receptionist. It made no sense to me. Severely tempted though I was to dish out Alkazi's 'betrayal' lecture to her verbatim, I desisted for I could see that theatre and acting and everything that was my life's blood had been for her, and in truth for most other NSD girls then, a means of merely hanging around there until a suitable boy, marriage proposal in hand, appeared on the horizon. She was not coming to Bombay to be with me but to shop for a husband. I decided I would try to woo her back nonetheless and make her believe that nothing could stop my career now. She had always told me she loved me but had also always told me she couldn't foresee a future together and she was intelligent and honest enough with herself to recognize that I was at that time incapable of giving her the kind of life she craved. I realized later she was right in believing this; she wanted to marry, settle down, have children; I was still in the process of building my career and of course 'in films there is no guarantee of regular work'. She believed love could not withstand an empty stomach, I believed it could withstand anything.

The following Friday I returned to Bombay to meet Shyam and was told that the colossal sum of 10,000 rupees would be mine in return for working in this film. I had a thought then which is still with me and it is this: actors who gain employment have to be fortune's favoured children. You are not only asked to do the work you would be willing to pay people to let you do, you are actually paid to do it. My eyes had never ever alighted on an amount like this and the thought that I was kind of a rich man now was really heady though it didn't feel terribly different from when I wasn't. The only thought in my head was whether I would be able to get a home in Bombay for that amount. If that happened the rest

would be a breeze, I assured myself. I was also given an air
ticket from Bombay to Hyderabad, where we were to shoot,
and told to guard it with my life. Never having seen an air
ticket before, much less having travelled by air, the fear of
losing the damn thing, as thick as a cheque book, made me
lodge it in my underpants for the journey back to Pune, then
safely in my cupboard under the newspaper lining on the shelf
containing my other pair of undies. I wrote to Baba and the
two Zs about this winning streak I seemed to be suddenly
hitting and received cautious congratulations. All of them
were vastly relieved that I was capable of actually earning
money with my obsession. They had no idea of the kind of
films that were starting to be made by Mr Benegal in Hindi
and which would soon flower into a mini movement; they had
never heard of Satyajit Ray, but had seen some of the regular
commercial Hindi films and I didn't blame them for feeling
uneasy at the thought of where I could possibly fit into one
of those. Ammi wrote me a letter advising me to be thrifty
with the money I would earn. Word of my great good fortune
had spread in the Institute by now. Jaspal said nothing but
smiled cynically every time we met and another close friend, a
student of direction, who during the strike had secretly sided
with the actors but lacked the courage then, or even now, to
openly speak up explained to me why: Jaspal believed I had
got the part as reward for having sold out the acting students.
What was more, he said he too believed it and what is even
more, he still believes it after all these years.

I suppose such people are actually convinced that selling
out is all that is required to get a start in life. I do not know and
do not care who else believes my getting the part in *Nishant*,
as it was later titled, was a reward for betraying my classmates.
In what way I betrayed them, however, I do not know and if
someone is paranoid enough to believe that I engineered the

entire strike in order to get a role in a film, then he certainly imagines me capable of Machiavellian collusions and I am not unflattered. I know for sure that no one was betrayed, the decisions conveyed to the administration were made by all acting students present, and on behalf of those not present, and what ultimately transpired was that I was the only one who continued, while a student, to refuse to be part of any diploma film.

And introducing . . .

Iignored Ammi's dictum right away. I felt like celebrating and got a seat in a taxi instead of a bus this time for the journey to Bombay to catch a flight to Hyderabad. Not willing to risk being late, I set off from Pune at midnight. Bombay being a four-hour drive from there, I was at Santa Cruz airport by 4.45 a.m. with a little over four hours to kill before my flight took off. I really savoured this part, and I needed time to check out a real airport as a passenger. The closest I'd come to one before this was seeing off Asha K. at Palam a few years ago, in a different lifetime. This was 1975, the pre-hijacks and bombings and terror-in-the-skies days, anyone could come and go at any time, no policemen everywhere, no metal detectors, no scrutiny of tickets or IDs at that hour or at any other.

Bottling my feverish excitement I sauntered in trying to look as if I was accustomed to all this. There were some dead neon signs, a few shuttered kiosks and abandoned check-in counters. Even without a soul in sight the place still looked grand compared to what I'd experienced in the name of travel so far. The concept of plastic bucket seats hadn't been imported yet; there were Rexine sofas with foam cushioning, on one of which I reclined in great style, lighting a cigarette and foreseeing a future where like Hugh Hefner I would have airports and airplanes to myself. Not difficult to imagine as that morning I actually had the airport to myself. I instructed imaginary staff to wake me when it was time and stretched out on the sofa, my suitcase under my head—no point taking a chance with all one's worldly possessions, and infinitely better than sitting on one's luggage on a railway platform. I liked travelling in comfort, I decided. I nodded off and awoke to see an enticing pair of legs clad in skintight white jeans walking past a few feet away from me and exactly in my line of sight. I realized on rubbing the sleep away that they belonged to a slightly known film star whose name I now struggle to recall, and she was headed to the check-in counter. Vikram Mehrotra who had travelled by air before had earlier briefed me thoroughly on the protocol, so I nervously approached the counter displaying 'Hyderabad', all the while reassuring myself that there couldn't possibly be anything wrong with my ticket. There wasn't, so I then sat clutching my boarding pass and worrying if my battered suitcase would also get to Hyderabad safely. By and by the other cast members who seemed to know their way around also assembled, and after introducing myself I tagged along and my suitcase and I both got to our destination without incident.

Being introduced to the cast and crew of the film was like entering a who's who of Indian theatre. First off there was Satyadev Dubey, enfant terrible and apart from IPTA (Indian People's Theatre Association) sole practitioner of Hindi theatre in Bombay for decades. Normally an obdurate and exasperating autodidact Dubeyji, who it transpired later had been hoping for the part I got and ended up playing the priest instead, was dismissive when I first met him, 'Alkazi's pupil' he sneered; even though he himself never failed to acknowledge Alkazi as a guru, being Alkazi's pupil was my shortcoming apparently. He and Alkazi shared a history which he happily divulged some time later, and in fact many times again in the course of working with him in the years that followed. Everyone interested in Dubeyji knows that story so I needn't go into it here. Apart from acting in the film, Dubeyji had written the dialogue, and I got to work with him right away on the spoken pieces and the dialect. Then of course there was Girish Karnad, Rhodes scholar, towering intellectual, pioneer of the art film movement in Karnataka, committed theatre worker, the author of two authentic contemporary Indian theatre masterpieces, *Tughlak* and *Hayavadana*, and all round Cool-Cat more known for his writing than his acting. The screenplay was by Vijay Tendulkar, another heavyweight whose incendiary and hugely popular writing greatly offended the right-wing in Maharashtra, caused a massive furore and irrevocably impacted the future of playwriting in that state. The costumes and art direction were by Shama Zaidi, an active member of the modern IPTA and daughter of Begum Qudsia Zaidi, one of the founding figures of the movement in the thirties. Playing central parts were the widely respected, gravel-voiced Amrish Puri who had trained under Dubeyji and in partnership with him had run their company Theatre Unit for many years; Mohan Agashe whose performance in Tendulkar's *Ghasiram Kotwal* I still consider one of the most perfect pieces of actor-blending-into-role that I have ever seen; Kulbhushan Kharbanda from Delhi whom I had not seen perform but who carried a big reputation in Delhi theatre circles. There was also Sadhu Meher, so convincing in Shyam's first film *Ankur* as the drunken husband to Shabana Azmi, who herself had achieved great success in it and was indisputably the star of this one as well. And the ebony-hued Smita Patil was cast as my neglected wife.

The only other time I had visited Hyderabad was some

four years previously on tour with NSD. We had stayed five
to a room in a crummy place in the old city called Shree
Venkateswara Lodge. As the van transporting us all entered
a vaguely familiar area, I had a sickening feeling that we
were headed for the same lodge, with all those memories,
hell! To my enormous relief we drove past it and alighted at
a slightly more upmarket one, Annapurna Lodge, in which
air-conditioned rooms awaited us. I was to share a room with
Kulbhushan K and so blissful was I about actually working
on a feature film and staying in a hotel room that for the first
week or so even KBK's snoring didn't disturb me. I'd pore over
the script at night and within a few days had all my scenes
memorized, not that any of them contained much dialogue.
There was a drunken scene I was terrified of and could not
think of how to perform except by resorting to the conventional
way, of which I had seen so much in Hindi cinema. Dubeyji
came to my rescue by telling me that when drunk it was not
how you stumbled but how you recovered that conveyed the
convincingly drunken quality I was after. He also pointed out
the difference between being stoned (to which I was much
too accustomed) and being drunk (to which I was not), and
to help me understand the latter shared a few drinks with me,
encouraging me to get hammered, but I could never consume
enough of the vile stuff he imbibed. In any case I had resolved
not to smoke dope at all for the duration of the shoot, I was
taking no chances. I knew this could be the last opportunity
I would ever have: if I blew this there would not be another.

I was instructed to shave daily, something I had never done,
and on Day One the village barber gave us all appropriate
haircuts. My unruly curly mop was sheared into a mushroom-
head, I was fitted out in kurta-dhoti, and a wormlike moustache
which I would much rather have grown had I been told to, was
glued on to my upper lip. The very same moustache despite

being used every single day of the shoot constantly caused some overhelpful type or other to inform me that 'today the mooch is looking little different'.

I was required on sets that very day. The first shot taken was from a scene in the first half of the film. Already attracted to the schoolmaster's wife I am trying to slink off to get another look at her when Amrish Puri, his muscles a-glisten at the well, calls out to me and asks what the matter is. In the conversation, unknown to me, the plot to kidnap the woman for me is laid. Despite being with an actor I had long admired I was not intimidated in the least, mainly because of Puri saab's kindly generous nature; but in any case I have never understood why actors get butterflies in the stomach when they act, particularly when it's with someone they look up to. I personally have always relished the thought of working with a superior actor; after all, acting is not a boxing match where one or the other has to be outdone, it's a game two people play together and both can and should win. It was easy transferring the feelings of awe and admiration I had for Agha Mamu on to Amrish Puri who, physically at least, was of the same personality mould, and being the slightly foolish youngest sibling and the butt of ridicule was also a feeling I was thoroughly familiar with. I had no trouble at all believing I was this person. On reflection, I know for sure that of all the parts I have done in cinema this is the one I have felt closest to. This character and I had many common qualities, I thought I knew this person well. I still consider it one of my more successful performances on film. I left nothing to chance, I knew what I was doing; no longer flailing in the dark, I was learning that giving a good performance has absolutely nothing to do with luck, and giving a good performance in a film was not dependent on the actor's skill alone but on the truth of the writing and the imaginativeness of the staging and the proper orchestration by the director of the actor's abilities. In short, if in cinema the director doesn't know his job, there is absolutely nothing a mere actor can do to salvage the situation. It seemed to explain why actors of universally acclaimed greatness have sometimes fared abysmally in poorly directed or poorly written films.

I submitted totally to Shyam; if for a shot he told me to stay still and do nothing then I did exactly that, sometimes I have to admit a bit resentfully, but observing those shots later I found them among the most effective in the film and it made me realize that an actor 'feeling right' about a shot cannot be trusted. A good performance in cinema can be assembled piece by piece in the same way as a carpenter cuts, then joins different pieces of wood to create a coherent aesthetic shape.

And Shyam came through for me in every way. His guidance was gentle, firm and caring, his craft at his fingertips and his knowledge of the milieu impeccable, but what affected me most was the trust he reposed in the actors, the assurance in dealing with them and his compassion for every character. I felt like a slightly spoilt child when, after a few days of shooting, one of the assistants informed me I was fast becoming Shyam's favourite on the sets. I resolved to make it stay that way, keeping away from the dope and giving a miss to the nightly post-shoot tippling, de rigueur on any outdoor shoot. I stayed in my room, practised my scenes for the next day, ate an early dinner and tried to get to sleep before KBK—once I was asleep even his snores couldn't wake me. A friendly rapport had by now been established with Dubeyji, I had obviously been forgiven, and he confessed to being pleasantly taken aback one day on overhearing me recite Professor Higgins's speeches from *My Fair Lady*, which I had thoroughly memorized years ago after having seen the film in college. This incident was fortuitous because it moved Dubeyji some years later to direct *Don Juan in Hell*, a piece by his idol G.B. Shaw, his first ever English-language production. But I am getting ahead of myself.

That month and a half of filming went by like the monsoon in Pune. Much too soon we were at the end. I had through those forty-five days abstained from all sorts of intoxicants except acting, and that has proved through my life to be not only the greatest high, but the cure for all ills as well. Not that I have continuously stayed away from other intoxicants! The staying away from being stoned I could bear, but after a month of tolerating the Vesuvian snores KBK produced in his sleep I cracked, and begged Shyam to transfer me to another room, any other room. He did, and I finally managed to sleep undisturbed through the remaining nights. There were, in the future, to be three more location shoots in which I would have the company and the dubious pleasure of KBK snoring the night away in the neighbouring bed. Once on a film by Girish Karnad, I was stranded in a room with not only KBK but two other thunderous snorers, Om Puri and Bajju bhai as well, and had had to shift my bedding to the corridor. Stroke of good fortune, therefore, that for the rest of that shoot we stayed in tents on location and I made sure my tent was as far from the others' as it could possibly be.

In the course of the filming of *Nishant*, staying much too unsure of my people skills and in any case never having been able to initiate friendships, I found only the sound technician Hitendra Ghosh and the chief assistants Deepak Parasher and Girish Ghanekar (both now sadly deceased) going out of their way to befriend me. I was a poor conversationalist as well and still carried the massive chip on my shoulder with regard to the world. Ill at ease in the company of almost anyone, I now had the feeling I was on probation and my every move was being observed with great interest. I was not far wrong in feeling that and I feel very gratified, even now, to report that I did not put a foot wrong all the way. Girish whose charismatic sex appeal had vanished behind a pair of full-moon spectacles, a pencil-thin moustache and a severe haircut was too preoccupied with his own performance to pay me much attention but the other senior actors Amrish, Shabana, Kulbhushan and Mohan were all encouraging and supportive and I ended the shoot in optimistic spirits and with full pockets. When the schedule wrapped I had my second taste of flying, I was beginning to enjoy it and was already getting better at the 'blasé flyer' act. We all went our separate ways, with Shyam expressing happiness at my contribution. Dubeyji as a parting present handed me two tabs of Purple Haze, hugged me warmly and told me to stay in touch. To get back to Pune, this time I hired a taxi to myself instead of just a seat and lolled in the back all the way. It didn't bother me that I was splurging—hell, it was my hard-earned money, I was capable of earning my living as an actor, I had just acted in my first film!

During the shoot there had been some talk of my perhaps adopting another name for the screen, my own being somewhat long and a trifle difficult to pronounce for some people; but I resolved that the one my parents had given me was good enough and finally it was Nira who made the definitive announcement that she 'liked the name Naseeruddin very much'. That settled the matter then and there. When the film came out six months or so later, Baba taking his daily constitutional along the Mall in Mussoorie caught sight of a poster with my name on it. Going straight to the Rialto he caught the first available show, then went home joyously to tell Ammi I had not changed my name. She was livid he had seen the film by himself, so he had to watch *Nishant* again when Ammi insisted on seeing it too; probably the only film in his life he ever saw twice. His relief that I had finally made good and was part of this unreal world made him write me the longest letter I ever got from him, saying he was 'happy' when he saw the title 'and Introducing Naseeruddin Shah', that he thought it was a good film but wondered if 'these were the sort of films nowadays and would they continue to be made'? Though after this, the relationship with Baba stayed somewhat more peaceful, we still never found an equation that would let us be ourselves when together. With no more chastisement in store for me, our discomfort in each other's company should have diminished but it didn't. Perhaps telling me off had by then become his only way of communicating with me.

R had arrived in Bombay by the time I returned from the shoot, still drunk on my luck. She was staying, she wrote, with friends in Cumballa Hill, a rather swish part of town. I didn't know she had any friends in the city. I then made one of the biggest mistakes of my life, arriving at this mansion-like place she was staying in sometime after dark without informing her. She must have stumbled upon a jackpot or something, I thought. My heart was breakdancing against my ribs as I walked up to the second floor and rang the bell. We were going to be together again. A friendly young man opened the door and informed me she hadn't returned but I could come in and wait for her. Somewhat puzzled as to who he could possibly be I demurred but left a note and was about to trudge away when she appeared, back from work—she had moved fast since landing in Bombay, had already managed a job and a cushy place to live in. Of all the scenarios of 'meeting again' my imagination had painted over the last two years, meeting her in my travel-soiled clothes, on the landing of the stairs to her fancy residence, was the most improbable. She didn't seem exactly overjoyed to see me, we didn't fly into each other's arms after all these years either; there was only a limp handshake before she produced a bunch of keys and let me into an apartment larger than any I had seen before. It had ornate Parsi furniture, a long hallway and spacious rooms on either side. There were about half a dozen thoroughly decent-looking young men present, all strangers to me but with all of whom she seemed to share an easy familiarity. What the fuck was going on here???

I suggested we go out somewhere instead but she didn't seem keen on that. I was mortified at the prospect of having to hobnob with a lot of people I didn't know at all, more so because all of them, though my age more or less, were total aliens with their nice haircuts, their polite conversation, their well-ironed shirts, their confident worldly air, and their banter about stocks and shares and people and things I had no inkling about. They were all in fact employees of Bank of America, I discovered later, and the apartment was company accommodation, where they all lived. There being a plethora of rooms, she was camping in one of them, and WITH one of them as well? I must have been a very sore thumb in that company, with nothing to contribute to the conversation. I wanted to be alone with her, something she didn't seem to reciprocate, and after a while my ardour was completely deflated by her pointed enquiry whether I was in Bombay for the weekend—the question put so obviously to establish that I was no one special, that all I could do was mumble a reply, feeling like I was swallowing a bag full of pointed screws. I got up to leave, she didn't stop me. I said my goodbyes, determined to return to Pune right away, I saw no point in staying. Outside the door as I was leaving she made me promise to come and meet her the next day, she would be free in the morning and she had something to tell me. Of course I immediately scrapped the plan of returning to Pune that night.

Next stop Colaba Causeway and Stiffles Hotel, the hippie hangout in those days, to score myself a tab of acid and survive till morning which, when it came, found my head still buzzing with paranoid visions. I picked up my bag and the two Pochampalli saris I'd brought for her from Hyderabad, and arrived once again at that forbidding doorstep. No one else was present, the other occupants presumably being at work. The opulence I had been so impressed by the night before now felt stifling. In the two or so jaw-clenching hours we spent together and during which I kept hallucinating looking at the curtains in the room, she didn't once enquire about the film I had just done, or about the Institute but explained at length that she now wanted to marry and raise a family. I was in no position, she reiterated, to give her the life she desired and she couldn't wait for things to improve for me. I agreed that I had no idea how long that might take. She was approaching her thirties, was concerned she would soon be past childbearing age, and was very keen on having children. She confirmed my suspicion that she had in fact met someone else with whom she reckoned it could go the distance. I listened, having to strongly hold back a totally unreasonable but irresistible urge to laugh, gave her the saris which she reluctantly accepted, and in a catatonic state caught a taxi back to Pune. I resolved I would never see her again though she had declared with certainty that she still considered me her dearest friend and if ever I needed anything . . . blah blah blah.

I managed to circumvent getting completely bogged down because when I got back to Pune there were more pressing matters to attend to: I had to act in my acting course short film and then find digs for myself in Bombay. There were about two months remaining before the Institute would no longer be home to us. In the interim, the diploma films had been shot and I was not in any of them. No skin off my nose, though, as I would soon have an entire feature film as my portfolio. Shyam was good enough to offer to come to Pune and direct the film which four of us had been allotted. He and Shama cobbled together a rather unfunny screenplay based on an Ismat Chughtai story. He shot, dubbed and edited it in three days flat.

Jaspal had already managed a room for himself in Bombay. Actors looking for accommodation in Bombay those days found it difficult to secure any, and for many good reasons: the unreliability of the profession, delays in paying the rent, odd hours, disreputable friends, noisy parties and women in their lives. Jaspal had therefore invented an alternative profession for himself—teacher in a municipal school—and secured paying guest accommodation, sharing with 'Paddy' A.M. Padmanabhan, a graduate in sound engineering passing off as an engineer. I decided I would be a journalist and Om who joined us later would run a small business manufacturing plastic toys. Dissembling thus, we all managed to find shelter over our heads in this mother of all cities. Now all we had to do was become movie stars.

To that end we decided to see some of the kind of films we should shortly be starring in and I decided to start with *Sholay*, then in its second week. I can confirm first-hand the many apocryphal stories of this film meeting with jeering and catcalls in its initial weeks. The nearest theatre showing it was the Ambar-Oscar complex in Andheri. Jaspal and I got delayed, bought tickets at the window, an achievement not many can claim, and entered a half-empty theatre. We missed

the first scene or two and the ones that followed seemed to
conform strictly to the abysmal pattern of so-called Indian
action movies. The guns no doubt were real and the clothes
the two heroes and the villain wore didn't look as if they had
just been laundered; some of the one-liners had the zinging
wit one encounters not infrequently in UP. But I could identify
the source of almost every single scene—not only Spaghetti
Westerns this time but blithe borrowings from Hollywood
classics as well, even Mr Chaplin was not spared. The action
scenes were competent but by no means breathtaking, I had
seen stunts of surpassing excellence in many a second-grade
Hollywood Western.

Now of course much is made of the impact of this 'cinematic
masterpiece', books are written about it, there are sociological
studies about it and deep meanings are being read into how
it and other equally shallow films reflected the 'mood of the
times'. The mood of the times in that case must have been
to greatly appreciate things that aspired Hollywoodwards.
What someone should research is what it was that caused this
failure to become the most successful Hindi movie of all time.
The cost of its making and the pre-release hype were both
unprecedented at that time and the poor initial reception it
got obviously sent tremors through the industry; there was so
much riding on it they couldn't afford to let it fail. A convenient
scapegoat was found: the newcomer who had played Gabbar
Singh the dacoit, in a manner the audiences were unfamiliar
with. Apparently the writers had wanted another actor who
was not available, so overriding their protests the director
cast the then unknown Amjad Khan, who was blessed with
enough confidence to fill a room by himself. I believe it was
Amjad bhai's contribution, and his gargantuan personality,
that helped shape the character as it finally appeared on
screen. I thought he was absolutely marvellous and yet the

entire industry was holding him to blame: his girth, his voice, all came in for flak.

It is supremely ironic that even today just the name of the film immediately evokes the reaction 'Gabbar Singh!', probably followed by 'Kitne aadmi thhe?' in almost anyone, but that day I saw with my own eyes the rejection by an audience of an effective actor in a movie because he was upstaging the ones they identified with. His later applause-inducing non sequiturs ('claptrap dialogue' in Hindi cinema parlance) were that day being greeted with stony silence or hostile rejection by the majority of the Dharmendra/Bachchan fan club present. It took a week or two for the audiences to cotton on to the fact that, hey, they had been rooting for the wrong guys all along. Gabbar was their man. And as if to atone for this judgemental lapse they went overboard in their worship of this new god. Gabbar Singh, though modelled closely on a couple of Sergio Leone villains, was suddenly hailed as 'the first of his kind' and the theatres running the movie began packing them in (with some 'feeding' by the producers, I daresay), and continued to do so, one actually for two years. With time the film's other virtues—the cinematography, the songs, the cool attitude of the heroes, the sharp dialogue—started becoming apparent and it seemed to become a habit with the audience to see the film every few weeks, there was so much bang for the buck in it, they realized.

Ramesh Konar, a Bachchan devotee who came into my household first to cook for me, then graduated to driver, then to Jeeves and has been a devoted family member for four decades now hated it at first, but being pressured by friends saw it again. Knowing what to expect this time he liked it a little and, deciding to give it one more chance, took some friends along for a third viewing and loved it this time. He has probably seen it more than once since, as have I in fact, and my initial opinion about it is still unchanged. While I do not dismiss for a moment the effort and time that went into it, I bristle every time it is included among the great Indian movies. Popular Hindi cinema is like a huge meal in which there is such a variety of food that the audience cannot and must not be able to devour every dish at one go, they must come back to taste what they missed out or couldn't fully savour the last time. That I suppose is what makes people see the same movie over and over again, even though the first time they saw it they knew exactly what would happen next and even though they may not even have liked it. And that, I suppose is what makes a hit.

Very soon after, I went looking for Dubeyji, never for a moment suspecting that meeting him was to result in the most serendipitous happening of my life. I needed to work and he was sure to be producing some play or other—he always was—and I thought I might land a part. I found out he would be at St Columba School in South Bombay, reading a new play. I immediately went to this address, for many years a rehearsal haven for Dubeyji and other practitioners of experimental Hindi and Marathi theatre, to learn he was not in town. But I did bump into Amol Palekar who was then on an upward trajectory to major stardom. Amol said he had heard complimentary things about me, and he probably meant Dubeyji who was not due to turn up that day. I wrote him a note, and asked Amol to give it to him. I was also informed that Dubeyji these days rehearsed in Bandra in the lobby of the Balgandharva Rangmandir, a monstrously huge, seldom used open-air auditorium (now razed, but immortalized on film in *Waqt* and my own *Jaane bhi do Yaaron*). The place was a stone's throw from Pamposh, my haunt of ten years ago, and

I was on my way there the next day when Dubeyji spotted me and treated me to a cold sugarcane juice at a roadside stall very near a bus stop outside National College where I had once spent a few nights years ago. He hadn't got my note but was in fact starting on a play he himself had written, called *Sambhog se Sanyas Tak*, translating roughly as 'From Fornication to Salvation', and there was a part in it for me.

This news was going down extremely well with the sugarcane juice when, to brighten my day further, a striking-looking girl who henceforth I could not keep my eyes off came up to Dubeyji and handed him a note, informing him it was 'from Amol Palekar'. It was the note I had written for Dubeyji! I took to her the moment I saw her, and really felt I'd like to get to know her. I even at once considered the possibility of spending my life with her, though after all these years she still refuses to believe that, but I did and it seemed like a jolly good idea, being on the rebound be damned. We had not yet spoken to each other and I knew nothing about her but somehow I felt certain that she was my kind of person. She looked flushed with the heat just then and her flawless complexion seemed to glow. I found her absolutely delicious. Dubeyji who had just had all his teeth surgically removed introduced us; his clarity of speech not being at its best she misheard my name as Shivendra Sinha, then a serious film-maker of some repute. My beard having grown back, I daresay I was once again looking like anything but an actor, an art-film maker possibly. I only later discovered her name was Ratna and she was the daughter of the formidable Dina Pathak, once a huge star on the Gujarati stage and screen and now a much-loved elder in Hindi movies.

Ratna was playing the central part in the play, an apsara who while doing whatever apsaras do in heaven, is unfaithful to her husband (me). Sparks and curses fly back and forth

and after being reborn on earth we are now labouring under
the weight of our own lives, she as maid to a sex-starved
princess and I as a poetry-spouting misogynist lout. I can
only dimly recall what else happens in this abstruse nonsense
but the plot was secondary to Dubeyji's chief intention in
writing and staging it: to deliver overwrought arguments
against conventional moralities and air his pet obsessions—
rebirth syndrome, reversal of sexual roles, woman fated to be
abandoned, hopeless man-woman-man-woman-man daisy-
chain, confusion of identities, sexual freedom. And there
were two recurring motifs, the menstrual cycle and women
writhing on the floor, in every play Dubey wrote and many
he directed.

Shishir Sharma and Sunil Shanbag, two close friends of
Ratna's, were also in the cast along with a whole lot of very
pretty girls. Jaspal also after a while was cast in it and ended
up doing a marvellous comic turn as the mad king. It was
stimulating to have found something apart from moping and
dreaming to do right away. The second half of every day was
thus taken care of. I in any case had no intentions of making
the rounds of producers' offices seeking work. I knew that the
only way work would generate itself would be if I grabbed
every opportunity I got and wrung it out till it screamed for
mercy. Work would come only if I could demonstrably deliver
the goods. If I couldn't, even being the son of the biggest gun
in Bombay wouldn't help.

Sambhog se Sanyas Tak was being produced by the IPTA,
by now a rather strait-laced company, its revolutionary fervour
a thing of the past. In a fit of misguided philanthropy the
IPTA people had entrusted Dubeyji with directing a play of
his choice for them; he promised them a comedy and came up
with this wicked parody of one. The scenes were set in forests
or palaces or the netherworld or nowhere, the characters often

just seemed to be there for the heck of it, and try as I might, all my efforts at empathizing with the part came to naught during the rehearsals of this play. If the scene was set in Heaven, it didn't do much good trying to imagine the geography of the place or where I was coming from or where I was going. There wasn't even any sort of intention this character had apart from just not wanting the woman. He could not be made believable by delving into what he had for breakfast and so forth.

Dubey enjoyed knocking my ideas of 'truthful acting' and advised me to find a voice and a walk for the character instead of trying to 'become' him. Caught between two half-digested techniques of acting, I floundered badly in this role, trying to bring believability to something that was patently a fairy tale. It took me many more years, and many more unsuccessful performances, before the very limiting nature of 'realistic acting' began to sink in. But at that point in time I had burnt most of my bridges with the NSD kind of acting and rebuilding them was a tough task I am still engaged in.

When this 'comedy' with its muddled sexual identities, a magical sex-changing pill, nubile maidens aching for sex, lusty men slavering for the same, heavenly apsaras reincarnated as humans, duelling nobles, a princess with a raging desire to lose her virginity, a king driven insane by satyriasis, a ghost guarding the virtue of the maidens and characters humping each other all over the place offstage of course, was finally staged, it was watched in apoplectic silence by the IPTA elders who, after staying in shock for a few days, promptly pulled the plug. Dubeyji, undeterred, took the production into his Theatre Unit stable and continued to perform it sporadically for a while, sometimes touring with it and reviving it much later with younger sets of actors whenever he was at a loss for something to stage. Ratna and I were thus able to stay in touch at that time and further our friendship. I had found a haven to cadge free meals from and I was introduced to the joys of pure vegetarian food.

Nishant was being dubbed when Shyam asked if I knew an actor who could voice Sadhu Meher, who was not available and who in any case had delivered a sub-par performance this time. I suggested Jaspal and he, no surprise but to his credit and to Shyam's great delight, brought an indifferent performance alive. Another thing I pride myself on, apart from my acting in the film, is the sound effects creatively and dutifully executed by Kulbhushan and myself. We'd sit at the microphone surrounded by small blocks of different surfaces and using various shoes and sandals would synchronically dub the sound of the various characters' footsteps—for bare feet we used our palms. Other instruments in our little orchestra were buckets empty and full, mugs, pots, plates, pans, spoons, cups, saucers, glasses, bottles, bangles, yards of cloth—every conceivable thing that would match the incidental sounds in the movie. We got paid a little extra for this job, it being above and beyond the call of duty, and it gave the sound effects firm of Kharbanda/Shah extra employment all the way till Shyam's sixth film, *Junoon*; by which time, having become somewhat well known (as actors not foley artists), both of us proved to be more of a distraction. But with our expert help *Nishant* was finally mixed and ready to release in September of that year, a month away. Even though Shabana Azmi in one of her moments of generosity had predicted that I would 'surely become a star after this film', I wasn't about to wager any money on that possibility. I had performed as well as I possibly could but knew only too well that this film world of Bombay had ever appreciated truth less than artifice. I wondered what kind of roles would come my way, looking as I did in the film.

As it happened, after its release I received not a single offer of work despite my performance being good and the film doing reasonable business at the box office. Every actor in the film, except yours truly, emerged with reputation enhanced and further employment gained. Shabana, already a star, reinforced her standing as a powerhouse performer, Smita was acclaimed the discovery of the decade, Amrish with his menacing mien and beautifully toned physique started making big money as the heavy in popular films, as did Girish who went on to play the lead in many he has now probably forgotten. Kulbhushan, Mohan Agashe, even Savita Bajaj all subsequently got cast in featured parts, but the only thing that came my way was a handful of glowing reviews. I can't say I had anticipated being deluged with offers but getting absolutely nothing was hard to take. The only money I made in the next year was for acting in a commercial, never seen, for a product (Gulab agarbatti) which in real life I hadn't ever and still haven't encountered, and in the shooting of which I greatly regretted not having attended the playback classes at FTII; and a comic one for Britannia Delite biscuits which ran very successfully in theatres for a couple of years, making me an object of great amusement when travelling by bus or local train. The earnings from these at least guaranteed two meals a day for a while because I had by now spent whatever remained of my *Nishant* earnings on a pretty humiliating haemorrhoid surgery I had needed for some time.

Ashok Ahuja, then in the final year of the direction course and preparing to make his diploma film, asked me if I would act in it. I had appeared in every one of Ashok's films made at FTII, and thought it fitting that if at all I did a diploma film it should be his. Besides, I was bowled over by the concept: two days in the life of an employment-seeking youth, in which, after meeting the girl he loves, he appears for an interview which is not shown, nor its outcome known when he phones the girl and asks her to marry him. She delightedly enquires if that means he has got the job. He replies he doesn't know but wants an answer to his question now. The film ends indeterminately, leaving the rest of the conversation and resultantly the relationship ambiguous, a common escape route for FTII direction students who seldom got down and dirty when it came to dealing with relationships. Instead of seeing people as people they tended to see them only as symbols of something (usually pretty arcane) that they were trying to convey. All they should have been doing was getting the nuts and bolts of film-making right, but instead they were hell-bent on making films of cosmic significance and conveniently resorting to ambiguity or abstraction when what was required was representation in truthful human terms. Ashok's film, called *The Proposal*, also suffered massively from this flaw but for the most obvious reasons I felt drawn to the story and I had always greatly enjoyed working with Ashok, so I went back to FTII for a week to act in my only diploma film.

The heavy-duty Mitchell movie cameras of those days were far from silent and every grain of the 'whirr' seemed to me to be costing money. As a student actor facing one of them, the sound would stiffen and immobilize my sinews. No live audience has ever had the effect on me that the sound of that camera had. Today's generation, whose every sound and action is recorded from the time of their birth, and for whom the camera is part of the family, will find it hard to understand how just being photographed was such a big deal for us but it was, and for me in particular, desperate as I was to see what I really looked like, a curiosity that was not stilled till

I saw my screen test for admission to FTII. Getting a picture taken when we were children was an event: everyone dressed up and posed stiffly, there was the delicious wait for the negatives to develop and then the bliss of seeing the pictures. Baba had a Kodak Brownie box camera he never used. The time I shelved my cricket dreams also coincided with *Sport & Pastime* folding up, so I started spending my pocket money on film rolls instead. Babar Mamu was an avid amateur photographer and had an Asahi Pentax 35mm camera which I was sometimes allowed to use after he had explained the principles of exposure and shutter speed, but I found the good old Brownie fascinating. It worked on the periscopic principle and you could see the subject being photographed, upside down on two little viewfinders on the sides, it only had to be aimed and clicked. The results, including one I took of myself in a mirror, would turn out really good but every botched picture was so much money down the drain, so film stock for me had always been synonymous with my life's entire fortune. This feeling had not left me through the shooting of whatever films I had done professionally either. I just had to crack this paradox actors face, of being simultaneously totally oblivious and completely aware of the observers; the observer in film work being the camera.

Before shooting *Nishant* Shyam had given me the most valuable piece of advice regarding film acting I have ever received: 'The camera is the eye of everyone watching the film,' he had said while explaining to me that it was essential to connect with the camera in the same way as one connects with a live audience. My terror of that camera sound, even after doing an entire feature film, had diluted but not disappeared, I discovered, when we started shooting Ashok's film at the Institute and the old anxiety about wasted footage started returning. Perhaps shooting on the same floor where the camera sound had given me such nightmares in the past provoked this Pavlovian response, but it bothered me that this should happen; the camera and I would have to coexist for the rest of my life, and I couldn't afford to stay thus terror-stricken. The last three days of the shoot were to be in one of the rooms in the hostel, not my old room but the one where I had been temporarily lodged. On the second day, we shot late into the night and when the unit wrapped up they decided to just leave the camera where it was, as we were to continue the scene early the next morning. I didn't notice the camera was pointing straight at the bed when I lay down to sleep, and being roused by one of those mid-sleep bladder protests I found myself nose to nose with Mr Mitchell who had been silently watching over me while I slept. I went back to sleep feeling comforted and not alone. In the morning when I woke up old Mitch and I were the best of friends and have stayed so; the still camera I continue to have problems with.

Just before *Nishant* premiered I got in touch with R and, not only for sentimental reasons but also wishing she should witness my day of glory asked her to attend it with me. I fished out and ironed the old suit, by now about as shiny with age as my polished cowboy boots. Dubeyji gallantly escorted Ratna and all the girls in the play to the premiere as well but our paths didn't cross that evening. R was really ill at ease by the time we got to Liberty cinema; matters were not helped by the blowout we'd had on the way, and she drifted away from me when we spotted the solitary photographer recording the event even though he didn't even know who I was and didn't bother photographing us. She either couldn't stomach my getting more attention than her or, because she also declined to be introduced to any of the team, she didn't want it to appear as if we were together. I was too high on what was about to happen to feel upset that she couldn't put such piffling considerations aside and share my happiness. I think I didn't really care for her any longer, I was just vindictively determined to prove my point and savour my victory. We watched the film; she said she liked my performance and the movie, but her hackles started rising again when after the show I got separated from her for a minute or two, being held back by the few people who had recognized me, even though now with a bushy beard I looked nothing like the character I had played. I wanted to hang around and gloat but she was in a desperate hurry to leave, so I didn't attend the after-celebration and dropped her to where she was staying. I did not look back as the taxi pulled away, and have never looked back at that relationship again. It was finally over, I was still alive, I had a future that didn't look at all bleak any more. I was not feeling quite as shell-shocked as the earlier time I had visited that place.

I had no further contact with her except for receiving an invitation to her wedding, which I did not attend; and we didn't in fact see each other again till the shooting of the film *Masoom* in Delhi many years later. She was by then happily married to one of the nice young men I had met that nightmarish evening at the bankers' residence and had two little daughters.

The churning

After the *Nishant* release I spent most of the time licking my various wounds so to say, including the most recent one of being rejected as newsreader in both Hindi and English on Doordarshan, where Smita who had made something of a name for herself in Marathi suggested I audition. Shishir and Sunil, both then living with their parents at walking distance from my pad, often generously welcomed me into their homes. I give thanks very often for the times such undemanding friendships and unselfish affection have come my way as with these two, and earlier with KC and Pearly in Sem, then with Asif and Jasdev in Aligarh.

While I was studying at FTII, the news that Mr Gulzar was planning a film on the life of Mirza Ghalib had created quite a buzz and Mr Sanjeev Kumar, one of Gulzar bhai's favourite actors, had been asked to play the part. Sanjeev Kumar, after a modest beginning in stunt movies, was now a highly acclaimed actor and a major star. After delivering some outstanding performances he seemed to have now developed a rather self-congratulatory way of performing and was thoroughly comfortable with the mannered acting habits typical of all stars. Even without having read more than a couplet of Ghalib's poetry, I felt sure Gulzar bhai was making a mistake: Sanjeev Kumar was wrong for the part. Then one day I read that he had been hospitalized and the shooting of the film delayed, so with Vikram Mehrotra's assistance I got hold of Gulzar bhai's address and wrote him a letter informing him I was the man he was looking for. I enumerated my qualifications: I belonged to Meerut (true), a place Ghalib had connections with; I had lived in Old Delhi's Gali Qasim Jaan where Ghalib had lived (false, I had only visited it); I spoke, wrote and read Urdu fluently (one-third true, I only spoke it); and I had studied the great man's work (totally false). I assured him he would not regret choosing me and that I was already a very good actor. I hadn't really expected a reply and didn't get one; I had no idea what effect my letter may have had, but at that stage there was nothing to lose by trying; surely my missive would have had some impact—even if it had only irritated him he would remember it and then perhaps he had seen *Nishant* by now. I secured an appointment, was warmly received by him at his Pali Hill office and complimented on my work in the film, but no mention was made about the possibility of my working for him. Asking him about my letter began to seem terribly presumptuous and neither of us made any mention of it nor of the *Mirza Ghalib* project. It was only much later when I was actually playing Ghalib in his TV series that I mustered up the courage to tell him the letter story—turned out he had never received it.

Time was going by in a haze of hashish smoke, attempts to procure LSD at Stiffles which either failed or ended in disastrously bad trips, inexpensive meals in a dhaba outside Khar station, occasional visits to Falkland Road and a steady succession of dreams, and once even a close shave with the police. Jaspal/Shah were sitting on the ledge of the wall around 'Aeroplane Park' in Juhu, rolling a joint, when two plainclothes cops materialized out of nowhere, grabbed us not very gently by the arms and suggested we accompany them to the police station. Assuming we were being hauled in for doing drugs we meekly complied and managed to slip out of our palms the moist tobacco/hash mixture we had been preparing. I even managed to chuck away the precious little sliver of hash in my pocket on the way to the cop station. The rather polite officer there who questioned us explained that there had been a child-lifting incident at that very spot a few days earlier and the police were conducting a watch, we had been taken in as possible suspects, the cops were not interested in two stoned guys. The officer it then turned out had seen *Nishant* and managed to identify me. We were given a cup of tea and let go.

I began to sense that things were not quite well between Jaspal/Shah and one morning around dawn, when we both were sliding down the slope of the rainbow, I asked him to sing something and he turned on me with a malevolence I had never seen in him. 'Why I should sing for you? You are special you think? All the time you are doing this to me you farking pancho sunawbeech! Fuckoff! @#^*^$! Come on if you are a man!' and other such hysterical nonsense. I was still reeling with stupefaction at this when he actually got up and dared me physically, a challenge I would have risen to had it not been hurled at a time when there were still violet clouds in my brain and all I felt like doing was listening to the Moody Blues. What Bajju bhai had said to me about Jaspal some years before immediately came back. I stayed out of his way for a while after this, but then one day we were summoned to Mr Benegal's office and told we would both be acting in the next film he was planning, a project that was to be funded by the Gujarat Milk Marketing Federation and was about the hugely successful cooperative milk-farming experiment in the state.

Shyam that day did not tell either of us what parts we would respectively be playing but assured us both of 'good roles' and told us to keep the months of February and March aside for the shoot which was to take place in a village near Rajkot in Gujarat. This film was to be made on an even smaller budget than *Nishant* and I was promised slightly less than I was paid on that one, but Shyam assured me that my part in it was a winner. The screenplay was by Vijay Tendulkar once again, but Dubeyji for some reason kept his distance from this project. Almost the entire *Nishant* cast once again assembled, with Girish Karnad playing the idealistic vet trying to set up a cooperative in the village, a character based on the real-life hero of the cooperative milk farmers' movement and the founder of Amul, Dr Verghese Kurien. The antagonist, Amrish Puri again, was the exploitative milk-contractor, and in the other pivotal parts were Smita Patil, Kulbhushan, Mohan Agashe, Savita Bajaj, Sadhu Meher (whose performance once again had to be bolstered by Jaspal's dubbing), myself and AP, a young lady with whom I had had a very brief dalliance while at FTII. I was not given a copy of the script beforehand nor even told very much about the story of the film or the character; Shyam just said he wanted me 'full of beans' through the shoot. I was to play a rebellious city-folk-hating village busybody who initially opposes the team trying to create awareness of the need for a co-op in the village, then changes his mind; and at the end, having recognized its benefits, takes up the gauntlet of running the cooperative after the team leaves in despair.

I flew to Rajkot with the other lead actors while the rest of the team, including Jaspal, travelled by train. The first day in my room at the guest house there, sharing with Kulbhushan yet again, I read the script, joyous at the great part I had landed, then delightedly passed it on to Jaspal, who in fact had just two or three scenes in the film. He glanced through it and to my disbelief tossed it aside with a maniacal celebratory laugh saying he had 'understood it all', and resumed attempting under the blanket to make a pass at AP who, though about as desperate for a relationship as he was, did not reciprocate, and his paranoia about me began to hit a new high.

When we started shooting on Day One with the scene where Girish, having just bailed me out from prison, is driving me back to the village, Jaspal was sitting close by and glaring at the goings-on. At first I thought he was admiring my acting; playing a villager, I had felt obliged to stay dressed and in character most of the time and was feeling rather pleased with the way I was looking. But then he started muttering first to himself, then gradually aloud, almost responding to what I was doing in the scene. This insistent aggressive disturbance not only threw me completely, it also made the unit uneasy enough for Shyam to ask him to leave. As he left, glaring back over his shoulder at me, I saw him mouthing the words 'Bastard! You have done it again! You have done it again! I'll get you!' the veins in his neck bulging, his face contorted with rage, his eyes aflame. I assume it was while watching this scene shot that he suddenly realized he was not doing the role which, in the course of having cursorily glanced at the script, he thought he would be; I was doing it instead and his muddled reasoning told him that I had somehow manipulated all this, just as I had manipulated the strike at FTII. The confusion of Jaspal/Shah's identity was taking its toll at last. The unit considered it a minor tiff between two close friends, but never having suspected him capable of this kind of behaviour, I felt a premonition of worse to come.

It came quite quickly. Though that evening, having scored

some local hashish, he came to my room and we smoked together, he didn't apologize, just laughed and said he had misunderstood the whole thing and patronizingly admitted I might also do well in the role that rightfully was his; but even in his small role he would show me anyway. He promised to thoroughly fuck my happiness with his brilliant acting. This was a joke that had often been exchanged between us in the past, but this time there was a blood-curdling conviction to the way he uttered these fantastical beliefs.

The next day, after he had done his first scene and rather well too, we were travelling back to Rajkot after the day's shoot. I was seated next to AP on the bus and from a far corner I could feel Jaspal's eyes on me. Then his muttering turned into a string of Punjabi swearing and, lathi in hand, he lunged at me. Fortunately a bit of distance and quite a few unit members separated us or I might have been taken by surprise. Even after he was subdued, he went on simmering, threatening to advance on me again. I could have taken him on and I wished the others would let him come at me—that would have settled matters for a while, though I didn't relish the thought of doing bodily harm to someone I had been close to. Shyam, who had not witnessed the incident in the bus, agreed to my suggestion that we had better be kept apart. I was totally clueless as to what had caused this outburst but if he tried it again I would retaliate. It took me a long time to learn that he was at the mercy of the chemicals bombarding his brain and scarcely in control of his actions, but then the thought that he should harbour such resentment and such impulses was hard to bear. Grateful to escape KBK's snoring and Jaspal's bad energy I shifted to the bungalow in the village where Shyam and the leading actors were staying. Jaspal remained in the guest house in Rajkot, only being called to the location if he was shooting, and since we had no scenes together I seldom saw him. Only a matter of time, though, before he tried wooing AP again, then vented on another unit member, got thoroughly thrashed and, on Shyam's instructions, was put on the next train back to Bombay, his one remaining scene having been scrapped.

Seeing the film *Manthan* now, one cannot help being struck by his performance, truncated though it is. There is an intensity in his presence that goes beyond acting, and there is the magnetism of a person completely sure of what he is doing and, paradoxically, completely out of control—a highly flammable combination. He had in fact become the character he was playing. This for me was a very early lesson in how undesirable it is for this to happen, and exposed the first of the many limitations naturalistic acting, in which I had devoutly believed so far, suffers from.

I often wonder how Jaspal's career would have gone had he managed to keep a grip on his feelings and consumed less mind-altering substances. While at NSD I had thought him a superior actor in many ways—he could sing, he could dance, he was good-looking in a rustic Punjabi way and his acting had verve and energy. Though not suffering from lack of self-esteem and always generous in his praise of my work, I guess he could see that my English education invariably put me at an advantage in many respects, and he would often wistfully say he wished he could speak English the way I did, or act the way I did. I greatly envied his singing abilities but never said so. Naturally I had not an inkling of what was going on inside him, I always believed we had a mutual admiration society, a friendship with no insecurities. Mohan Agashe, acting in the film but by profession a psychiatrist, later tried to explain to me that these symptoms were typical of an ailment in which the close identification of oneself with an admired person can become so acute that it results in the complete immersion of one personality into another; and the confusion of identities becomes so total that the afflicted person can actually not see his own reflection in a mirror. This evidently is what the man who shot and killed John Lennon suffered from; believing HE was actually Lennon, he was only getting this impostor who was usurping all the credit out of the way. All this was too terrifying to comprehend and caused a miserable distraction right at the start of a film I felt was going to be significant for me. I tried to put it behind me and tore into the part with every physical, mental and emotional resource I had.

My efforts to behave as much like a villager as possible started with trying to mimic the posture of the Gujarati shepherds, the 'Bharwads' whose lathis are part of their bodies, whose sexy, graceful attire and eloquent body language are impossible to approximate without years of practice. So I did the next best thing: I stayed in costume all the time, slept on the floor, learnt to wash and milk a buffalo. All this, though vastly amusing to my fellow actors, was necessary to reawaken in my muscles the memory of people I had seen earlier in Sardhana. And though looking back on it I now cringe at the thought of the kind of song and dance about my commitment to the part I made in this film and later in Shyam's *Junoon*, I was in a phase where I needed to do it. I had quite a bit to say in this film so I was constantly going over my lines as well. I did in fact end up trying too hard to shine in both these parts instead of understanding that the ideas they represented were far more important than the characters themselves, and no one had bothered to explain this to me yet. So in both *Manthan* and *Junoon*, despite Shyam's injunction not to play the role 'as you see it in your head but as it is written', I did precisely what I should not have done, but didn't manage to completely ruin either film with my misguided energy. That is why both these performances, despite generating more work for me and bringing me continued acclaim, are not among my personal favourites.

Manthan however is a unique film, in that it had 5,00,000 financiers, all of them members of the Gujarat Co-operative Milk Marketing Federation who paid two rupees each, to amass a figure of 10,00,000 rupees—more than enough at that time to make a film of that kind with a large cast, on location. In later years of course there were films I acted in, shot in Bombay, on starvation budgets like 3,50,000 rupees, but *Manthan* was probably the first Indian film to be financed by a cooperative. When it was released after quite a delay— 'a film about milk farmers?? Who the hell will see it??'—it astounded everybody by running to full houses in Gemini, Bandra and other 'single screen' theatres—there were no multiplexes then—for a good ten weeks, and was considered one of the sleeper successes of the year. By that time of course Shyam, indefatigable as ever, had already embarked on his next film.

Getting back to the city and once again being able to cadge meals at Ratna's or Sunil's or Shishir's homes felt very good. Dubeyji promised me one of the central roles in Vijay Tendulkar's new play, *Baby*, a rather morbid piece about a film extra, opposite Bhakti Barve who I still consider the finest female theatre actor I have seen in my life. But he reneged and did the part himself. Shama Zaidi, then embarking on a Hindi translation of the new Satish Alekar play *Maha-Nirvan*, asked me if I would act in it. I readily agreed and didn't object when she cast Jaspal in the central singing role. I still hoped the relationship could repair itself and figured it might be therapeutic for him to do a part where he could really shine. Shama during the shoot had been sympathetic to Jaspal's situation and so, despite Dubeyji's strong reservations, went ahead with this ill-fated enterprise which fell apart within three weeks of rehearsal. Jaspal, instead of appreciating the opportunity to be the star, in fact started behaving like one: swaggering around telling us all what we should do, directing by proxy when Shama was not around which was often. Shama, unable in any case to handle the situation, was present when another ugly situation developed one day between us, resulting in Jaspal being asked to leave the project. He was hurriedly replaced and in another week this shoddy production was staged and closed after one performance. Dubeyji came to see it and all he said was, 'I told you so.'

The lodging I had managed was a room with three others in Martinville, an ancient Ango-Indian bungalow in Santa Cruz, the very house where Jaspal had earlier found accommodation. I then graduated, with an increase in rent of course, to a room with two others; and finally with a further rent hike to a room with only Tika Singh, a Nepali classmate from FTII, who after an unhappy and fruitless time trying to get acting jobs in Bombay later went home. There was no question of waiting for the phone to ring in Martinville, there was no telephone there, but summonses of any kind were also not forthcoming. In any case, the telephone had not ceased to be an object of some wonder for me ever since the Ajmer days where when it rang, which was seldom, there would be a race between the three of us to get to it first. None of us dared make a call to anyone though, because you had to deal with a no-nonsense operator enquiring, 'Number please?' and we were scared she would tell on us. I still had a phobia about phones and Ratna could not understand why I didn't call her up more often. I would ask what I should call up about and she didn't seem to understand how difficult it is saying sweet nothings on a public phone with people waiting in a queue breathing down your neck.

The one summons that did come was from a big production house for a multi-starrer in which I was being offered a tiny part. Big production house I thought, so big money too, and promptly went to the meeting. I had earlier been narrated the part and didn't really feel like doing it but the thought of the money got me. And so to the big man behind the desk I daringly quoted a sum the like of which I had not dreamt of receiving so far. 'Fifty,' said I. There was a short pause during which he smilingly doodled on a pad, then looked me straight in the eye and said, 'Thousand?' I nodded, holding back another stronger response that was on the tip of my tongue. He doodled some more for what seemed like an interminable while, then looked back at me and pointedly drew a cross on the pad. Not another word was going to be spoken, it seemed, so I took my leave, much to the consternation of the director of the film who had told me he 'really wanted' me in the part.

Ratna was then in her second year of college. There was a seven-year difference in our ages and our backgrounds were as different from each other's as they could possibly be. We made no attempt to hide the relationship when it developed, and I had to manfully ignore the snide whispers of 'cradle snatcher'. Dina, her mother, who seemed to have a special antenna for these things, was uneasy about me from the start but was charming and diplomatic when I was around. Little sis Supriya however was staunchly on my side and Ratna's friends, most of them Parsi, thought I looked just like one of them so I was happily taken into the fold. It was some years though, after successfully portraying a number of

Parsi characters in various films, before I actually became an honorary Parsi (Nazru Dinshaw).

There was a 'no girlfriends visiting' rule in Martinville which Mrs Martin, the near-sighted and friendly landlady, did not rigorously enforce in my case—my picture had appeared in a couple of magazines, her niece had happened to see *Nishant*, and by now I had been classified as 'a decent boy' so I was not chastised about having deceived her by posing as a journalist nor was I asked to leave. Old Mrs Martin was actually quite thrilled that she now knew a film actor in real life and I got somewhat special treatment after that. Ratna and I met every day either at her place or mine, depending on whether her parents were home or not. Tika would tactfully disappear when she arrived, usually around lunchtime, straight from college, and we would then just hang around together. I loved going to the movies, she didn't mind. She loved going to art galleries, I hated it but would tag along. She loved wandering around and looking at things in shops while I talked to her incessantly mostly about acting and about my past, which took a while to relate in full. She made me feel great, listening intently, already sharing my enthusiasm for cinema and theatre and later learning to tolerate my love for tennis and cricket as well. She wasn't quite as obsessed with acting as I was, but wanted to be an actor and was pretty good too, her clarity of voice and her diction were particularly impressive. I had always found her terribly attractive and now a deeper friendship, a mutual admiration and fondness, began to grow. Despite Dina's vociferous objections, and the more subdued ones of her father Baldev, pretty soon we both knew for certain that we wished to spend the rest of our lives together. One evening at Juhu beach when she and I had strolled off, much to the consternation of Shishir and Sunil who feared we might have been mugged, I asked her if she would marry me when it was feasible to do so and she accepted without a moment's hesitation. I wonder if she was brave or foolhardy: I had no work, very little money, not many prospects, nothing even dimly on the horizon and she agreed to share my life. That faith was one of the major battery-chargers through the stress and uncertainty of the extremely fallow succeeding year or two in which, though big-league players like Manoj Kumar, Yash Chopra, Javed Akhtar called me to meet them, I again received no offer of solid work.

During all this time Ratna had been fighting off her parents to keep the relationship going; and even though we had by now reached the stage of ferocious arguments neither of us, I am pretty sure, even once considered severing ties. With no inkling of what the future had in store, we were both at the moment happy enough to have found our 'missing halves'. After trying for a while to wean me off my hashish habit she realized it was hardly a threat to her and gave up. Dina's problem with my smoking though continued right to the end; her nose would scrunch up almost on its own accord and her first reflex was 'something is burning' every time I lit up. I tried many times to persuade her to have a puff or two, arguing it would make her less uptight, and I was only half-joking.

Ratna's home had a television set and so I got the perfect excuse to spend all my time there if a Test match or Wimbledon was on; those were the days of the two-channel black-and-white Doordarshan in India, on which a Wimbledon final was once stopped near match point for a telecast of 'Parliament News'. She shared my fascination for Borg and McEnroe but could not quite comprehend what could be so engrossing about every single delivery in a five-day cricket match. She had never played the game, so I couldn't explain, but to her credit she tolerated my cricket mania and would watch with me most of the time. Even though I could never successfully explain to her the difference between off and leg, she eventually developed an interest in the game, maybe because of the Pakistani hunks or maybe because, years later, she saw me help my sons with their addition, multiplication and division sums, not to mention averages and percentages (rest in peace Miss Perry) using cricket scores.

But at that time, college was ending in a few months for her and she had to decide what to do—marriage for us was still very far away, the resident rodent in the poorest church had more put away than I had, and she didn't fancy acting in the Gujarati theatre or commercial Hindi cinema. Her dad's stylish tailoring establishment 'Shriman' which had once catered to the biggest stars had fallen from favour, there was no point trying to run that, and in any case she was keener on theatre than on designing men's clothing. She began to consider the possibility of going to study at NSD and so we thought we would fatten her résumé by attempting some plays on our own.

There were two problems with that though: we had no director and nowhere to perform. Though there were many Western plays that I hoped to do in the future, nearly all of them were impossible to attempt at that point, so we decided to start small. Prithvi Theatre would take another five years to come into our lives, and the NCPA's sixty-seater Little Theatre was rarely made available to beginners. The only venue that the 'un-commercial' Hindi and Marathi theatre workers could afford was located in a very downmarket middle-class Marathi-medium school Chhabildas, tucked away in one of the by-lanes that snake around all sides of Dadar station. Persuaded by the wonderfully persistent theatre couple Sulabha and Arvind Deshpande, the management of this school agreed to grant use of the school hall to theatre companies to perform in, charging a rent so minimal it was practically a gift. The Deshpandes were convinced there was an audience for serious theatre in that area and pioneered the crazy scheme of performing there with their company Aavishkar helmed by the indefatigable Arun Kakde kaka. Dubeyji quickly joined forces with them, as did some others, and for almost two decades Chhabildas enjoyed, among the vernacular intelligentsia, a smallish cult status as the haven of experimental theatre in Marathi and Hindi. Audiences were small and losses were invariably incurred at every show but the few intrepid souls who had made Chhabildas's reputation persevered until Arvind suddenly passed away, Dubeyji started exploring newer venues and many of the actors and directors who had worked there had to move on when the school management decided it was more profitable to let the hall out for wedding receptions.

No one had attempted an English play at Chhabildas, there was no audience for English in that neighbourhood we were told, so though even that venue seemed closed to us we decided to go ahead and perform there. It was the only place we could afford and I somewhat neatly resolved the 'director' dilemma by deciding on two pieces I had done before, Ionesco's *The Lesson* which, not knowing French, I had been itching to do in English; and a stunning 10-minute piece by Jorge Diaz on US war atrocities, called *Man Does Not Die by Bread Alone*. I directed the latter and Ketan Mehta directed *The Lesson*. The show, with Ratna as the Pupil, opened in a hall at the Alliance Française, courtesy Asha Kasbekar, who played the maid, then did more than one performance at Chhabildas, sometimes with audiences of ten or twelve. We later went on to revive *Zoo Story* and staged it with Chekhov's *The Bear*, again two pieces I had done before—I was obviously dying to show off. The performances happened in all sorts of places apart from Chhabildas: in the open air at various institutes, in hotels, in friends' drawing rooms or terraces, once even on a badminton court. All this time I cadged as many meals as I could at Ratna's home. Babi bai, her cook, had taken to me when I first met her and by now had made it her responsibility to stuff me thoroughly every time I ate there. Things seemed to be glancing upwards ever so slightly at last. Dina who had been dialect consultant on the dubbing of *Manthan*, and who despite herself was impressed with my work, had begun to tolerate my presence, Baldev was seldom home and Shyam Benegal's next film, a biopic on the Marathi star Hansa Wadkar, had taken shape and I had been told I would be featuring in it.

Of admen and film-makers

I hadn't ever heard of Hansa Wadkar who was in her prime in the forties. The only Maharashtrian actors I knew were those who had worked in Hindi cinema as well. Shyam, greatly obsessed with the idea of filming Wadkar's life, often talked of it as his dream project. His reputation as an auteur whose films also made money was now firm, and *Manthan*, when finally released commercially, further consolidated his standing as one of India's most exciting film-makers so he had no trouble at all raising funds for this somewhat ambitious and not really 'saleable' project set in the film world of the forties.

A superstition still exists in the film industry that films about films do not run, just as there was the equally absurd notion that films on cricket do not run, though until *Lagaan* no one who knew anything about the game had bothered to make a film about it. Films about films still do not run. I will leave you to ponder the question why. What was particularly admired about Shyam was his handling of actors, so the project even in its nascent stage aroused great curiosity in the acting fraternity; and the question of who would play the tour-de-force central part must surely have created many swirls of anxiety, even though Shyam had long since decided upon

Smita. I was to play a film-maker who seduces and abandons the lady, a brief part requiring just a week's work, and I would be paid more than I had ever been paid before!

Bhumika was produced by Blaze, the company that had made big profits and an even bigger reputation backing Shyam's first two films, so this time round he was not as strapped as he used to be, and to compensate for the small payments we'd received on *Manthan* was extremely generous. All the stalwarts of Shyam's stable were to be there: Amrish, Kulbhushan, Mohan Agashe, Anant Nag, along with prize catch Amol Palekar who had graduated to stardom much before any of the others. It was a heavyweight cast, and for trivia-lovers the film also features Om Puri under heavy make-up in a tiny part, his very first in cinema. Happy as I was at the prospect of more work and more earning, I was not overly thrilled about this film. I don't think there's been a single film made on Indian movies which rings true. They are all either determinedly arcane or thickly sugar-coated, and most of them end up pandering to the industry's own self-congratulatory image of itself. If a truthful, cutting-edge film were to be made about the Indian film industry it would out-Fellini Fellini. But I daresay it is futile hoping for that to happen.

Shyam's office in Jyoti Studios at Grant Road was a place I had by now visited several times. It was the very studio where the first Indian talkie *Alam Ara* was filmed, though the Shooting Lot was now decrepit and almost never used. Half its compound housed a car-repair garage but the place was redolent with history. I loved it. Actors I had seen in fleeting parts would drift by, there was evidence everywhere of an age long gone; the chairs had accommodated a thousand bums, the equipment looked like it should be in a museum, the architecture of the place, the decor, the banisters, the worn wooden steps, had been neither maintained nor replaced. A myriad ghosts hid in the nooks and crannies of the editing rooms. If I remember right the first scene of *Bhumika* was shot in this studio, at least my first scene was. Smita and I, having just been mutually smitten in a Holi celebration, go roaring out of the studio, doubling as a studio, in an antique Bugatti Thunderbird.

Shyam's only instruction to me for this part was that I should 'look dapper and cool' so to that end I had neatly trimmed my beard, which he approved of, then added a pair of rimless glasses and a crisp kurta-pyjama outfit. The effect was not un-dapper except that my driving skills not being the best I looked anything but cool as we zigzagged off in a cloud of dust, leaving the Parsi owner of the car in real life looking mighty worried. Luckily my expression of terror at the prospect of totaling an obviously very expensive antique car does not quite register. Except for a couple of steamy scenes with the gorgeous Smita and the perk of having Shyam take Kulbhushan and myself along for the schedule in Goa even though neither of us was required, I didn't enjoy acting in this film too much. And soon enough something, apart from having to be rescued by Rekha Sabnis from an air mattress that had drifted too far into the sea at the deserted Anjuna Beach, was to happen that would further mess up my head.

I had finally been able to afford a room to myself just across the road from Martinville in an apartment owned by a Mrs Remedios, a large and formidable-looking lady until you noticed the merry look in her eyes. She too initially laid down the no-girlfriends rule, then met Ratna, got bowled over and the rule was amended to 'okay, but no locking the door hunh?' Jaspal, Paddy, Tika and Om were still staying at Martinville.

About a hundred metres from the front of Khar West station was a little place called Sindh Punjab Dhaba where all of us often ate dinner. It was a reasonably priced eatery where dal was served free if you ordered another dish, usually vegetarian, and chapattis. A totally satisfying meal in Sindh Punjab cost about four rupees, a sumptuous one cost a little more and the taste of the food belied the ridiculously low pricing.

While the *Bhumika* shooting was on, Om and I were in the middle of dinner when Jaspal, whom I had kept well away from for some time now, also entered and greeted Om. We ignored each other but, eyes fixed on me, he passed to sit at another table behind me, so I thought. I was by now accustomed to this menacing attitude and muttered threats every time I was anywhere around and continued eating. After a while I was reminded of his presence by what felt like a short sharp punch in the middle of my back. I started to rise, wearily preparing myself for another free-for-all. Before I could move, Om, with a strangled cry, lunged at something behind me. I turned to see Jaspal holding a small knife, its point dripping blood, his hand raised to strike again, and Om and two others grappling to subdue him. The strength suddenly seemed to leave my legs but a desperate attempt to get out of range caused me to lurch forward, upsetting the table, sending plates and their contents flying. On the floor I was aware of feet running past, shouting, and sounds of violence behind. Someone was helping me to my feet as I heard the manager of the place telephonically informing the police that there had been a fight and one man had been stabbed. Om returned to inform me that Jaspal had been taken to the kitchen and was being given the treatment. He wanted to take me to a doctor, but was thwarted by the restaurant staff refusing to let us move till the police arrived. A sizeable crowd had collected by now, the muscles in my back were beginning to go into spasm, blood was soaking my shirt-back and had begun its progress down my trouser seat. I was breathless and desperately thirsty, I wanted to lie down but Om didn't think that a good idea, and the gaping crowd had gotten thicker.

Two constables on a bicycle stopped and after making some off-hand enquiries one of them escorted Jaspal away in a taxi. I wonder if that cabbie ever got paid. These cops in any case had gotten unwittingly co-opted—they were not responding to the phone call, they seemed to just be passing by, and pretty soon a Black Maria carrying a whole posse with its siren at full blast came screeching around the corner, making the crowd disappear like smoke. The constabulary swarming out of the van hungry for action, nightsticks at the ready, were somewhat deflated when pointed in my direction: one injured guy sitting there looking pretty helpless. Before anyone could explain anything to them I was hauled up by my scruff, a hard hand or two landing on the back of my head along with admonitions about fighting in the street; the morals of my sister and mother were questioned and I was not exactly kicked into the van but just about. Om made the cardinal error of climbing in as well without permission and managed to rile the boss-man there by asking the cops to be gentle with me. He was ordered to get off and after considerable pleading with the goon in charge was allowed to stay. Neither of us had any idea where we were headed but I prayed it was not to the police station. The bleeding hadn't ceased, the pain was getting intense and these cops obviously hadn't quite understood the situation. After a few cursory questions to us and some garbled transmissions over the radio in Marathi, we arrived at Cooper Hospital in Juhu, by which time all those present had been apprised of what had happened and I was not unsympathetically helped by the cops to alight, finally laid on a stretcher and taken in to be stitched up. It has taken years for my visceral hatred of the khaki uniform to subside.

I was supposed to shoot in the morning so obviously Shyam had to be the first to be informed. It was almost midnight and I didn't know if it was possible for Om to take the liberty of calling his residence at that time, so Govind Nihalani who lived nearby was asked to tell Shyam the news and also to lend me a shirt. Sunil Shanbag informed Ratna and the whole lot turned up early next morning, with Shyam deciding I should shift to Jaslok Hospital at his expense. The shoot naturally was suspended for a while.

While recuperating I learnt that Jaspal, after spending two nights in custody, had been bailed out by Saeed Mirza in whose film *Arvind Desai* he had replaced me when I was unable to find the time for it. Saeed had always been hugely biased towards Jaspal since our FTII days and was now sheltering him in his own home; I hoped he knew what he was doing. After a luxurious three days, my first stay in a five-star hospital, Nira and Shyam took me to their home, where I was tended to by these foster parents.

I wasn't famous enough for the news to make it to the papers and there was no relentless TV coverage of every fart, burp and nose-pick by actors, so Baba who I think quite enjoyed having more things to worry about, didn't get wind of the incident and he and Ammi were spared this time. It was a day after I moved back to my pad in New Light building on SV Road that the full impact of what had occurred began to sink in. The sonofabitch had tried to kill me and I suppose I should thank my guardian angel yet again that Om had been there and that Jaspal didn't know a thing about handling a knife. If he had, he would have gone for my throat from behind; as it happened the knife entered an inch into what are probably the most resilient muscles in the back, and the X-rays showed it had missed my spine by a whisker.

I was dozing one afternoon when the doorbell rang. Opening the door to find Jaspal standing there with a smile that didn't reach his eyes I froze, too scared to do or say anything. He entered, stretched out his hand to shake, helped himself to a cigarette and made himself comfortable as I stood there gaping. He didn't enquire after my well-being, nor did he make an apologetic sound. Instead, with a slightly hysterical chuckle he explained that what had happened was 'nothing personal' (he had earlier been deeply affected by Al Pacino's *Godfather* performance), 'it's a class war, Saeed has explained it all to me'. Saeed Mirza had always been the high priest of Marxism at FTII; 'Marx-Pravachans' as they were cynically called regularly took place in his room there, and though I was not actually surprised at Saeed holding this opinion, it could easily have been an invention of Jaspal's fevered brain as well. An extremely tense five or ten minutes followed, during which I kept standing at the ready in case he went for me again, though I would have been far from able to defend myself. Eventually, when I asked him to leave, he seemed genuinely astonished but didn't protest and got up mumbling something about 'no need to still be angry yaar, I haven't been well', before I shut the door in his face and continued to hear him calling out from the window for a while before he left. A week or so later we met again at the petty-crimes court, I did not press charges and the judge declared the matter closed as Jaspal stood grinning in the dock.

The shooting of *Bhumika* was barely done when Girish Karnad turned up in town, invited Om and me to breakfast at the Sun 'n' Sand Hotel and told us he was casting us both in a film he was planning to make in Bangalore. Based on the celebrated novel *Tabbaliyu Neenade Magane* by S.L. Bhyrappa, it was to be in both Kannada and Hindi, with the two of us in the Hindi version. I was to play a pedantic Brahmin priest and Girish asked if for the part I would shave my head to which I instantly agreed, and if I could put on a bit of a paunch which proved an utter impossibility. Bajju bhai too was to be closely involved in the Hindi version as an adviser.

Manthan was about to be released and Ratna and I were seeing each other daily. She had been around all the time I was recuperating from the stab, and her parents started getting seriously worried that things were getting out of hand. It was time for them to take action and make her lose this drug-addled mongrel she was becoming increasingly fond of and for whom, on the odd occasion, she had even defied them. A plan was hatched to send her to London, ostensibly as reward for having successfully graduated from university but actually to get her out of my clutches and in the hope that she might develop some interest in a good Wembley-based Gujarati boy. Turned out her visit to London was to coincide exactly with my shoot in Bangalore, so off she went to England's freezing winter while I made my way, now with complete assurance by air, to Bangalore and thence to Mahimapura, a village just off the Mysore highway, to act in my fourth film. After spending two days in a hotel in Bangalore (the encounter with the three fearsome snorers together occurred here) and having my head shaved, we were driving to the location when Girish informed me that the actor playing the priest in the Kannada version had suddenly made himself unavailable and would I do the Kannada version as well? Not knowing a word of the language I baulked but was reassured by the promise of extra payment, and this time I stayed awake many a night not because of Kulbhushan's snoring but in trying with Bajju bhai's help to memorize my Kannada dialogue. The Hindi version of this film *Godhuli* seems to have vanished without a trace but the Kannada version still exists. My pathetic pronunciation in it, however, necessitated my voice being dubbed by a Kannada-speaking actor.

Both versions were shot simultaneously and directed by Girish and B.V. Karanth. The two, after making a couple of films in tandem, had made one each on their own and probably to affirm their commitment to each other went into this, their final effort together which in fact was Karanth's last at film-making. The lead was played by Kulbhushan, cast against type as a suave 'England return' toting a white wife (Paula Lindsay) whose ideas prove too modern for his village; in the Kannada version the part was being played by another actor Manappa who later died tragically in a road accident. Paula and Laxmi Krishnamurthy playing the mother were also common to both versions and neither of them spoke Kannada either; but since the former had to speak only English and the latter, a deaf mute character, nothing at all, neither of these ladies had to undergo the kind of nightmares I had memorizing words I hadn't heard before and whose meaning I barely understood. I had to resort to mnemonics to remember the lines most of the time, but I muddled through. Many years later, doing a Malayalam film and realizing that Kannada had been a cakewalk in comparison, I completely abandoned any attempt to speak it after a while and resorted to reciting numbers instead of dialogue. I had also by then somewhat lost the burning enthusiasm I had at the time of *Godhuli*, to believe in myself as the character, to stay in costume, to sleep on an iron cot in a tent, to be served a boiled egg for breakfast with my name in pencil on it, to be paid a pittance, but at that time it hadn't seemed so bad.

In fact one morning I got a reminder that my lot could

actually have been much worse. After having jogged up to the temple that was our main location, I was somewhat impatiently awaiting the arrival of breakfast, when I heard a clanking, huffing sound emerging from the direction of the roughly two hundred steep and uneven stone steps leading up the hill. The sound got closer before I realized it was a spotboy, maybe sixteen years old, ascending the slope I had laboured up carrying only myself. Half a dozen chairs were piled on his head, he had a kettle of tea in one hand and some cups in the other. Though the glaring disparity between the various echelons of workers who comprise the film industry has been illustrated to me many times over in the course of forty years, it has never manifested itself in so affecting a sight as this.

After a twenty-five-day schedule we had a fortnight's break and returned to the city. Initially terribly self-conscious of the shaved head I took to wearing a cap, but then decided what the hell, it looked rather enigmatic. I threw away the cap and began to enjoy flaunting it. In this break I was summoned by Alyque Padamsee who, the rumours now confirmed, was planning to film Girish Karnad's play based on the life of Mohammad bin Tughlaq, the eccentric fourteenth-century Sultan of Delhi, who assassinated his father, introduced copper currency and ended his reign in despair after unsuccessfully trying to shift his capital from Delhi to Daulatabad. Mr Padamsee had earlier produced *Tughlaq* in English on the Bombay stage to massive acclaim. I had seen it and had not come away impressed. Kabir Bedi played the title part and the production seemed more interested in flaunting his oily beefcake than focusing on the issues in the play. The mincing diva playing the stepmother seemed to be drooling so over those gorgeous pectorals, at times I wasn't quite sure this wasn't

Oedipus Rex I was watching. At NSD I had acted in Alkazi's Urdu version of *Tughlaq*, playing two or three minor parts and feeling terribly cheated that I wasn't considered for the title role—I felt I could play it as no one had. The possibility of getting it in a movie I had fantasized about, but I assumed Mr Bedi had already been cast. However, I told myself there were plenty of other good parts in it and maybe Alyque had seen *Manthan* by now.

Mr Padamsee, at that time head honcho of Lintas, the advertising concern, had a secretary called Miss Pope, the better I suppose to savour the appellation 'God' by which he was referred to in ad circles, and she ushered me into God's presence right away, the first sign that things were going to go terribly right at this meeting. I had never met the man, only seen some of his theatre productions, which seemed impressive until I saw the original versions later when I started travelling abroad. He said he liked the 'raw-boned' quality of my face and that he was looking for an actor with my kind of intensity. He had just seen *Manthan* and after hemming and hawing for quite a while he finally said he thought I was 'right for the part of [it seemed an eternity before he said it] Tughlaq'. My heart by then was hammering so hard I could barely hear him speak. Swallowing resolutely a couple of times I refocused on God. I needed to grow a beard, start pumping up and learn to ride, he was saying. Apparently he wanted me to look as much like Kabir Bedi as I could; I didn't waste time wondering why Mr Bedi himself hadn't been cast. I was given money to obtain membership in the Amateur Riding Club at Mahalaxmi and enrol in a gymnasium. Even though my excitement was practically bursting out of my ears, I knew by now that talking about a film before it is actually released is foolishness, and in any case there was no one, apart from Ratna, to whom this news would matter, and she was on her way back from London, not having met the good Gujarati boy of Dina's dreams.

The future now had a distinctly rosier glow. I had landed the eponymous role in what promised to be a seriously high-profile project. It was to be in Urdu but 'on an international scale' so Alyque promised, was to be shot on location in Rajasthan and Gwalior, and was to have a massive budget—until my fee was discussed that is, when it would suddenly become a 'small film'. Simi Garewal evidently had been signed to play Tughlaq's stepmother and Jalal Agha was to play the other protagonist, Aziz.

By the time I ended my work on *Godhuli* and returned to Bombay, *Manthan* had garnered not only great praise but healthy box office returns as well. A message awaited me from Rajshri Productions, the producers from another lifetime of the film *Dosti*, asking for a meeting. It transpired that one of the clutch of film-makers they had on their roster had seen *Hero* (my acting course film made at FTII by Shyam) and had got it into his head to remake Chaplin's *City Lights* with me as the tramp. The script was being worked on, they said, and would I be agreeable? Since it was put that way I decided to lay down a stipulation—only if it was to be shot in one stretch, something they promptly agreed to. But first I had *Tughlaq* on my brain. Before my hair started growing back I was religiously working out in the gymnasium every morning, and every alternate afternoon brushing up on the rudimentary riding abilities I had picked up in Aligarh.

Even though I never received a monetary advance for *Tughlaq*, I no longer had to scrounge meals, I could now even pay the bills when Ratna and I lunched together. The workouts were severe and the brain-dead trainers at the gym advised me on diet but not about the need worked-out muscles have for rest on alternate days. So my regimen consisted of pumping all muscles every day in a two-and-a-half-hour session that would leave me feeling limp. Fortunately my body was young enough to take that sort of punishment. Soon my shirts started going tight around the shoulders and my trousers at the thighs. I was quickly able to recover my not quite forgotten riding abilities, got promoted out of the circle of beginners and was allowed to venture round the race track on my own, resulting in my turning a little more confident than was good for me and taking a tumble at full gallop that resulted in a shifted vertebra and forty-five days flat on my back, not allowed to rise or even turn over. As I was falling, all I thought was, 'Hell! There goes *Tughlaq*, and here comes the bedpan.' It had in any case been almost six months since I had come on board and there had been absolutely no movement on that project except that I was expected to turn up at God's office whenever called and he, after leaning back in his chair, scratching his goatee, examining my by now not unmuscular body, would nod ever so slowly and inform me of a further postponement in the schedule.

Now that the fractured vertebra had put paid to my workouts and pushed the film further away, I considered going into a depression but decided not to. Govind Nihalani who was to be director of photography on *Tughlaq*, told me not to lose any sleep, the project was still pretty far off, even though Alyque kept insisting it would happen soon. A cyclostyled schedule was actually distributed, detailing every shooting location with exact dates right up to the day the film would be re-recorded and the date, time and location of the first screening for the cast and crew! I was within that year to become educated on the vast gulf between good advertising and actual film-making. I also made the monumental discovery while in hospital that there is one position in which it is impossible to roll a joint—flat on your back. Ratna and Om who visited frequently were closely instructed on how to do this essential job for me.

Bobby, now a major in the Armoured Corps and in town for some military matter, unexpectedly visited me in hospital, bearing the news that he and his long-time sweetheart Sabeeha were planning to tie the knot soon and I was expected to attend. Ratna had already met my brothers and their wives and won them all over completely, so naturally she was included in the invite. Agha Mamu, who had chosen another girl for Bobby and had without consulting anyone at all given his word to her family, was furious at the prospect of egg on his face. He threatened to not only boycott the event but to cut Bobby off without a cent if he went ahead. If it had been held in Meerut he might even have disrupted it, guns blazing; so Bobby and Sabeeha's family had decided Bombay was the safest recourse. An uncle of hers made available a picturesque cottage his company owned at Madh Island and there the banns were to be held. Agha Mamu stayed away but Bobby and I were convinced that with time the old man would come round, after all even my father had; and Bobby had always shared a much closer relationship with his father than I had with mine. Besides he had been a dutiful son, always toeing the line, always obedient, always compliant; now for the first time in his life he had defied a diktat and asserted himself. Agha Mamu, if he truly wished to 'make Bobby a man' as he claimed, should have been proud of the new backbone his son had grown but his ego was too huge to allow that. Through the remainder of his life not once did he ever come close to melting, never forgiving Bobby's solitary act of defiance, nursing his imaginary wound, even refusing to acknowledge his grandsons when they were taken to seek his blessings. I, who according to him had always been a 'bad influence' on Bobby, now having made a bit of a name for myself had, not so surprisingly, risen in his esteem. I received a letter from him telling me to advise Bobby against 'this rash and unwise step', which I did not bother to do; and Ratna and I happily attended the wedding held with no one present except us, Bobby's sister Mohib and Sabeeha's parents. It was the loveliest wedding I have ever been to, on a gorgeous day by the sea, devoid of the heartburn, backbiting and stress always present on such occasions. The beard and long hair I now sported got me mistaken for the 'qazi' when we arrived at the wedding location, and Ratna and I that day decided that when we wed it had to be by the sea.

Shooting on the *Tughlaq* project had been postponed so often it was becoming a bit of a joke; the bulk I had put on preparing for the part now became an impediment in the rehabilitation of my injured back. All form of exercise except lower-back therapy being forbidden for the time being, I could only look on in wonder at the bulges around my waist that hadn't been there before. *Tughlaq* was looking more and more like a mirage but Shyam had decided upon his next, based on a Ruskin Bond short story called *A Flight of Pigeons* set around the 1857 War of Independence and I was cast in the part of a mutineer. The riding skills I had picked up came in useful for this film instead of for the other on which, tiring of Alyque's constant procrastination, the producers ultimately pulled the plug.

Mrs Remedios came into my room one morning to wake me, something she never did, waving a telegram. She stood by as I tore it open; it was from Zaheer and it said 'Baba died stop burial in Sardhana today.'

Breeng the shit

The word hijack had by now fully entered the lexicon: the first mid-air incidents had occurred, planes had been blown up and security screens were being tightened at airports the world over. I borrowed the airfare to Delhi (then around 500 rupees) from Ratna, and went to the airport hoping to get on a late morning flight and catch a bus to Sardhana before evening. There were no seats available, I was informed in the not-so-incomprehensibly rude manner in which Indian Airlines ground staff treated passengers those days. Ratna had told me I would get a seat if I showed them the telegram to confirm that my need for a ticket was genuine and urgent, but because of new security rules she couldn't accompany me into the airport to do the talking; and the desk clerk's dismissiveness so incensed me that far from telling him about my father's death and pleading for a seat I felt like slamming him in the face. Besides, if there was no seat available how on earth could he have got me one? So I didn't plead or produce the telegram and I didn't get on the flight and I wasn't present when Baba joined his ancestors that evening. His body had been brought to Sardhana by truck from Allahabad where, staying with Zaheer, his ulcer—a source of trouble for him always—finally got him. Zameer, posted in the North-East, had not managed to turn up in time either. Though all present knew Baba's condition was grave, he instructed them not to inform me so I had no news until the telegram arrived. He either felt my time would not be my own or he didn't want me to see him in that condition. On hearing later of the physical agony he went through, I feel thankful I was spared from witnessing his loss of dignity.

Ammi was remarkably composed when I met her—her last thirty years had gone by sharing his life and serving him ceaselessly; now the pivot of her existence was gone, the three of us were able to spare less and less time for her, she hadn't another involvement she could immerse herself in, yet she was holding back on the lamentation. We knew though how deeply grieved she actually was and that suppressing one's grief is not always good. We feared she wouldn't last long after him but the old girl had more spunk than any of us gave her credit for. She not only squared her frail little shoulders and tackled life on her own terms, she outlived him by almost twenty years and had the time of her life revelling in her children's successes.

The day I arrived in Sardhana I visited the mound of earth that was Baba now and we had the first of the many easy conversations I was later to have with him. That day I talked to him about the film I had just done, felt his amusement at my playing a shaven-headed Hindu priest. I told him about the one I was going to do, playing Sarfaraz the mutineer, and that I was modelling the way I would look in the film on portraits of Dada Jan Fishan Khan, my Afghan ancestor. I could virtually hear him chuckle. I told him about my dreams and my doubts, about Ratna whom he had never met, about how much I was now earning, anything that came into my head. I knew he was listening and responding. This was an actual conversation in which I took the initiative. I suddenly began to feel the weight of all I had lost out on and would never regain and

I was surprised by how much I suddenly missed him. A few years later, I had a dream in which I see myself seated as for a job interview, at a long, polished table. Seated on the other side of the table is the interviewer, Baba looking beatifically happy, and he says to me, 'Tell me about your father.' I proceed to enumerate the ways he had failed me, how I had never felt loved or appreciated by him, how I never got what I wanted, how I hated his judgemental nature, his narrow worldview, his negativity, etc. etc. As I, quite unemotionally, poured out in a steady stream all I had in life never been foolhardy enough to say to him, he quietly listened, not saying a word and looking unflinchingly into my eyes, as if understanding perfectly what I was talking about. Through his life he had never seemed so much himself, so approachable, as he was in that dream. When I awoke I felt as if my troubled relationship with Baba had achieved closure to some extent.

When I returned to sin-city after the burial, Zaheer insisted on taking Ammi with him to Allahabad and she complied, but only for a couple of weeks before heading back to Mussoorie where she continued to live perfectly content for the next fifteen or so years, only coming down to Sardhana or to one of our homes if the cold got troublesome. If one of us compelled her to leave Mussoorie she'd often angrily acquiesce, and though we all really tried to keep her happy, she was never at peace anywhere except in those two places, in her 'own home'. Many a rainy night in Bombay did I wonder how she was managing in Mussoorie. She was always desirous of being sociable, loved meeting people, but with Baba being the way he was she had always had to put that desire on hold. Through her remaining days she spent much time in Mussoorie alone or with people she liked, or with one of the three of us alternately and as briefly as she could, though she seldom had much to say.

I wanted to lose the beard and hair I had grown for *Tughlaq* but was told they would be required in Shyam's new film, and the longer the better. This one was to have a much bigger budget than any of his earlier ones and I would be paid twice as much as I was for my first film. Mr Shashi Kapoor, tasting major commercial success those days, had not only decided with his wife Jennifer Kendal's goading to build a theatre in his late father Mr Prithviraj Kapoor's memory, he had also formed Film-valas to produce what he hoped would be memorable popular films, and to that end had signed up nearly every 'different' film-maker of those days. Shyam was the first to be taken on and his next two films (the first one *Junoon* was the first of four such ventures) were to launch the company. Mr Kapoor was in huge demand in the popular cinema, so common sense dictated that his coming on board as an actor as well would open up a whole new audience for Shyam. He was cast, much to my chagrin, as the lovelorn Pathan reluctant to join the war. I had read the original story and had always fancied myself in the part. Shyam, knowing I was feeling short-changed, gave me a stern talking to about how 'the film was more important than individual parts', and I should enter into it with the same spirit I had so far displayed. He also assured me the part he had created for me was pivotal and the most dramatic of all. I naturally assumed that in that case my job was to outdo everyone in the movie and proceeded to attempt to do that instead of playing as a team man.

The film was to be shot in Kakori and Malihabad near Lucknow, and we repaired thence. Staying at the Clark's Awadh, the city's only five-star hotel, I got a room to myself and so, glory be, did Kulbhushan at the other end of the corridor. Ratna, now at NSD, came down to Lucknow for a few days and amusedly witnessed my frantic efforts to stay in character all the time. I very slowly recovered my confidence with horses, and began once more to love it so much, I would have ridden back to the hotel every day if I could. It didn't occur to me that less could be more and I went through this film straining every nerve and every sinew carrying a banner proclaiming how hard I was working at becoming the character. All totally unnecessary, but hell, it was fun being that guy, red-bearded and turbaned, muzzle-loader slung over shoulder, gunpowder pouch at waist, sword in hand, charging at the British soldiers like a messenger from Hades.

The film viewed now, despite the excellence of its making, appears like an acting contest and the only one who emerges with any laurels at all is a non-actor in a tiny part, Ismat Chughtai the celebrated writer, and that's because she's the only one of us not trying to ACT everyone else under the table.

The third day of the shoot, whom should I see standing in the lobby of the hotel with Jennifer but Mr and Mrs Kendal. This should not have been surprising considering they were her parents, but they were there because English actors were going to be needed for the film—somehow I just hadn't joined the dots. Jennifer, who knew of my fascination with Shakespeareana, introduced me to them and I shook hands with 'him' for the second time. My twenty-year dream of acting with him was about to come true.

He was playing a priest delivering a sermon in a church when it is attacked. I am the leader of the attackers. After waiting one score years for this day, the only acting I get to do with him is to walk up to him and cut him down with a sword. But in the few days he was in Lucknow, finding him actually very approachable, I did corner him and talk to him. I soon eliminated the compliments—he would embarrassedly brush them aside anyway. I asked him one day if he didn't feel regret at not having stayed on in England and becoming a Knight or Lord; I considered him no less than any of those actors who had. 'Regret?' he growled. 'I did what I chose to do. I'm not an actor, I'm a missionary and my mission is to spread Shakespeare.'

A few years later, pungent irony, he and I were simultaneous recipients of the Sangeet Natak Akademi award for services rendered to Indian theatre. I was seated next to him at the ceremony and could not help wondering how much all this really mattered to him. This recognition by the Indian government was too damn late. But surely he felt honoured. I don't think any Indian has done half as much to spread theatre awareness among schoolchildren in Asia as the Kendals.

I was able finally to tell Mr Kendal about my dream of joining Shakespeareana and in return he asked me if I would act in a production of *Gaslight* he was planning for the Prithvi. But three things conspired against it: a) he himself was not going to act, only direct, b) I was not free at the time he needed to rehearse, and c) I thought the rest of the cast totally unsuitable. The production was staged sometime later and I have to say I didn't care for it.

The *Filmfare* awards were announced while we were in Lucknow, Ratna called me up from Delhi to tell me that she'd heard I had won something. I had no idea I had even been nominated. I imagined it might be for 'best supporting actor' and felt pretty pleased—my picture would start appearing in *Filmfare* at last and the next fortnight it did. I had been awarded a special prize for my performance in *Manthan*. Dr Shriram Lagoo won Best Supporting Actor that year, something I didn't at all resent. What had happened was that the jury members, probably wanting to reward my efforts but not being able to find a category, had decided to curtsy to the fact that *Manthan* had succeeded critically and commercially, both factors being essential criteria in winning one of those ridiculous statuettes which Smita, while smiling straight at the cameras, presented to me at the function. Except that it felt exactly as heavy as the ones in Mr Dilip Kumar's drawing room, the whole affair was a frantic letdown.

Barabanki had always been just a word for me. It had no memories or associations at all since I had spent only the first six months or so of my life there. But during the shoot, with Ammi deciding to visit Lucknow to meet her youngest sister Nikhat, and with Ratna discovering that Barabanki was barely an hour's drive from Lucknow, we undertook a visit there. Ammi who normally could get lost in a phone booth was as sharp as I have ever seen her and guided the car unerringly through the by-lanes of Barabanki to the gate of Jahangirabad House where they lived when I was born. 'The old house', as Mr Tom Jones once sang, was 'still standing, though the paint is cracked and dry'. The bungalow stood forlorn in a large unkempt compound which, knowing Baba's fondness for roses, must once have had a garden in it. There weren't many other dwellings around. It had a small gate of the kind one used to see at railway crossings and a short driveway leading up to a low, pillared veranda. The place was locked and looked uninhabited so we walked around; Ammi pointed out the room where my eyes first opened to the world. I didn't have a camera so we took no pictures but I revisited Jahangirabad House some thirty-five years later to find it completely hidden from view amidst a teeming colony. All around where it stood, alone and somewhat grand, were clusters of newly built shops and houses for miles around. Half the house had fallen down, including 'my room'; and there were some people, presumably squatting, in the remaining section. We were welcomed in and I saw a smallish drawing room, walls now stripped of plaster, and a tiny fireplace. I tried imagining Baba lighting the fire or Ammi sitting by it while I lay in my crib but it didn't work. We were soon surrounded by a mob of gawking onlookers. But I now think of that house very often, surely it being the very first place I set eyes on has had some effect.

Rajshri Films, the makers of small, clean family entertainers, had been assiduously wooing me for a while, and with some misgivings I agreed to do their film *Sunaina*, a reworking of *City Lights*, even though the script when I heard it gave me a dyspeptic attack. I was to play the Chaplin part and an FTII classmate and friend, Rameshwari, who had always generously bailed me out with small loans and who despite being the unlikeliest of candidates had hit pay dirt with her first film, was to play the blind flower girl. Shooting was to commence the day I finished *Junoon*, but they gave in to my request for two weeks off before starting. Rajshri Films was nothing if not polite. Vastly relieved to exorcise the demons of 1857 I got a shave and haircut, stopped glowering at the world and started practising the 'churmeeng ismaaile' that the Bengali director of *Sunaina*, Mr Hiren Nag, wanted me to employ in almost every scene. Whatever little excitement I had felt about getting to reprise a part created by the greatest actor ever vanished the day we started shooting, and the little fact that Mr Chaplin himself would not be writing and directing this film really sank in.

The ghosts who passed off as the writers of this film obviously had been dissatisfied with Mr Chaplin's effort and instead of just copying faithfully were intent on improving upon his mastery and control over every aspect of everything in his films: the tenderest subtlety and the broadest pratfall; his ability to manipulate the audience's feelings in a flash, from the quiet smile to the belly laugh to the silent tear. Chaplin's worldview, his spare elegant wit, had transmogrified into unfunny situations labouring for laughs or lachrymose self-pitying nonsense. There were endless pages of turgid dialogue instead of the silences or just the looks that say volumes in Chaplin's work. Worst of all, his somewhat grotesque but deeply perceptive characterizations had become boring prudes, and a self-congratulatory morality had replaced the master's frequently bawdy sense of fun.

All this, needless to say, is par for the course in Hindi cinema, which seems to pride itself on churning out ghastly adaptations of much-loved Hollywood movies. I feared a bad trip coming on but foolhardily believed that I could surmount it by bringing authenticity to my performance. Besides, I was committed and had received a signing amount. There was no escape.

Rajshri Productions was vegetarian in the strictest sense: not only would there be nothing non-veg on the daily menu, the characters in their films could not consume meat even as part of a shot. Evil characters smoked and drank of course but the actual showing of either on screen was a taboo placed by the wonderfully old-fashioned paterfamilias, Mr Tarachand Barjatya, who had created and nurtured the company. I wondered what the suicidal drunk in the film would be consuming before throwing himself off the pier—grief, I reckoned, probably accompanied by a song. Then I heard the songs, both solos I had to perform to but mercifully not sing myself. They were not bad as Hindi film songs go, one of them is still heard occasionally, but the thought of being cast in the lead in a commercial film, singing those songs, probably dancing around trees, didn't exactly thrill me because I didn't know the first thing about how to do a song and a tree can't make its partner look good.

The bravado that had carried me through actually singing on the stage in NSD was no longer part of my personality and I was now having trouble even faking the singing. All I thought I had to do was lip-synch perfectly, I felt it would be passable if it seemed like I was actually singing and that was all I practised. What in fact I should have done was study the songs in Shammi Kapoor's movies and attempt to get somewhere remotely close to what he did. It's what every male actor and every choreographer in Bombay post-Shammi has done—with varying degrees of success, of course. It took me years before I learnt the difference between merely singing a song and 'performing' it. But I was always slow.

One of the mistakes I had made in the preceding five years had been giving up on popular Hindi movies, both as audience and acting aspirant. I was convinced that there was absolutely nothing to be gained by seeing them and futile hoping to act in them—I just was not that kind of actor. Besides, there were no more Dara Singh films and the stars I had grown up loving—Dilip K, Shammi K, Dev Anand—all were way past their sell-by date as leading men and were being replaced by another less charismatic and infinitely shallower generation. I did attempt to see the odd so-called classics—*Reshma aur Shera, Upkaar, Mera Naam Joker, Abhimaan*—but none of them really blew me away. My attitude to Hindi cinema turned even more condescending, possibly because I couldn't see myself fitting in in it. I was resentful in advance of being cast in roles it would hurt my ego to have to play. So I gave Hindi cinema a very wide berth even at FTII, quite seriously believing that I'd never have to act in such movies and that I'd get my due in the newer kind of cinema now being made, films like *Ankur*. Though I have to say the thought that I was not qualified to be the lead in popular movies pinched greatly, so this reaction was very possibly my defence mechanism working in advance to counter the rejection I anticipated. And now here I was, having to deliver the goods in the kind of movie wild horses could not have dragged me to see.

I was dimly aware that there would be a difference of approach in the acting in such movies but just not being able to zero in on what it was, decided to give it my usual kitchen-sink treatment. In retrospect I could probably have done this part without breaking a sweat when I was twenty and had my brief fling with Hindi cinema. But a decade and more later I was thrashing in the dark to find my own way of expressing, and I was also hampered by the hang-up that I could never be a popular star (even the girl who loved me had been cynical about my chances). I could no longer appreciate the kind of narcissistic, scenery-chewing, upstaging approach to performing required by popular films.

Since studying at FTII, I had worked assiduously at removing all that I began to consider as 'larger-than-life' nonsense from my performances and indeed from my personality, and the task of trying to recover it now was not only offensive to my newly acquired sensibility, it felt unachievable.

I tried misguidedly to apply the method as I understood it: insisting, much to the director's disapproval, on wearing my own used clothes, the same set for the entire movie, and looking unshaven and sloppy throughout—after all, that's what Chaplin did, I figured. Instead of drawing on the equivalent of the music-hall tradition from which the great man had devised his act, I just tried to be real in a film where everything—the characters, the story, the settings, the costumes, the situations—was screaming out its falseness in neon hues.

Not only did *Sunaina* fail to break new ground in the depiction of the Hindi film hero as I had hoped it would, it was dead on arrival. Taher Bahadur Khan, who had by now attached himself to me as manager, kept insisting 'Hit hai Naseer bhai!' but in actuality nobody went to see it from the day it came out. One critic described me as being 'unfortunately no Amol Palekar' and my performance, which in any case I had hated when I saw the film in a trial show, was completely underwhelming. I looked wrong even to myself, I found myself wondering what a guy who looked like that was doing in a film of this kind, and I feared the majority of the audience would share this view, so I didn't gather the gumption to check it out in the theatre. Having heckled actors on screen several times myself, I was terrified at what I would hear from the audience about my shambling efforts to be real which, it was now confirmed, had only resulted in my looking grimy, unappetizing and out of place; fatal for a Hindi film hero who must always be clean cut, honourable and wholesome. I had not yet encountered the priceless gem 'even the ugly character has to be handsome ugly', passed on to me sometime later by Mr Subhash Ghai.

In addition to looking simply ugly there was nothing I did in the film that was heroic or even remotely funny. The director's sense of humour was stuck in a time warp somewhere in the forties, and my suggestions were received with bewilderment. I just didn't feel that I was getting through to anyone at all. Through the shoot, and particularly while performing the songs, I was a child in a new school finding everything unfamiliar and ominous and being asked questions the answers to which he has not the faintest clue about. My confidence during this seemingly unending shoot was not exactly spilling over and almost reached depletion point when one day, at the door to the set, dressed in full costume, I was refused entry by the doorman. The only diverting moment came when Mr Nag, greatly hassled and in need of the dialogue sheet, was yelling at his assistant to 'Breeng the shit! Phor habben sak breeng the shit so I ken bhwark in piss!!'

New wave or old hat?

Two more films in quick succession followed the release of *Junoon* in which my overheated performance received moderate praise. But these two, *Shaayad* and *Khwaab*, were such pure cat-vomit that the critics, who so far had been singing hosannas to this 'exciting new talent', began now to wonder whether they had been hasty in their assessment.

I knew even when shooting them that I was performing abominably and I hadn't a solution for it, so despite trying to do exactly what the directors asked for, just couldn't get it right. I have never felt so incompetent as an actor except perhaps when trying out for the Sem choir. In fact, the feeling has returned every time I have been part of a movie in which conviction necessarily has to be tempered with elan and not a little self-love, where being visibly synthetic, trumping the other actors and maintaining a certain detachment from the part while connecting closely with the audience are essential requirements. You can't be real, the audience must never forget it's you up there, they must not think you've become that guy you're playing. The hordes of (mainly male) *monstres sacré* in our films clinging on to vestiges of what they did well in their youth unwittingly bear testimony to this—botoxed or bewigged gents actually endorsing skin tonics or hair oils; darkening their remaining hair, then whitening it to play age, taking great care that the white looks as false as possible. I thought that trying to perform in that manner was an impediment to the kind of acting I really wanted to do. Playing scenes that had appeared a gazillion times in other films, and singing songs and fighting bad guys and doing it all very badly didn't seem to me to be the reason I had become an actor, so I continued vainly attempting to bring believability instead of attractiveness to the parts I played in these popular movies. It didn't work and I just couldn't take these movies seriously anyway, so I never quite got the hang of the kind of acting that was needed in them. I don't, however, know if that's a loss or a gain.

The very tangible benefit of doing *Khwaab*, apart from the money, was the discovery, when I was asked to match steps with Mithun Chakravarty, that I had an extra left foot. Both these films sank with barely a gurgle, but facilitated the purchase of my first car so I suppose they too were worth it. A second-hand Premier Padmini costing 18,000 rupees being what I could afford, I went for it even though it was a hideous shade of blue. I dubbed her 'Miss Mary'.

That winter Vikram Mehrotra, Tahir and I toodled off in this hideous turquoise apparition all the way to Delhi where I was to shoot a film, *Sparsh*, which proved to be a great energizer and a strong antidote to the rubbish I had recently found myself in. Most of the shooting was to be done on the precincts of the Blind Relief Association, in a school for visually impaired children whose headmaster, Mr Mittal, evidently was the model for the character I was playing, also a headmaster whose relationship with a colleague was based loosely on Mr Mittal's own experience in wooing the lovely lady he wed shortly after the film was done. Ratna was in NSD now and when Miss Mary brought her cargo into Delhi, the first stop was the school to surprise her with my new acquisition. She made no secret that she thought I had blundered badly and she was bang on the button—the 600-kilometre journey had taken a lot out of the tired old machine; before long she began to limp and sputter, and through most of the shoot stayed in a garage.

The script of this film, centring on the love of a sighted woman and a sightless man played respectively by Shabana and myself (our third outing together), was an incisively observed piece of writing by Sai Paranjpye, who was also to direct it. A total deviation from the stock portrayal of sightless characters in Indian cinema, the story centred around these two, one very much his own man, treating the word disabled with disdain; and the other a grieving widow, disabled by society. Justifying his aggressive rejection of help, knowing that pity is only a step behind, the script was a startling depiction of the fact that being deprived of one sense necessarily means being compensated thoroughly by nature in the others, including in the sense of ego. The story, extremely moving in itself, was also an intense rumination on the prejudices faced by those who would have no problem of self-esteem if they were to receive the same regard and treatment as so-called normal people.

The thought that I would have to act as a sightless person with children who were actually sightless and acting as themselves took me as close to butterflies in the stomach as I have ever been. I was up against it this time, but at least on my own turf, I reminded myself, so managed to short circuit the inhibitions and anxieties that had returned with full force while shooting the previous two movies. The fear of being shown up disappeared the moment I started working on the script. On first hearing it, I knew how I was definitely NOT going to play the part—the way it always is in Hindi cinema: eyes fixed in a frontal gaze, stumbling around arms outstretched, bumping into walls, referring to oneself as 'main bechaara laachaar' and such nonsense. The script did not require me to do that anyway and Sai, bless her, forbade me from wearing dark glasses: 'Mr Mittal has the most beautiful eyes I have seen,' she told me.

I had also keenly observed a few sightless people including Nani Baji, the great Sardhana storyteller, and two classmates in Aligarh, because I found their physical manner intriguing: I had by now figured out that the key to it was that they directed their ears and not their eyes at the point they were addressing, and that caused their sometimes ungainly bodily posture, which, having absolutely no self-consciousness, they were oblivious to. I also spent quite some time watching Mr Mittal operate, chatting with him, and found that sightless people use the verb to 'see' quite freely and in the same sense as the rest of us. The day before the shoot began Mr Mittal and I spent a most entertaining and educative evening with a friend of his, a Mr Advani, also sightless and an undersecretary in the Ministry of Education who had invited us to dinner. After enquiring from Mr Mittal his preference, I loaded a plate for him, placed a fork in it and offered it to him. He accepted the plate but didn't start eating with the rest of us nor did he respond to my puzzled enquiries, just sat there with the plate until his fiancée who was a little late arrived and replaced the fork with a spoon. Turned out sightless people never use forks.

It also turned out sightless people can thoroughly enjoy a drink, they do have dreams, they have a concept of the primary colours, they never keep pets (a guide dog does not qualify as a pet), and they possess a sense that operates above the waist which is why they do not bump into lamp posts or trees but do trip over low-lying objects. Post-dinner, we were headed down the steps when a power failure turned everything pitch black. Everyone except Mr Mittal stopped dead in their tracks. When told why, he continued down the steps chuckling, 'Well, follow me then!'

I did a few sessions blindfolded, helped by sighted instructors, but I didn't kill myself practising 'how a blind man moves' or trying to understand the psychology of the sightless; in any case this was a person I was playing, not an idea. I just had to empathize, to put myself in his shoes, not 'become' him or anything. Earlier, as practice, I had acquired a pair of very high-powered contact lenses to simulate the feeling of not being able to see, and actually attempted to navigate in my neighbourhood wearing them, but still being able to see hazily through them, I decided to just go with my imagination. I had always been able anyway to shut out all aural stimuli whenever I had felt like it, but shutting off all visual stimuli proved equally easy. Luckily my instincts were on the right track; and in any case Sai's beautifully accurate script had already done the difficult work for me; all I had to do was submit to it and embody the character. She went along, trusting me all the way, and it must have been fun for her to watch her creation come alive.

Performing in this film was totally painless and totally pleasurable, without any sense of competition or frazzled egos or insecurities, something I can only say about a small handful of my films. Shabana was wonderfully supportive and encouraging, as she has always been to me through my career. I am very proud of this performance and even though the film didn't come out for another two years it fetched me a National Award, but neither for me was as significant as the, no pun intended, eye-opening time I spent in the company of Mr Mittal and the students of the school. Their gentle, unhurried approach to life, their ready laughter, their willingness to enjoy life, the pride they take in their achievements, their acceptance of and ability to cope with permanent darkness was inspiring in a way few other things have been. In a heart-breaking moment, one of the boys playing a major part in the film asked me if he would 'be able to see it' and just as I was about to assure him that of course he would, it struck me that he mightn't be able to identify himself when he did 'see' it; his voice would have been dubbed. Watching the way these boys (girls had a separate school of course, sightless people's lives depending so much on touch) could identify people not just by sound or touch but by footsteps even, watching them play cricket or dial a phone or quite simply just go about their lives was a mind-expanding acting lesson. From Mr Mittal I learnt how a sightless person knows the traffic lights have changed, how he can regain his sense of direction if lost, how he lights a cigarette, how he signs his name. Braille was beyond me, though, despite learning the alphabet; Mr Mittal kindly explained that it is impossible for a sighted person to read Braille with his hands; the fingertips just do not have that kind of sensitivity.

The producer of the film, Basu Bhattacharya, could have done with some sensitivity himself. After having struck gold when his first film *Teesri Kasam* was belatedly hailed, he had made a reputation as a maker of very small-budget off-beat cinema. Notorious for paying absolutely no one in his unit, he probably turned delirious at the prospect of so many enthusiastic hands, most of them Delhi-based, happy to work for a pittance, and actors unhesitatingly coming on board without discussing fees or laying down conditions. He was getting a really good film, which also promised to be popular, made on less than a sandal-string budget.

Arriving in Delhi, I not only discovered that Shabana and I were to stay in a house belonging to a friend of his but that the schedule had been planned around being able to use my car for production duties. Miss Mary's convalescence, which cost me almost as much as she had cost to buy, however, nipped that in the bud.

The car was now ready to undertake the return journey to Bombay with a different set of passengers—the absolutely wonderful Renu Saluja and motormouth Vidhu Vinod Chopra, who was then married to her. That return journey turned out to be somewhat more exhausting than the forty-five-day shoot had been, as anyone who has had to listen to Vinod Chopra non-stop for a couple of days will promptly attest. The absence throughout the shoot of any kind of stress, exasperation or exhaustion was thoroughly compensated for in that two-day journey.

The work itself had been such fun that the thought that I hadn't been paid anything didn't occur to me until I returned to Bombay and Taher learnt of it. A burly fellow who stood no nonsense and had begun to love me deeply, he promised to get Mr Bhattacharya to cough up, and to that end religiously turned up at the latter's house every morning, disturbing his morning ritual, whatever it was, to politely remind him about 'Naseer bhai payment Dada'. The persistence and the 'I take no shit' air made the immovable object give way ultimately, and Taher one day produced a wad of 10,000 rupees plus another 2000 for petrol charges from Dada, who finally decided he preferred having his breakfast without Taher around. Dealing with Mr Bhattacharya, though a good first lesson in filmi financial negotiations, did not mean I never had to sit through the 'no money' ritual enacted by the popular film-makers time and time again, causing me to wonder why only guys with no money made movies. This charade was also resorted to very often by the 'serious' types, resulting ultimately in my having to sever ties with most of them.

Om Puri so far had appeared in a few supporting parts in movies, including *Sparsh*. He wasn't having an easy time but was enterprising enough to get a play and a company, Majma, together. His first attempt, a Hindi translation of Govind Deshpande's *Udhwastha Dharmshala*, received tremendous acclaim and Om began to be known in his own right. The play, done mainly with raw young actors and put together under great financial strain, also inaugurated the Prithvi Theatre which, now complete, opened with great fanfare. I played a small part in *UD* for the opening show and various other walk-ons as and when required, as did Ratna. Meanwhile Benjamin Gilani and I had found a lot of common ground during *Junoon*, and had launched, at his insistence, into *Waiting for Godot*, a play I had had an allergy to since having ploughed through it on Zahida apa's insistence in Aligarh, and against which I had written a vituperative essay which nearly got me failed at NSD—a play I would never ever have attempted but for Benjamin. When, after struggling with it for about a year, we finally felt it was stage-worthy, Om generously offered us the Majma banner for the opening show of *Godot* on 29 July 1979. It was only later that Ben formed the Motley company, which survives to the present day, as does the production which finally began to make sense to us once we stopped trying to understand it.

Om's blazing salt-of-the-earth intensity finally caught the eye of many a film-maker but it was Govind Nihalani who first recognized the magnetic simplicity in his screen presence and cast him in *Aakrosh* as the anguished silent Adivasi, wrongly accused of his wife's murder, Om's definitive film performance. I was to play the defence lawyer and Amrish Puri the prosecutor. I got barely a day's break between arriving in Bombay and leaving for Alibag for this shoot. It was a wrench coming from the gentle dreamlike world of *Sparsh* to this hard-edged portrayal of small-town corruption and its constant progenitors—lust and politics.

In the one day I was in Bombay, barely had I cleared Vinod Chopra's voice out of my head than I was called to meet with one A.V. Mohan, a B-grade film-maker who had produced various horrors in the past. This time he promised me 'a trudy fhantaastic fildum and hero rolde saar' so I went along, my mind jingling to the tune of plenty more change in my pocket and a 'hero' role, not the namby-pamby of *Sunaina*. Mr Mohan who, for some reason, prefixed or interspersed anything he said with the words 'mutlubmutlub' went straight to the heart of the matter. 'You know Holdyvud fildum *Jhorba Grik* saar? Mutlubmutlub ve making dat wondly. Amjad bhai pdaying Grik mans you mutlubmutlub pdaying young hero.' Taher was yet to pull his act with Basuda, I had been told I was going to get nothing at all for *Aakrosh*, petrol costs money and the pay packet this time was 30,000 rupees, so I didn't take any time at all to say yes.

That being settled, there remained the small matter of the script itself. Imtiyaz Khan, elder brother of Amjad Khan, who was to direct walked in shortly after and proceeded to narrate a script that the final film not only bore absolutely no resemblance to, it was one of the most delightfully entertaining and moving scripts for a popular Hindi film I have heard to date. I went away deliriously deluded that my breakthrough in popular cinema had finally arrived. I now badly wanted a home of my own and this film could start to do that for me. I had loved *Zorba the Greek* anyway, I always enjoyed watching Anthony Quinn; and Amjad Khan, now quite a phenomenon, and I were to co-star and I was to play the Alan Bates part, with the dance on the beach replaced by a fight on the beach, of course.

This film, after a mind-bogglingly disorganized, incompetent, troubled shoot and a half-dozen title changes, disappeared so fast no one took any notice of it, so my career didn't receive another body blow, but had I had the faintest inkling what I was in for during its making, even the prospect of getting a home to myself would not have made me accept.

The first alarm bell went off when in the middle of the *Aakrosh* schedule Imtiyaz Khan and his entire unit turned up without warning in Alibag, to shoot a song sequence. Since I was supposed to sing some of that damn song and since I was there already, he would need a few hours every day with me to do it, he told me. We were in the midst of shooting the harrowing scenes with Om in the prison, I was stupefied at the man's presumptuousness, but when he pleaded with Govind that we just had to help him out, that this two-day shoot with me just HAD to be done now—he quoted completion and release dates and the mess he'd be in if he didn't deliver the film within a month and a half—Govind, probably sympathetic to a fellow film-maker's plight, gave in. When the schedule of *Aakrosh* got extended by a week, however, and I was required to stay on in Alibag, he was not to receive any reciprocal gesture from Mr Khan who insisted on proceeding with his schedule in Bombay. But he was shooting nights, so in the day I could shoot for Govind. As a result, I got my first taste of shooting double shifts, having to shuttle between Alibag and Film City for seven days in a row, since *Amaan aur Ajab Khan* (as it was first titled, then amended to *Loha aur Lahoo*, then to *Maan Gaye Ustad*, then to *Dushman Dost*, then to something else) couldn't possibly be held up: release date was already fixed, you see. I made the mistake of taking Imtiyaz Khan seriously, having so far worked only on films where my work and the entire film were completed in one go start to finish. I fully expected the same to happen here, in fact had been assured it would. I was about to get my first taste of this kind of film: the kind that gets made only because a star is doing it a favour by being in it so naturally the whole scheme of things depends on the star's whims. If he has somewhat reluctantly joined in, real trouble is in store. Thus, after having dutifully driven in from Alibag every evening, I often spent the night sleeping in the green room awaiting my call, and not infrequently being woken in the morning and driving back, not having done a single shot all night.

Through this, all I remember doing is waiting endlessly for Amjad bhai who was dealing with a hundred other films and a humongous new-found celebrity status and was always 'about to arrive'. To his credit he actually did, sometimes. Despite all this industriousness, the shooting of *Pyaara Dost*, as it was finally called, dragged on for the next two years, for reasons too complicated to go into here. That song I enacted in Alibag, seeing before me Om's disapproving face instead of the heroine's, was not even used. And Imtiyaz Khan, being strictly a nightbird, made me do the accursed graveyard shift for him along with whatever project I happened to be currently involved in. I swore that in the future whatever the monetary inducement, I would never shoot double shifts again. This particular bum-trip doesn't merit further mention other than that it was the first of the films I acted in that I never bothered to see. Quite a few more I never ever saw were to follow, though: *Haadsa*, *Tajurba*, *Swami Dada*, *Kanhaiya*, *Shatrutaa*. My career was barely five years old, and along with some critically acclaimed stuff I also had an impressive roster of truly execrable films.

When Saeed Mirza was making his *Arvind Desai ki Ajeeb Dastan* I was to be in it until I learnt that so was not only Jaspal but AP, the lady from *Manthan*, as well, and we were all to share screen space which would mean spending time together on the sets. I didn't want to take any more chances and withdrew. But *Arvind Desai* was now history; despite being a quite exquisite piece of work it stayed unreleased, and Saeed now embarked on his next, titled *Albert Pinto ko Gussa Kyun Aata Hai* and asked me to play Albert. For such a dynamic title the script seemed strangely somnambulistic to me, but I thought it would be fun playing this Anglo-Indian character whose alienation from the working classes and apathetic attitude to life gradually turn into a growing political awareness. Finally shedding the communal identity about which he is so vain he eventually merges whole-heartedly with the mainstream. The positioning of the minorities in the larger scheme was obviously close to Saeed's heart; he himself is a Muslim married to a Goan Christian, and this film is his dreamscape about the dawning of a political awareness. Believing that it would be significant and also pretty keen that his work should be seen, and being basically an adman, Saeed was canny enough to ask Shabana if she would play Albert's girlfriend Stella, not a large part, which she very sportingly accepted even though she wasn't (if Shabana will forgive me) strictly speaking ideal for it. In fact neither was I, as Shyam reminded me—I had gone all Elvis Presley and James Dean when it was street-cred that was required. Mine is an immature self-adulatory performance but Shabana's presence added great oomph to the project and certainly was one of the factors that helped make the film widely known, even though there are probably more people who have heard the title than have actually seen the film.

Shabana and I over the decades have worked together in more films than you can shake a script at. Her dramatic abilities are too well documented to need a testimonial from me so I won't go there, except to say that but for the somewhat smug reverence she has for her own acting and her tendency to perform with background music playing in her head not to mention the eccentric preference for her right profile over her left (or is it the other way around?) I have never found her to be anything but a consummate professional and the most confident, generous, sane and positive female co-actor I have ever worked with in films. Playing off her has always been non-competitive, full of mutual regard and trust and, therefore, a great joy. Our views differ drastically on many subjects but whatever we may think of one another's opinions and one another as people, I have while working with her always felt safe. Evidently so has she, and on the solitary occasion that we didn't enjoy working together, it had nothing to do with her! Never once while working have I seen her at the mercy of her moods or indulging in displays of temperament; something I, on the other hand, have often been guilty of. I had looked up to her ever since she had conducted a class in speech in our first year at the Film Institute, and receiving her encouragement and approval now was a great high. Many of my personal favourites among the films I have done are the ones with Shabana; films it was generous of her, a mainstream star, to consent to do with me—a nobody.

I believe it was also not only coincidence that we happened to be paired together so often; I think we carried similar energies and a similar attitude to the table. This helped us both bring out the best in each other. I suppose that's what 'good chemistry' is all about. For whatever they are worth I could not have done those performances without her, I know that for sure. I'd like to believe the reverse is also the case but one never knows.

Despite spending so much time together, we have somehow escaped becoming close on a personal level, which I am inclined to think is not a bad thing. We do consider each other to be friends, but visit each other's homes on an average once every two years or so. The roles in our real-life relationship are not at all defined so when we meet there are no expectations, and when we approach two characters at work it's like drawing those people on a clean slate, the baggage of things personal does not intrude. I believe the danger of that happening is greater in cinema than in the theatre; the camera may not be 'able to look into your soul', as they say, but the fact is it can catch you with your metaphorical pants down, and if a personal relationship is involved there are bound to be unguarded moments, which can sometimes embellish, but more often mar, the content of the scenes. That is probably why there have been many legendary husband–wife acting teams in the theatre but not in cinema. In some cases a close personal equation between actors may have resulted in charming or believable behaviour on screen, but only when those actors were playing parts that conformed to their real-life relationship. It is equally true, though, that personal animosity between actors has often been the cause of incurably bad acting. For the avid 'listener', the things unspoken between characters in popular cinema are sometimes more audible and engrossing than what is actually being said. In fact, my only reason for watching Hindi potboilers now is to catch the subtexts passing between the actors.

I received an unexpected lesson in the politics of the Hindi film industry in the midst of shooting *Albert*. Called for a meeting by a writer duo of some recent blockbusters, I went to meet them, heart bouncing with joy. These two gentlemen had earlier been extremely warm in their praise of my work, had made many polite noises and the usual vague promises. Now I was being urgently summoned and I had visions of a part like the one a few years ago in which they had seen the potential in an unconventional actor and it had paid off big-time. I learnt later of course that the 'unconventional actor' had been their third or fourth choice and he was only cast when the stars they wanted turned down the part. I decided I wouldn't mind one little bit being the third or fourth choice provided I got a part like that one. Arriving at the plush seaside residence where the meeting was it didn't take me long to figure that I was dealing with very big brass here. The legendary director, who mostly kept silent or looked suitably harassed, was there, so were the producers with their shiny briefcases and, as was unfailingly mentioned, the 'stunt coordinators from Hollywood'; also a journalist or two; and everyone got up to greet me.

Polite chat filled the room for a while as I sat there silently squirming, and finally a few subtle signals and quick looks shot around the gathering and one of the writer gentlemen came out with it: prima-donna attitude from one of the stars in the massive film they were shooting at the moment had made them decide to replace the gentleman in question with yours truly, and I should make myself available from next week. I wasn't asked, I was told. My stunned reply that I was already in the midst of a shoot ending in three weeks was met with an incredulous guffaw. 'What film yaar? Who is going to see it?' I desisted from naming it, not wanting to create further merriment, so got bombarded with advice that was not without a certain friendliness: 'This is the chance of a lifetime for you', 'think of your career', 'forget that film whatever it is'. I have to say that this carrot-on-a-stick they dangled, far from tempting me, made me wonder what kind of people these were, for whom nothing else mattered except having their way immediately, for whom no other film in the world apart from the one bringing them big bucks quickly was of any importance. I had absolutely no intention of saying yes, there seemed more to this whole thing than met the eye anyway, and secondly, I just didn't think I'd be right for the part they briefly described—I knew I was no good at this larger-than-life stuff. My temperature was rising but I put a lid on it and continued listening silently. Even though the producers sitting there were itching to instantly hand me a cheque and I was being paid nothing for *Albert*, there was not the slightest dilemma in my mind. I could only stare in disbelief at these rich, arrogant poseurs and wished I could tell them all where they got off; but I only stammered and excused myself, saying I would think about it. That was also greeted with garrulous disbelief and I took my leave. I didn't bother to re-establish contact. In a day or two the unconfirmed news that I was in the film broke anyway, and in yet another few days the news that I was not, and that all had been amicably settled also appeared and so prima donna and I were both back where we belonged. And fate decreed that this 'colossal extravaganza' on which I had missed out sank leaving barely a trace, taking with it some big reputations and at least a couple of fledgling careers (mine without a doubt would have been one) and it now rests secure in the musty pantheon of forgotten biggies while the tiny *Albert Pinto ko Gussa Kyun Aata Hai* is still remembered if only for its title.

To counter this event, something else happened around the same time, almost as if to illustrate to me that the film industry is not completely full of self-importance. With nothing much to do, I was snoozing one afternoon when Ramesh who had been looking after the kitchen for about a year came and woke me, looking as if he had seen a ghost. 'P.. P... Pr..... Prraaannn!' his voice was trembling as he frantically gesticulated towards the outside room, 'Pran saab is there!' Only half registering what he meant, I went out and snakes alive! There was Mr Pran Sikand himself, wearing a pair of horn-rimmed spectacles, grey trousers and white shirt sitting cross-legged, shoes off, on the huge mattress on my living room floor. Pran! He of the riding crop and breeches, of the evil eyes, of the pencil moustache, of the blood-curdling half-smile half-leer, was sitting in my living room looking as timid as a vacuum cleaner salesman.

Mr Pran had so defined the concept of villainy in Hindi movies that I suppose something in me expected to see him in felt hat and trench coat, nonchalantly blowing smoke rings; to see this side of a star of his magnitude was a revelation, it actually took me a few seconds to recognize him. He had come to invite me to play in a film-stars' festival cricket match, but being pretty allergic to these things, I made an excuse and declined. He took the refusal in good spirit and, while leaving, remarked that I reminded him a great deal of his elder son, and he hoped we would work together some day. Through the time he was there, sharing a cup of tea and Shrewsbury biscuits with me (he had quit smoking though), he graciously said he admired my work. Thinking it too obvious to return the compliment, I gratefully swallowed his praises, not quite believing who they were coming from. I did get to work with him much later and discovered he loved being praised. He would be overjoyed, Mithun once told me, if he were in make-up and you walked past not recognizing—or rather, pretending not to recognize— him. Your subsequent fake apologies, 'Pran saab, kya fantastic get-up hai! Main to pehchana hi nahin!' would literally make him blush. I tried it and it worked! So punctual you could set your watch by him, always ready bang on time in full costume and make-up, usually pretty elaborate make-up, never leaving the set between shots, retiring to his green room only for lunch, then right back to the set in full battle readiness. This was something the entire old-time brigade of supporting actors, a breed that has vanished, had in common.

There was a survey conducted once which uncovered the disconcerting statistic that on an average five hundred young boys/girls arrive in Bombay every day to become actors. No one has ever researched the number of moneyed people who arrive here every day, hoping to produce films to multiply their investments and of course get photographed with the star, preferably the female star, but my guess is that that number too would be staggering. Among that legion was a multi-millionaire shipping magnate from Hong Kong who decided he wanted to be a movie mogul as well. While staying in the wings he had quietly financed the film *Shaayad* with a frontman acting as producer, and having tested the waters and decided they were to his taste, he had now decided to make a big noise to herald his arrival in the film world. He wanted his pictures in the glossies, he had had enough of being invisible and shelling out piddling amounts to make 'Naseeruddin Shah type of serious movies'; he now wanted to scatter the stuff about and sign up the biggest stars he could buy, to appear in thoroughly commercial fare. 'Money can get anything done' being his motto, the overambitious gent formed a film production company and in four full-page ads in *Screen* announced four medium-to-large movies, all four to be shot simultaneously, at least two with big-name directors and each with a different star-cast. The only common factor was the presence, in a leading capacity, of Om Puri in each of them; in fact one of the films was to star Rajesh Khanna and Om Puri. The fourth, never made, was also announced thus, 'Production no. 4 starring Om Puri'. Govind Nihalani had not spotted Om yet, he was not really known, so many assumed that this was a new leading lady being introduced. By the time these films got under way Om was gainfully employed elsewhere and to my knowledge, he didn't actually appear in any of them.

I did, in one of the three, an adaptation of *Oliver!* and I did a bad imitation of Ron Moody's Fagin, one of my favourite

performances. Amjad Khan played Bill Sikes and this film did
to the Carol Reed classic what many Hindi films have done
and continue to do to classics to this day. Though, as in the
original, the film's title was the child's name (*Kanhaiya*) the ads
screamed out 'Amjad Khan as Kanhaiya', a marketing ploy that
fooled no one. The mainstream audience didn't know who I was
but Amjad bhai's massive fan following also decided to give
this one a miss. The other two films produced by the company,
starring some marquee names, plodded along for a few years
then also died of natural causes at the box office. The shipping
magnate, after being repeatedly taken to the cleaners by the
film industry's charlatans, was barely heard of after that and I
have a bad feeling about those ships.

Still fancying myself to be leading-man material I initially
turned down the part Ketan Mehta asked me to do in his
gorgeous allegorical film of a folk tale, *Bhavni Bhavai*, but I
hadn't anticipated his persistence. I didn't want to do it mainly
because I wasn't looking forward to a repeat of the kind of run-
ins we'd had when he had directed *The Lesson* for us. In that
production, apart from one stunning visual idea for the set—
four gigantic books suspended by invisible wires from the four
corners of the stage—he had had precious little by way of nuts-
and-bolts help to give the actors and would constantly resort
to unfathomable abstractions instead of tangible guidance:
'a spiral turn is needed here' , 'you must show the character's
contradictions' and so forth; or when at a loss he would
tauntingly toss the ball into my court: 'Tum actor ho yaar kuch
jadoo karo, kuch khelo!' I would be halfway up the wall, and our
friendship was seriously endangered by hysterical arguments
occurring too often for my liking in the course of rehearsal.

I seriously thought I'd never work with the man again, and
now he wanted me to play a bumbling Raja in a film that would
be seen by many more people than had seen *The Lesson*. I had

an immediate premonition that this film would work but the thought of playing a foolish character was not appetizing. I opted for a shorter, heroic role but Ketan would have none of it and coerced me into agreeing to do the Raja and am I glad he did. I look back on it with great affection and pride, not least because the splendid look of the film, for which Archana Shah and Mira Lakhia must get complete credit, belies its impossibly small budget. It was produced by a cooperative of which I was a member and everyone in the unit treated it as their own baby: no one in the unit was paid a penny, some of us even travelled to the location at our own expense, but despite it all, a group of friends mucking in together to create something, with the odds heavily stacked against them, created such joyous energy that all of us who acted in it, and are still alive, look back on it with great affection.

This film also helped illustrate what Mr Brecht had been saying all this time and which so far had made little impression on me who was dying to 'become' every character I ever played. Ketan's vision for the acting in the film was that it should be like the behaviour of the characters in the *Asterix* comics, which on reading the delightful script made complete sense. Om was cast as the Untouchable who, in the best tradition of fairy tales, discovers and rears the baby prince. Benjamin was playing the Prime Minister; Suhasini Mulay on whom I had had a crush ever since *Bhuvan Shome* was the Queen; another dear friend, Mohan Gokhale, was the abandoned Prince; and Smita was his love interest. Another pivotal part, the Chorus, who narrates the story mostly in song, had not yet been cast. Ketan dearly wanted B.V. Karanth, something of a guru to him, to play it but Karanthji was unavailable and so crisis Number One hit us on the first day itself. A brainstorming session was held to discuss possibilities and inevitably Jaspal's name cropped up—he could sing, reasoned Ketan, and working would do him good. So he was informed and called to the location, something I had major misgivings about but was assured we would be kept apart, and in any case we were never in the same frame together.

When he arrived for the shoot, staying true to his current form he proved impossible to handle, and had to be asked to leave. The man for all seasons, Om Puri, who couldn't sing a note, took over and played both the narrator as well as one of the chief protagonists. I desisted from any I told you so's because I was really disappointed. I knew that Jaspal had blown this as well; he wouldn't now have another chance to redeem himself. This was the last chapter in which I was to figure in his long and extremely sad story. We never met at the location, and subsequently I had no more direct contact with him, just kept hearing bizarre, disturbing and often contradictory reports about his doings first in Delhi and then Patiala, whence apparently he returned when Ketan's misguided plan to help him backfired.

TWO SPECIES OF FIGHTING BANTAM

Junoon

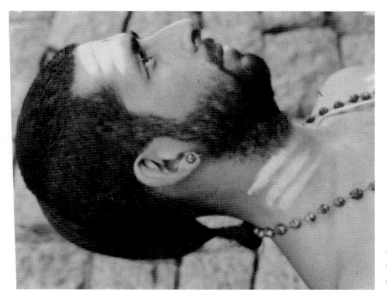

Godhuli

Among the village folk who appeared in *Manthan*.

Shooting the motorcycle scene in *Albert Pinto ko Gussa Kyun Aata Hai*:
Virendra Saini with the camera, Kundan Shah behind him.

On the sets of *Bhumika*, trying hard to look dapper driving the
expensive antique car; Shyam and Smita *(behind)* seem unconcerned.

The unit of *Bhavni Bhavai*, awaiting a sunset;
Ketan Mehta *(extreme left)*, Archana Shah *(extreme right)*.

My Spike Milliganish tribute to
Sunaina, Shaayad and *Dil Aakhir Dil Hai*

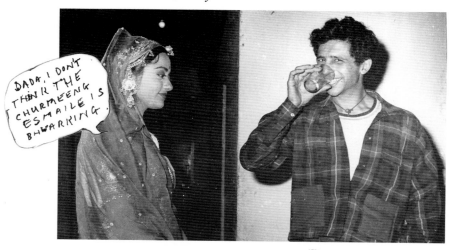

Poor theatre, moneyed film

When Motley was formed, Benjamin and I, its nucleus, both had a wish list of plays we would have loved to do, but didn't have the resources to attempt, so starting small, we staged a series of two-handers in English after *Godot* had fallen into place. Not into the kind of bedroom farces always so popular in Bombay, we wanted to include only the few people we knew well, who we enjoyed being with and who shared our love for theatre. Tom Alter, Kenny Desai, Aakash Khurana and of course Ratna when she ended her NSD course gradually began to form the core of the company. Like every other actor in the world, I too had often fantasized about playing Hamlet but suspected that mounting it was beyond me.

I often dreamt of grand glittering productions Alkazi could be proud of, but on the other hand there was Dubeyji's example. Having directed many of the same plays Alkazi had, Dubeyji demonstrated that being hamstrung financially was no impediment; his productions could be as effective, if not more so, than the Old Man's. With no resources and no agenda, political or otherwise, we had nothing to 'say'; we were in the theatre only because of an unreasonable love for it. After some confusion as to the direction Motley should take, and not having access to even a thousandth of the kind of funding

NSD received, I had to abandon my dreams of attempting an 'Alkazi' and settled for working with what we had, and Dubey's route seemed the one to take. In any case I had been unable to hit upon a solitary insight that would make *Hamlet* say more than it already has over the centuries—portions of it baffle me still. I wished, quite simply, to do it only in order to play Hamlet and that didn't seem a good enough reason. This is a thought that over the years has grown and hardened into an unshakeable conviction and has in a way contributed to my being able finally to arrive at a somewhat satisfactory equation theatre-wise.

Motley didn't do much initially. The corporates had yet to make serious theatre fashionable and every show we attempted on our own put us further in the red. Of the plays I really wanted to do, there weren't many that wouldn't be merely exercises in vanity, so I thought I'd just be patient until a director who wished to do any of these saw in me the potential to play Macbeth or Lear. No one did, but I am pleased to report that getting to play neither did not devastate me because I was beginning to feel I might be on the verge of discovering a reason for doing theatre, other than to strut on the stage and lap up the applause. I felt I owed something more to theatre than tired re-enactments of well-known dramas or popular comedies. At one point, before my ideas had had time to germinate, and fed up of not being able to produce the kind of classy stuff I wanted to, I decided Motley would make some money by going popular with Neil Simon's *The Odd Couple*, but the audience stayed away in droves. Benjamin then attempted Shaw's *Arms and the Man* and both met the fate of many an early Motley production—closure after a dozen or so poorly attended shows. The headache of organizing and dealing with the real props in *The Odd Couple* made me resolve never ever again to try anything naturalistic onstage; and doing the Shaw play made it clear that one should never attempt his work unless the actors' tongue muscles are flexible enough to handle the musical notes his dialogue demands.

Jerzy Grotowski's concept of a theatre sans illusion began to make a little more sense: after all the audience never forgets they are in a theatre; they only need to glance away from your face to see the lights and the curtains. Attempting to convince them that what they are seeing is actually happening is futile and according to Brecht, undesirable; they must in fact be reminded that they are witnessing an enactment. This contention too began to seem extremely valid, but we plodded along for a while, doing other short pieces by Beckett, Pinter, Chekhov.

I next played Oedipus for another company in a production that received much acclaim and I witnessed for the first time at Prithvi a queue for tickets extending almost into the street. I have no idea what it was that so attracted audiences to this show—my presence could hardly have been the cause, else there should have been such a response for every play I appeared in and that was certainly not the case. I lost my voice on the fourth or fifth day of the run and the production was just this side of competent, but people who saw it were going away delirious. I guess the idea of a guy marrying his own mother is a tad titillating, and certainly *Oedipus Rex* is one of the most cracking whodunits ever written. Logistics problems made the play close after two stints of ten shows each, but in the course of it Ratna and I made friends we have stayed close to.

An earlier attempt at reading Jerzy Grotowski's book *Towards a Poor Theatre* at NSD had not worked, but finding it staring at me accusingly in the face in a bookshop one day, I glanced through the Foreword in which he argues that poverty of resources should be theatre's strength not its weakness, and decided to give it another crack. Profoundly influenced by Kathakali and the Balinese Mask Dance, and disillusioned by all Western theatre which, he felt, was at that time moving in the wrong direction (and incidentally still is) by becoming more and more illusory and technical, in fact attempting to create the hallucinatory quality of cinema—something which goes against its very nature—he originated the concept of a theatre comprising only the absolutely essential elements: actors and a text. Eliminating everything extraneous, decorative or suggestive, he zeroed in on the actor as the central tool of communication. There were no sets, actors performed on a bare stage wearing only bare minimum clothing, and he often even replaced the text with what he called 'primal sounds'. Ritualistic/religious connotations were evoked, the performance space was 'hallowed', the terms 'state of grace', 'holy Actor', 'exchange of energies between Actor and Audience' were used. All this, apart from sounding pretty far out and well-nigh impossible to attain seemed also to demand an exceptional degree of commitment and physical skill, neither of which I suspected I had. Then in a passage on actor-training, I came upon the statement that created a paradigm shift in my ideas on learning how to act. His intention was not 'to burden the Actor with skills, the skills must be taken for granted'; what he said he tried to do was 'rid the Actor of everything that prevents him from being himself'. I don't think the problem of learning acting has ever been put so succinctly, I knew that this training was what I needed if I wished to grow. There was no one around me who would even understand what I was talking about, let alone help with it; and I had a suspicion that neither the kind of 'popular' movies that were now coming my way nor the so-called serious cinema being made here would do it.

As if to vindicate this feeling I then got offered in quick succession a mixed bag of both kinds of films, some enjoyable but all in various ways somewhat unsatisfying: *Saza-e–Maut* (also called 'Saza-e–Mouth'), *Katha*, *Chakra*, *Hum Paanch*, *Bezubaan*, *Woh Saat Din*, *Bazaar*, *Holi* and *Aadharshila*—in which I had to be respectively put-upon hero, lovable loser, lecherous street thug, buddy of the hero, smooth blackmailer, dutiful husband, alcoholic poet, upright professor and passionate film-maker. It was almost as if nature had benevolently decided to give me more time to decide which kind was my cup of tea, and also to ensure that I make some money. While the first and last three named films (until I saw them, that is) were the result of wishing desperately to be involved in the new kind of cinema, the others provided the bacon, so to say. And somewhere along the way between the lot of them, I moved at last from a rented apartment to one I owned. Miss Mary was proving too much trouble to maintain so I had to flog her and bought myself a Royal Enfield, my resources having exhausted themselves buying myself a home in Sherly Village, which then was actually a village with little thatched cottages, paddy fields and a profusion of coconut trees. Only the occasional high-rise had disturbed the equanimity of the place but all of it still had the wonderful laid-back energy that pervades the air in a coastal town. When Ratna and I married, it was the first home we made together.

Then one day in 1981 the playwright Mahesh Elkunchwar who knew of my desire to study under Grotowski called to tell me that the man himself was in town and would I like to meet him? Assuring me he wasn't in jest, Mahesh gave me the address I should go to—Rekha Sabnis's house, in fact, which I happened to know. I wasn't sure what Grotowski looked like,

I had seen only one photograph of him, looking somewhat robust, black-suited, hair short, eyes hidden behind dark glasses. It was obviously an old picture: he was now reed thin with a straggly beard and matted hair; dark glasses, however, were firmly in place. Barefoot, wearing a crumpled kurta, dirty jeans he smoked bidis incessantly; and well into the evening though it was, he seemed to have just awoken. He asked a few questions about why I wanted to come to Poland, I told him that his book and what I knew of his work had opened a few windows for me and I wished to undergo the training he could provide. In reply he said 'the window opens inward, not outward'. Seeing I wasn't too sure what he meant, he spoke in plain language: 'It all might not turn out as you expect.' I assured him I was prepared for anything, which in retrospect became an idle boast when I actually got there.

I did not know that Grotowski's theatre ideas and practice had grown radically since he wrote that book. He had in fact abandoned performance altogether. Theatre in any case had been analogous to life for him and he had now decided to dispense with an audience as well, and was involved in a search for what he termed 'the Primal State'. 'One Actor, one Audience with the roles interchangeable' had now become 'Actor and Audience are one'.

The next day I received a note informing me I had been selected to participate in the 'Theatre of Sources' workshop to be conducted in Wroclaw where his Institute for Research into Acting was situated. The earnings from some of the above-mentioned movies helped me secure a ticket on Swissair to Warsaw via Vienna and I got ready to travel overseas for the first time. I was able to withdraw with some difficulty from one film I had taken on, was unable to withdraw from the other—I was unable to repay the money they had already given, having spent it on my ticket, and to trusty Taher's complete incomprehension I told him I was going to a country he had never heard of. As far as he could see I was getting plenty of work and I was taking a chance with my career, but the fact was my acting abilities had come to a standstill, I was actually finding myself tiring of the whole business and had begun to fear that this was the mediocrity I was condemned to for the rest of my life. With no guidance, I was not growing. I was finding neither the commercial nor the art-house fare stimulating, I wasn't getting the popular films I'd have liked to do and many of the serious types had already been shown up as money-grabbing idea appropriators who kept making the same film over and over, and not too well at that—a situation which didn't seem to be heading to a resolution I liked. Well, I figured, if I can't help my career at least I can help myself by acquiring new abilities, and from someone who knows and doesn't mind sharing.

Also selected and travelling with me was Grotowski's host in Bombay, Rekha Sabnis, though I still fail to see what he detected in common between us. I had flown within India quite often by now but I was really nervous at the prospect of an international flight. Ratna came to see me off and said later she'd had a bad feeling about this trip from the start. Rekha having travelled abroad before knew the ropes; she practically held my hand and guided me to the aircraft. It was the first night I spent in an aeroplane and I didn't sleep a wink; in fact my heart hadn't slowed one bit by the time Vienna hove into view. Some two decades later I spent some more time in that magical city, touring with Peter Brook's *Hamlet*, and my appetite for architectural beauty was not only thoroughly satiated, it reached saturation point. The surfeit of aesthetics everywhere began to give me indigestion and to behold a faceless rectangular apartment block there was actually a relief.

We spent the morning taking in the sights within range

of the airport, telephoning a friend of Rekha's who lived in the Vienna Woods, getting set to go there, then remembering she had misplaced her passport, retracing our steps, managing to locate it, and after being fairly comprehensively swindled changing dollars on the street, getting on the Warsaw flight. Poland was at that time, like most East European countries, a fairly depressing place to be in and the biting wind and rain welcoming us there seemed entirely appropriate. Our destination, Wroclaw, was an hour's flight away, and since we weren't pre-booked, we thought we'd do the journey by train instead. We struggled to explain to the ticket clerk that we needed two seats on the train to Wroclaw (pronounced Vrotslav) and he, nodding vigorously in comprehension, slipped us two tickets to Bratislava, an error we managed to rectify just in time. There was no rail connection to Wroclaw so we boarded a very bumpy forty-five-minute flight to our destination.

We landed just as it was turning dark. There was no one to receive us, naturally, and without a clue where to go kept calling the two phone numbers we had and neither one responded. In a taxi we found our way to the institute, which had an almost unnoticeable front entrance bearing no sign, just a number. The door was locked and as we sat shivering in the porch I began to have serious second thoughts about this whole enterprise: being alone, friendless and hungry in a foreign land which made me almost decide to head straight back to the airport and catch the next plane back. The numerous complications involved in such a journey, however, made me desist, and just after I had rung the bell for the fiftieth time and even considered kicking down the door, someone passing by enquired what we wanted. He turned out to be one of the instructors at the institute, and he sheltered and fed us in his home that night. He was maddeningly evasive when we enquired when the work would begin or where we would stay and would just smile mysteriously when we asked when we would get to meet Grotowski—'maybe tomorrow . . . maybe not'. I would soon discover to what extent this mythologization of the man would go, and that it too was part of the experiment he was conducting.

Next morning all the participants, about fifty of us of every nationality, assembled and we were finally admitted into the mysterious portals of the institute, to a huge room where about half of us would spend that night before heading the next day into the forest where the work was to be conducted. Grotowski came in and addressed us for about an hour. I am not quite sure what he said because I didn't understand most of it, save when he spoke of the need to unlock potential, and that our so-called truthful behaviour is actually no more than a series of 'conditioned responses'; therefore the need to discover the 'primal condition'. He preceded and interspersed every remark with pauses long enough to let the silent anticipation of the listeners grow so thick I thought his spectacles would fog over. The rest of what he said sounded so convolutedly esoteric he might have been talking in code, and I wondered what his reply would be if I asked him the time but no questions were allowed and we were given no inkling what the work would actually consist of, but were made to practically take an oath never to divulge anything to anyone about it and also not to discuss it among ourselves. We were also informed that consuming narcotics would not be permitted during our stay. I have no idea about the others but my unease certainly grew.

There were three other Indians apart from Rekha and myself. They were all from Calcutta—Deepak Mazumdar and Probir Guha, both theatre practitioners, and Gaur 'Khepa', a Baul singer of great repute. The verdant, pristine forest we drove into next morning evoked Andrzej Wajda's films, the pines glistening in the morning dew, the seemingly manicured meadows glowing in the sun, an occasional horned stag bounding past kind of thing. In the heart of the forest was a clearing where two newly built barn-like cottages stood. We unloaded our things, found spots to sleep in and were introduced to the work, if I can call it that. I was prepared for rigorous exercises in physical control and voice work to start with; I had no idea what else would follow. Instead we were divided into groups of five, each with an instructor, and after doing some ritualistic unrhythmic kind of dance which was totally uncoordinated and stayed so as long as I participated, we'd sit in a circle, palms almost but not quite touching the person on either side, and were told to experience the vibrations, while the instructor, in an almost inaudible tone talked of being aware of the grass and the earth beneath it and asking us to feel the sun and the breeze. I was straining so hard to hear what he was saying that all I could do was give thanks it wasn't raining.

At various times different groups of five would go off among the trees and return looking worn out, sometimes drenched, sometimes muddied but always deliriously disturbed. Nourishment consisted of bread and cheese, cold meat, potatoes and, if you were quick enough, eggs. These had to suffice at all mealtimes.

The days went very slowly past trying to comprehend—while running down a forest path to a clearing, doing some incomprehensible ritual and running back; or wading across a chilly stream, or rotating blindfolded on a sawed-off trunk, or listening to the same repetitive percussion played for hours every night—what connection all this had with what I had come to learn. Discussing it with the others was forbidden anyway and in any case they all seemed happy enough submitting to the restrictions. I was perplexed, not least because we hadn't even had the benefit of interacting with Grot at all through the week. The prospect of a session with him was always tantalizingly held out to us but he never showed up. I was reminded of Amjad Khan. In the course of one of these exercises, however, fearing for my life while swaying precariously atop a towering pine, I caught sight of him sitting all by himself in a clearing some distance away. I hadn't even known he was around. Somehow the suspicion that he had planned this appearance just didn't go away, particularly as he still refused to have anything to do with any of us. Every question asked of the instructors would elicit either silence or an incomprehensible profundity, which actually said 'I'm not telling'. After a week we were given a break, taken back to civilization and eatable food for two days. I enquired if, while we were here, it was possible to attend a performance at the institute and was greeted with a sigh, a sideways glance and a smiling reply, 'No more performance.'

My burning desire to see Grotowski's work remained unfulfilled and we were not even permitted anywhere near what used to be the performance space. When he did perform, apparently even witnessing a rehearsal was not possible; he now no longer had audiences and the place was unused except for workshop sessions by some of his ex-students, but we were barred even from attending these. The previous week's experience in the forest and now this 'secret ceremony' attitude was making absolutely no sense, and the condescending attitude of the instructors didn't help. Gaur 'Khepa' moodily informed me he had wanted to leave almost as soon as he arrived but in an ominous twist had his passport taken away, and he was being practically compelled to stay on. I was baffled and disturbed by the goings-on, but he detested the whole affair and resolutely refused to take part in any of the exercises. Laughing continuously through the phlegm in

his chest and calling it all 'mano chodan' (mind fucking) he
would emit clouds of smoke, sadly only of tobacco, from his
chillum, hoist his ektara and go off into orbit for hours. I had
no such outlet. We were not permitted even to read.

The second session in the forest was the same old thing
with some additional stuff, which I will respect the oath I
took and not talk about, except to say that Grotowski took
part occasionally and some of it was pretty scary and it still
made no sense whatsoever. I had an eerie sensation of being
initiated into some sort of a cult and knew this was not what I
had come here for. The resolutely unquestioning way all were
going about what was asked of them unnerved me. I decided
that since I couldn't read and was not participating any more,
to write about this whole experience which I started to do,
only to discover to my disbelief all those pages torn out of my
diary a few days later. Deciding I had had quite enough of this
concentration camp with Big Brother watching all the time, I
booked myself a ticket back to Bombay via Warsaw and quit
the workshop after twenty days.

The feeling that I was losing my bearings would start turning
more acute after another week in that forest, that was for sure.
Waiting at Warsaw airport for my flight back, I saw a Sikh
gentleman for the first time in Poland and I felt grounded again
and halfway home already. I had had no telephonic contact
with Ratna all this time and I wasn't supposed to return for
another month, so all were duly astonished when I reappeared,
sans my luggage which Lot Airlines had misplaced and which
finally got to me a month later. This whole misadventure didn't
have too many after-effects except for a foot infection and the
dawning of the realization that no one at all could in fact help,
and whatever I wanted to learn I'd have to do on my own.

For quite a while I kept grappling with what the scenario
might have been had I stayed on; I even kicked myself a

couple of times. Had I chickened out? Was I not ready for Grotowski? Did I need to evolve much more before I could comprehend what he was doing? The fact that Grotowski after he passed away sometime later left no lasting legacy except a bunch of very well-equipped but pathetically ill-adjusted actors banished from my mind any doubt I may have had about having missed an opportunity to grow. My own world was where I belonged and it had begun to seem like a mirage. This whole misadventure had turned out a foolish waste of hard-earned money and, more important, time. Whatever it was they were trying to impart to us in that forest, I knew it was of absolutely no use to me. After achieving the primal state, what? Does one then try to cohabit with bears in the jungle? And I was not looking for a guru who would provide answers if you waited long enough. I didn't need any answers, I needed to hone my craft. And if physical prowess was what this was about then I had, even before coming to Poland, waded in enough streams and climbed enough trees and wandered in enough forests to be able to find anything new and elevating in all that.

I had gone there looking to gain some insight into my work which I was, by and large, happy in and which I intended to continue doing. Here I felt I was losing my wits and it was not a comforting thought; no way did I want to lose touch with my reality, there was too much there that I loved. The 'primal state' and 'conditioned responses' part had made sense, though, and I was dimly aware that if I could shed the second and gain the first or get somewhere close, that could be of enormous help in my acting, but this seemed to be more than just that. This had the smell of proselytization and prophet-building. The unquestioning submission asked of us I just did not take to, nor the air of mystery created around everything. I have to say I had visions of another

Jonestown. Setting himself up as a guru and withholding information from disciples is all that Grotowski seemed to have assimilated from the Indian guru–shishya tradition, with the difference that in return for this loyalty he actually gave back nothing the way a guru does and should, he seemed only to be taking; putting us into situations, observing us, probably reaching some conclusions which none of us at least were privy to. I felt like a guinea pig must feel in an experiment. (This feeling came upon me again with full force when playing Rosencrantz in Grotowski's most celebrated disciple Peter Brook's *Hamlet* in Paris in the year 2001. Peter was equally intent on mythologizing himself and had not only never bothered to learn how to pronounce the word 'Mahabharata', he turned out to be easily the vainest, most self-absorbed person I have ever met. Never once coming anywhere near to divulging any insight into theatre work or the meaning of the play, he stayed completely oblivious to all of us except the leading actor.)

My attempts in Poland to delve into what it was that those who seemed adjusted found stimulating had elicited only vague responses like 'it's so liberating', 'I'm just experiencing the energy', 'it's enough just to know he is around', 'my life has expanded' and so on. I wondered then how many of them could actually relate any of it to their work, and wonder now how many of them came away with anything tangible. I do know, however, that two of them from India who thus far had been pretty active in the theatre never ever attempted another play again, nor anything else as far as I know; one of them continues to do whatever it is he does, in a forest near Calcutta, and Gaur passed away shortly after. So bizarre was this whole experience that I was almost grateful to start shooting a Hindi commercial potboiler again—the one I hadn't been able to pull out of before leaving—and wallowed in the perks that go with a job of that kind, including first-class travel to Dubai, five-star comfort there and the heavenly Helen sitting on my lap (in a scene, of course!)

The news of Richard Attenborough's dream project—to film Gandhiji's life—had been circulating in India since I was a child in school. I had even read a news item about his having attended a film festival in India to announce this intention. The person slated to play the part then was Sir Alec Guinness but at that time it was just an announcement. Over the intervening years many other respected thespian names were floated: Tom Courtenay, Donald Pleasence, Anthony Hopkins, Brian Blessed, John Hurt. And just around the time that *Aakrosh* came out, the news broke that an Indian actor would be chosen to play the part and Sir Richard was to visit Bombay shortly to look for such an actor. My antenna vibrated madly, I thought I was in with a pretty good chance. When I had first learnt of the prospective film (1964 I think it was) I didn't give a thought to the possibility of playing the role—hell, I was fourteen, I wanted to play Zorro not Gandhi; but now closing in on thirty, I thought the prospect was worth pursuing. I thought I could age convincingly, I had done it several times onstage, but getting the eponymous role in a huge Hollywood biopic—it all seemed too unreal to actually happen but reason told me it wasn't impossible at all. Which European actor would be able to get Gandhi's body language, I thought vainly; and there weren't too many other accomplished actors in India either who could manage the physical resemblance. Nature had given me a slight physique and a funny face for this reason alone! If it were to be an Indian actor, it had to be me.

Not suspecting that the dice was loaded, I got an

appointment to meet Sir Richard, friendliness itself. He had just seen *Aakrosh*, waxed eloquent about my work and kept addressing me as 'maestro'. I told him I had admired his acting in a couple of little-known films, *The Angry Silence* and *Guns at Batasi*. He seemed to have forgotten them and was indifferent, but we hit it off rather well and he said we should meet again. Every second actor in Bombay was making the rounds of the Taj Hotel where he was staying, in the hope of a meeting, but I secured another one at which he asked me if I would like to travel to London for a screen test. I was growing a beard for a forthcoming movie but hastily got rid of it, leaving the moustache, got into one of the new suits I had by now acquired and embarked for Vilayat for the first time, travelling executive class along with Smita Patil, Bhakti Barve and Rohini Hattangady, all contenders for the part of Kasturba Gandhi. Two Rolls-Royces with the personalized registration numbers RA 1 and RA 2 awaited us and we rode in splendour to Oxford Street where we were lodged in rooms that had TV. Having no clue of the bill I would later be hit with, I telephoned Ratna and she told me that news had already appeared in the Indian papers that I had been cast. My spirits soaring like the clouds on that gorgeous summer day, I swaggered down Oxford Street, soaking London in. I was in England at last and again I realized I was missing Baba.

Next morning at Shepperton Studios, the first sight that greeted me in the corridor was the back of Ben Kingsley's head and my heart sank. He turned around as we were introduced and it went further down somewhere near my ankles. The man already looked more like Gandhi than I ever could. I had been too smug in my belief that there couldn't be an English actor who could manage the resemblance but here he was right in front of my eyes. The other 'contender', also present, with calf-muscles like a tennis player, was John Hurt. I later deduced that

Ben had in fact already been cast, as had Rohini, and this whole business of tom-tomming all of us being tested and sneaking the news to the press in India that I had been chosen was a masquerade conducted to pre-empt objections that inevitably would have arisen if a white actor were announced straight away. And of course it had to be a white actor—the Oscar campaign had probably begun even before the shoot started.

In fact almost immediately on returning, I saw a news heading, 'Indian Actor to Play Gandhi', but the picture beneath it was of Mr Kingsley. I was crushed but not entirely taken by surprise. I had gone to London fully expecting to have to shave my head for the test but no such thing had happened. I was 'tested' with Rohini in a scene as the young Gandhi; then to my bewilderment as Nehru in another one with Kingsley as Gandhi; and I could not run away from the fact that he was better equipped to play the part. In any case I wasn't given a chance to display my wares. It's a pungent irony that in my entire career this is the one part I went after and it eluded me. I don't know if I was so eager to play the part itself or eager for the worldwide exposure it would involve. I did think though, when I saw it, that Ben was quite wonderful, he got everything right except Gandhiji's ear-to-ear smile. I was not at that time skilled enough to have pulled it off the way he did, though. My curiosity to know if I could, however, was finally stilled many years later when I played Gandhi on the stage in a hugely successful production; and merely repeated that performance in a film with so much prosthetic on my face it could have made a Mongolian actor resemble Gandhi if his head were shaved and he wore granny glasses.

Search for a voice

Dubeyji, meanwhile, had written another play, *Apratyashita* (Unexpected), which he wanted to do with Amrish Puri and a few others, myself included. Much as I disliked this perverse piece about an unorthodox relationship I was keen once again to participate in what I understood as theatre and went into it with whatever zest I could summon. If Grotowski had shed no other light, at least he had made me see that I should make do with what was available instead of chasing the end of the rainbow. It was while doing this play that the irony of the actor's job being completely dependent on other factors became clear to me. Why the very same person could be brilliant in one job and atrocious in another no longer remained a mystery; an actor can only be as good as the work he is in. The categorization of actors into 'good' and 'bad' began to seem a bit of an injustice, even though there are undeniably some who should not be in the profession at all, and even to call those ones 'bad' would be a compliment.

An actor's output hinges totally on being cast right, on how the scene is written, what the character is asked to do, how he is guided to do it, often even on how he is lit. There is no way an actor can salvage a faulty scene, and this play had them in abundance. It was another ghastly production, and I again performed uncomprehendingly. I seriously began to wonder if Dubey in the theatre was all he was cracked up to be. As a student, I had been hugely impressed with the precision and intensity of his theatre work and the performances by Sulabha and Arvind Deshpande in the luminous film he had made of Tendulkar's *Shantata! Court Chaalu Aahe*, but working with him thus far had given me no real charge. I was offended by his aversion to what I considered my way of working, and he was determined to make me see that truthful impulses were not all that was required to make an action stage-worthy. It took me a while to come around to his view. He however continued to claim he saw no validity in mine and greatly enjoyed knocking it. He did however continue to cast me, so I guess I was doing something right.

Dubey was accustomed to plotting out the characters' moves in advance, and after the actors were instructed it was left to them to inject meaning into what he had devised, very much like Alkazi, whose work and personality Dubey had a marked aversion to, though both could scream hysterically at actors equally well. I was at the stage where I felt that exploring possibilities before deciding on a move or an intonation was the way I liked to work, but I could see that Dubey's technique just like Alkazi's, despite both being terrible hams as actors themselves, had by now, because of all their years of constructing stage actions, gotten distilled into an infallible instinct for knowing what looked right onstage and what didn't. Dubey, like Alkazi, had an inbuilt shit-detector and no patience at all with 'fancy concepts like exploring'. Unlike Alkazi however he was concerned not with the aesthetics but the guts of a scene. All that notwithstanding, my experiences of working with Dubey thus far, and later also—including in Girish Karnad's *Bali*, Mahesh Elkunchwar's *Pratibimb* and Dharamveer Bharti's *Andha Yug*—were dissatisfying. I presume that had I been at the same stage of evolution when I worked with Alkazi I may have found him equally wanting.

As the years went by I grew further and further away from Alkazi's kind of theatre, and it was when working with Dubey on his beloved Shaw (*Village Wooing, Don Juan in Hell* and *Dear Liar*) that I finally managed to get on to his bandwidth and discovered that his lifelong obsession with perfect diction and clarity of speech was no idle whim, it was as important as the 'true feelings' I had always been after.

Dubey's contention was that in Shaw's prose, as in the best poetry, the music of the word-sounds contains all the feelings; the words do not need any embellishment, only purity of pronunciation. The same however is not true of Shakespeare, whose worldview or absence of it Dubey also had an issue with and thus did not hold the bard in as high esteem as he did Mr Shaw. I was perplexed at someone scoffing at Shakespeare, but what Dubey said sounded valid.

In Shakespeare the incisive psychological studies of characters at war with themselves are expressed in the most sublime poetry but the plots are hardly worth writing home about; they are in fact utterly predictable. Most of them are borrowed from older works or myth, and he takes major liberties with history. The irresistible P.G. Wodehouse claims (only in jest?) 'the old bird's spelling was not quite up to par, neither was his grammar'. I had in any case never found any of his 'comedies' funny, but listening to Dubey it began to dawn on me that the action of even the 'tragic' or 'historical' plays seems to be pushing not towards an accurate representation of, or a significant statement about a society, a people or an era or even an individual, but towards a resolution which more often than not strains credibility, but attempts to be as dramatically entertaining as possible. That is perhaps why the Hindi filmwalas have helped themselves to such humongous doses of Shakespeare—there is no cliché in Hindi cinema that is not borrowed from the man, and I often wonder what popular Hindi cinema would have been like without Shakespeare's source material. *Julius Caesar* was the first of his plays I'd read and I had many ideas for a production of it. It was, first of all, not a tour de force for a single actor as most of Shakespeare's great plays are, and unlike any of his other works (the oft-borrowed *Romeo and Juliet* being an exception) seemed to represent the state of affairs in India and elsewhere pretty accurately as well, so I didn't consider adapting or Indianizing it in order to present it. Humbled at the thought of doing it myself, I tried without success to persuade Dubeyji. Ultimately, many years later, around 1985, I plunged into it myself.

After six months of yelling at the actors, or the light designer or the backstage crew, on opening night my voice disappeared along with my hopes that this production would receive great acclaim. It was an unexpected lesson on how we in India love creating gods and cannot tolerate anything we consider a desecration of them. That so many in the audience were offended by the changes in the script taught me that Mr WS is more revered in India than in his own country, and it really is hard not to smell a cultural conspiracy here, still working after all these decades. Much as I loved the play ever since I'd studied it in Class 9 in Sem, I'd always felt there was something wrong with it. The two halves seem written by two different people. While the initial section is crisp, racy and engrossing, the post-oratory part feels like another play altogether; it refuses even to allude to Caesar's assassins, all of whom except Brutus and Cassius vanish from the scene without explanation and are replaced by another set of characters who you do not know and care nothing about. Convinced that the conspirators should be shown getting their comeuppance, I altered major portions of the second half of the play including Brutus's suicide. We were greeted with incomprehension or jeering, which I suspect would have happened even if I had not changed a word of the text. The audiences, such as they were, had come either to be entertained or to see something they thought they knew, and were well and truly baffled. While the real flaw of the production lay mostly in the actors' diction, and I am not defending it for a moment, I was stupefied by the accusations of 'blasphemy', no less, that were hurled at us by teachers of various schools whose students we had hoped to tap as potential audience. They all promised to forbid their students from ever seeing our production. And because I had eliminated all the soliloquies and made them part of conversations, to my disbelief, I was confronted by an irate teacher who accused me of 'confusing the students in their understanding of reference to context'.

The laryngeal problem I'd had all these years still bothered me, and the stress of mounting a seventy-strong production and playing Brutus in it as well (Benjamin was a wonderfully wily Cassius and Aakash a rotund Caesar), and seeing it not only collapse on its face but be thoroughly roasted, resulted from the second show onward in a forced intake of steroids to restore my vocal chords to normal. After performing *Lear* in school my voice had taken a week to mend; the same had happened after shows of *The Chairs* in Aligarh and *Chalk Circle* at NSD and in almost every play I'd done since, and no one so far had been able to offer anything close to a reason as to why it happened or a solution to remedy it. All they said was 'stop smoking' as if that was a magical panacea. Every performance onstage ended with my voice in a whisper. While shooting and dubbing both *Manthan* and *Junoon* I had suffered greatly from this malady and schedules had sometimes to be rearranged. I dwelt much on the thought that my voice would get in the way of performing every night when I went to London to act on the West End, as I surely would some day.

While performing *Don Juan* which had some hair-raisingly wordy passages, the old demon began to reappear. Dubeyji advised me not to speak excitedly in life to start with, to relax and try to discover my own voice, then went further with his analogies to Shaw's words: 'They are musical notes,' he said, 'you have to hit the right key. In order to discover how a piece should be broken up when spoken, first of all one must respect the punctuation, the right key will follow.' My desire to overpower audiences with sheer volume had bred in me the habit of straining too hard in performance; that had to be checked. He told me to speak at the pitch the words demanded; it was only necessary for the character you were speaking to to hear you really—that was as loud as you needed to go. And he kept reminding me that I had a breathing problem, but it was only after *Julius Caesar* that I encountered another person who actually suggested concrete steps to help. Till then I hadn't suspected that one had to learn how to breathe.

I have always had doubts about the existence of God but I do believe in the power of prayer; praying not as in grovelling for something but exuding positive energy, and the prayer is answered by receiving it in return. This person, a Dr Raj Kumar, I sincerely believe, appeared in answer to my prayer and after curing my voice vanished without a trace like the Lone Ranger. A voice and speech therapist who witnessed my whispered performance as Brutus, he came backstage after the show, introduced himself and warned me that my vocal chords would be in serious trouble if I went on thus misusing them. Seeing I could do with help, he offered it. The next morning he was at my house at seven on the dot, and with absolutely no mention of fees commenced the exercises that I had the benefit of for the next six months. Turning up every alternate day, he patiently took me through the technique of breathing with the help of the diaphragm, exhaling in a way to relax the vocal equipment and then, with the exhalation, trying to produce the softest sound the voice is capable of and slowly, painstakingly, enlarging that sound while staying on the right note. The NSD acting teacher's exhortations to 'speak from here!' while slapping her ample midriff had only confused me further; how can one speak from there and so on. She, poor misguided soul, though herself a singer, had never so much as mentioned the words 'diaphragm' or 'resonators' or even 'lungs', and was probably one of those lucky ones who never had the kind of trouble I had. I have met many such actors, who instinctively knew how to use their voices. I, however, had to learn.

It was Dr Raj Kumar who helped me lose my colossal hang-up about not being able to hold a note and persuaded me that there is no such thing as a bad or unmusical voice; every sound box, unless it has a physical disability, is and should be capable of every sound. All of us are born with the ability to sing, most of us lose it as we grow, but it can be recovered. There can be no voice that is by nature off-key. Practising the basic notes on the harmonium, part of the therapy, helped me begin to understand the importance of listening closely to my voice and understanding its mechanics. And now the face of the poor, defeated singing instructor at NSD started flashing before my eyes—I wished I could telepathically reach him. To my unending delight, I can now not only manage to stay in key through the basic notes, and actually travel through three scales, I can tell when I've lost the key but continue to grope till it's found again. I have also, while acting, not lost my voice again in these years—and I've had to do plenty of shouting. 'Listen to the involuntary way your voice sounds when you sneeze or yawn,' Dr Raj Kumar said, 'that is your natural timbre.' He insisted that clearing the throat, as people mistakenly keep doing, is actually damaging to the voice if it has gone hoarse; it does not clear anything, it only makes the vocal equipment clash against itself and worsens the condition. What the vocal chords need, then, is the equivalent of a massage and that has everything to do with breath control, which no one in either of the two acting courses I had undergone had even talked about.

His prognosis of my problem was simple actually: I was neglecting to breathe in when the resonant voice which I hoped to constantly produce demanded full lungs, which I did not have, and the technique to control the outflow of breath, which I had to learn. Dying to make an immediate impact onstage the moment I opened my mouth I was exhausting my breath in the first few words of a sentence. Being unable to replenish my lungs while speaking, my body's backup system was kicking in to help me continue speaking with the precious reserves of breath remaining, and sometimes without any at all. Since voice, as I learnt, is nothing but breath brushing past and vibrating the vocal chords, the backup system too without any breath at all has to give up sooner or later. I had no choice but to keep performing with a bad voice and thus I'd strain harder, not only inflicting further damage but also at times experiencing strange sharp twinges of pain in my ribs and around my kidneys, which I should have known were warning signs that I was doing something wrong. And sure enough, I had been doing it wrong all this time, as the good doctor pointed out on the first day after asking me to demonstrate how I breathed onstage. Having performed this rescue Dr Raj Kumar made me promise I'd continue the exercises on my own and vanished from my life. I was unable to reach him at the only number he left.

Some five years later he reappeared in the green room of a theatre in Boston where I had just performed the part of Mahatma Gandhi in a play, he congratulated me on the progress I had made, and gave me another number on which again I was never able to reach him. But then the ways of guardian angels must never be subjected to human scrutiny, I suppose.

My reputation as a theatre worker and an actor in 'serious' movies was growing, though earnings from both were negligible. It was the 'non-serious' movies, as I suppose I should call them, which came my way that kept the kitchen fires alight. My bank account was now pretty respectable. I tried very hard to do only one film at a time but without the clout of stardom which makes such conditions acceptable to others and feasible for oneself, I had to give in. What I did manage though was never doing double shifts again and not getting stuck in the same kind of part in movie after movie. Nature played a strong hand in that by not granting me a single box office hit either as hero or as villain or as anything else, so the industry, not knowing where to slot me, continued to offer me roles that no other actor either would or could play.

This part of my plan too was turning out as I had foreseen: I was getting work in films not because I was 'saleable' or popular but because it was thought I could deliver the goods; but in 'story pitcher' only of course. Hindi cinema, according to its core audience (the stalls), comes in three varieties: the aforementioned 'story pitcher', 'faiting pitcher' and 'famly pitcher'. I was never considered for 'faiting pitchers', but got more than my due in the other kinds, though none of them made any impression at all, and I thus escaped what I imagine must be the utterly nightmarish situation of losing sleep over next week's box office collections, which if healthy create the equally traumatic scenario of upping one's fee for the next project. I never felt any need to do that, I was earning enough to keep me happy; and hell, an alphonso or an ice cream wasn't going to taste any better if I had a few more zeroes pickling away in the bank. I had always desired only as much money as I would need and that was happening now. Nature perhaps did a favour by saving me from stardom and the kind of pressures those who achieve it have to navigate through, I could not have handled them. Moreover, not being a star allowed me to persevere with the things I always loved or have grown to love doing: acting in the theatre or a film I connect with, workshopping with actors, playing tennis or cricket and watching them on TV, revelling in my children as they grow, going to the movies or simply doing nothing at all. It was very good fortune also that I have never needed to do a film only for the money; though the money was not a small consideration, I did only the films I felt like doing. Sometimes, though, after a few days of shooting, I did wonder WHY I had felt like doing this particular film but since I had chosen to do it of my own free will, and had no one to blame, would hold my peace as long as I could, which according to many was not long at all.

I think I had also unwittingly acquired the reputation of a snob and a troublesome actor, which didn't bother me unnecessarily. I began to realize that being so appallingly bad in my early commercial movies was not entirely my fault. The only two who could make the schmaltzy Hindi film dialogue and ersatz situations believable were Dilip Kumar and Amitabh Bachchan and I was nowhere in their league. Being effective in popular movies requires a certain kind of sensibility and an unshakeable belief in them, neither of which I possessed. While it is true that what I was offered was hardly the cream of the crop—that went to the actors who could ensure bums on seats—it is also true that my reputation as a crabby bitch on the sets was acquired because of my dissatisfaction with what I was asked to do and my futile insistence on trying to do it my way. So I found myself turning increasingly cynical, having to learn to act while 'facing', once actually having a director testily tell me, 'Naseerji this is not an art film, here you have to ACT!' It was also because of being frustrated in most suggestions I made, about having sometimes to rewrite the unspeakable dialogue I was given and at other times encountering directors who wouldn't stand even a 'yes' being changed to a 'hmm', about having to enact totally superfluous scenes of great passion, simply because I supposedly did such scenes well, and invariably finding they had to be left on the editing room floor. Scarcely ever was I convinced, but trying to do the scenes the way I imagined they should be done often meant a total overhaul even of the conception of the scene and resulted in worse confusion. And in any case I was not at all equipped to think in Hindi film terms, so I sometimes suffered silently and sometimes not silently at all.

I had by now quite digested the bitter pill that I was not really cut out for mainstream cinema, but since I was continuously offered work in it, and having always been circumspect about the stock parts that in both Hollywood and Bombay invariably go to 'respected' actors from the theatre, I tried to carefully choose the projects I thought might be fun to do. The tragedy of great thespians like Shreeram Lagoo and Nilu Phule being remembered only for their performances in films thoroughly unworthy of them was a guide as to the kind of parts I should definitely avoid. I was grateful I didn't have to work for the money and I was determined that my career would not meet with such a fate. The happy thought that some of the films I'd already done would surely ensure that was punctured on remembering that both Dr Lagoo and Nilu bhau had done significant work in the serious Marathi cinema as well, yet the rest of the country knew them only as the kind of excessive character actors they were compelled to be in popular Hindi cinema. People unfamiliar with the output of these two theatre giants would be unable to imagine what they were capable of and had done on the stage.

Luckily, as an actor seeking employment I had been at the right place at the right time and been greatly aided by the momentum of the other kind of cinema with which I continued to be identified, and which first gained me something of a reputation. These films seemed to be flourishing and the offers to act in them were plentiful as well, so I now found myself in a whirl of shootings. It seemed I had the best of two worlds and the opportunity to make a mark in both, so despite being chary about my chances I thought I'd continue to have a crack at mainstream movies as well. Earning the kind of money they brought certainly didn't hurt and how long could the odds continue to be stacked against me? I began to feel I had a good thing going which would take a lot of doing to blow, but I almost managed it.

Finding my spot

If it is true that 'an actor's talent lies in his choices', I must confess I had absolutely no talent at all. I did not choose to begin my career in art-house films, I was lucky enough to be offered a leading part by a reputed director in a great script, at a time when I would have accepted the part of the third dead body in a film by I.S. Johar. I just happened to be around when actors like me were needed in Shyam's films and I claim no credit for choosing that kind of cinema—it chose me. But for some reason I could never quite fathom, I continued to be needed in the 'popular' films as well, and my choices there were mostly nothing short of disastrous. I turned down some which went on to be huge and chose some that were dogs, including one made by a pair of dilettante brothers, with a small reputation as screenplay writers. The theme of their film, titled *Misaal*, sounded really novel to me, there was tons of the usual masala to balance it, and I thought I'd finally bust the box office with this one. I was to play a meek young man who flees, leaving his girl at the mercy of rapists who always in Hindi films go about their job in the most unlikely spots and with unabashed glee. He later sings a few songs, joins the police force, redeems himself, inspires a younger man, played by one of the director brothers, and they then go about doing

the usual heroics. I had done some 'faiting' for the first time in
a film called *Hum Paanch* and sprained my back on the very
first day trying to make it look real. The action choreographer
had not been impressed. When Ratna saw the film she pointed
out that I seemed to be trying too hard to create the effect of
actually being in a brawl when effortless haymakers and an
easy attitude of 'Is that all you got?' were required of a Hindi
film hero. This role seemed like a chance to get that right at
last. There was to be 'lots of faiting', and I was also tempted
by the prospect of being the 'solo hero' in a film in which I
thought I stood a chance of being noticed and this time I was.

Early in its very brief run I sneaked into a theatre
showing it, to see mostly empty seats and the silhouettes
of a few heads in the stalls, either unresponsive or hooting
derisively every time I appeared on screen. I also discovered
that instead of playing the main character, I was in fact part
of a subplot, while one of the brothers-duo had promoted
himself to central protagonist. In the interval, attempting to
sneak out unnoticed, I was accosted by an audience member
who slapped me on the back and asked why I'd kept my
hair so short in the film, I told him I was playing a police
officer and he laughed and said, 'Chhodo yaar, hero hero
jaisa dikhna chahiye.' This was not the first time a script had
turned out not at all as narrated nor indeed would it be the
last, but seeing this film created in me sufficient suspicion
about mainstream cinema to turn me totally paranoid and
quite ruin the experience of the next few films I did including
one with big-name stars, *Ghulami*, about which, despite for
the first time getting paid in six figures, I remained cynical
through the shoot. It actually turned out pretty good, a big
success at the box office as well, and undid some of the harm
inflicted by *Misaal* which had gained me really imaginative
profanities wherever I was spotted by the 'common man' who

blows his precious money every Friday in the hope of being transported to paradise for a few hours.

Unnerving as it was hearing taunts of 'O bhadwe!' and much worse at the cinema itself, from passers-by, from beggars at traffic lights in response to what I considered a sincere performance, for the only time in my life I regretted having become an actor when, in a traffic jam under the Khar subway, Ratna and I returning from our wedding celebration and still in our wedding clothes had our car surrounded by a dozen guys who for at least ten minutes filled our ears with the most surreal invective I have ever heard. It was a reminder of how seriously the Hindi film audience takes their dreams, and what piffling dreams these actually are, and how deeply they have bought into the sham world these movies create.

Let's not drag out the long-exhausted argument that the common man needs these films to get away from his own drudgery etc.; what I find terrifying is the degree of dumbing down of the audience that these films have managed to achieve, I daresay intentionally. A habit for consuming junk has over the years been created in the audience. They are now irrevocably hooked on that taste, they crave it so they swallow anything that comes thus packaged, and ironically they are blamed for having to be pandered to. The films we make reflect no one's inherent taste but our own. Every few months when some nonsensical multi-starrer flops, everybody assumes the audience has finally come of age but very soon they flock right back to something else equally shallow. It's impossible to explain.

The incident was also a reminder of how dangerous it can be to take celebrityhood seriously and how utterly disastrous it can be to consider oneself entitled and take it for granted. There are too many stories anyway about the flopping of the 'don't you know who I am?' approach. Film stars, when they

MADH ISLAND
All Fools' Day, 1982

(left to right, front row) Davinder Ahuja, Carol Alter, Jamie Alter, Ratna, Medha Kapur, Neelam Shukla; *(back row)* Saeed Mirza, Tom Alter, Shekhar Kapur, Me, Benjamin Gilani, Vikram Mehrotra, Ashok Ahuja, Vinay Shukla.

Hammered groom
arrives astride equally
hammered best man.

Revellers at the wedding *(left to right)*: Bakul and Kundan Shah, Vidhu
Vinod Chopra, Rameshwari, Ketan Mehta, Paresh Mehta, Vinay Shukla
and Javed Akhtar.

Escorting Ammi to the wedding.

Signed, sealed and delivered.

The mothers tuck into the wedding lunch.

Ratna as she looked when
I first saw her...

and on our wedding day.

And we lived happily ever after.

thank their fans for making them what they are and for their love, are basically indulging in what a star must do—play to the galleries. Stars who believe that the mobs going ape outside their windows actually love them are in for bruised shins sooner or later. Nature very kindly continued giving me small doses of fame, almost as if testing whether I could take it or not. I decided I had trouble digesting it, not because I dislike being told that my work is good or because my 'precious privacy' is being invaded or anything like that—I have been able to guard my privacy without any trouble—but because I am convinced that someone who cares for you would not make himself a nuisance when he can see that you would rather be alone.

It is being considered public property that gets my hackles up, when strangers try to put their arm on my shoulder, when they aggressively approach me for a photograph, when they feel they can disturb my meal. Not having and not desiring the security cordon that now surrounds most Hindi film actors, I am often subjected to looks of 'What are you doing on our turf?' or observations in my hearing of 'Who does he think he is?' on refusing to oblige autograph hunters while trying to retrieve my luggage at airports. Once, for *Albert Pinto* we were trying with a hidden camera to sneak in a shot of Shabana and me in the midst of the crowd at the Mount Mary fair. Of course she was instantly recognized; much jostling and misbehaviour followed, ending with Shabana spiritedly delivering a roundhouse whack on the face of a guy who was a particular pest. Things immediately got heated, and I had to step into the melee desperately holding on to my temper. In danger of being lynched if I lost it, I attempted reason and was greeted with more jeering and a response that left me dumbfounded, 'Why she has to come here then?'

I cannot deny the paradox in my behaviour that my

motivation for becoming an actor was not to uncover the secrets of the craft or to serve meaningful work or to make my contribution to society but to be noticed. I wanted to be known, I wanted to be rich, I wanted to be looked at, talked about; and when that started to happen in a serious way I found myself shying away. I hated being accosted and treated with familiarity by strangers and I could no longer take compliments seriously—they came to me even for some very inferior work. I had always thought I'd love signing autographs, in fact had dreamed of the day I would and had practised half a dozen different ones when I was in school. But when it started to happen, and I was often handed crumpled scraps of paper extracted from wallets or visiting cards with no space on them or even tissue paper, and not infrequently after signing was asked what my name was, I decided I hated this utterly meaningless exercise. I am still often mistaken for Om Puri or Girish Karnad or Nana Patekar and congratulated on the work they did in their films. Who they get mistaken for, I don't know. To none of them do I bear the slightest physical resemblance but I suppose many viewers just lump us all into one category and can't really tell us apart. When people at an airport (I am very good at the blasé flyer act now, by the way) or a restaurant come up and say they like my films, I appreciate it and would appreciate it more if they'd say it and go away because I am never quite sure they didn't mean *Arth* or *Swami* or *Ankur*, none of which I was in.

It had been about twelve years since I had last seen Heeba, I knew that she was in Iran and one day received a letter from her in Farsi, which I could not decipher and had no one to help in doing so. Fortunately, along with it was a note from Purveen curtly informing me, 'Your daughter wants to visit you if you will permit it.' Ammi was staying with me those days so I got her to write a reply in Urdu permitting it. I was intrigued and anxious at the thought of meeting this child I had barely seen and who I knew not at all.

Ratna and I were also beginning to feel it would be a really good idea to live together now—I wouldn't have to drop her home every night, for one thing. She was now through with NSD, and with absolutely no accountancy training had single-handedly sorted out the considerable financial mess her father had left behind when he passed away suddenly and much before his time. She spent months poring over accounts, meeting accountants, clearing debts and vainly attempting to collect unpaid dues from some rather big film-industry names. Much before we married, she had also taken over managing my monetary matters and continues to do so, much to my relief. I have only a rough idea how much I earn or how much I pay in taxes and the sight of a balance sheet still unfocuses my eyes, but she knows the numbers. Very quickly I realized my life could do with her kind of balanced approach, it badly needed organizing.

The distinction that I was a slob and she always immaculately turned out apart, we were alike in many ways. I was hot-tempered and impetuous, she was hot-tempered and rational. I found we had similar ideas about what we wanted from life. She made me aware of the worth of family, and her intervention actually brought me closer to Ammi and my brothers with all of whom she formed relationships completely independent of me, and in all of whom I then discovered aspects I had not known before. Besides, not only was she absolutely scrumptious in every way, her calm acceptance of Heeba's existence testified to her absolutely solid citizen status. I knew I would be safe in her hands and I was right.

Ammi knew how long the relationship had already lasted

and had been quite bowled over by the regard and affection with which Ratna always treated her. When I first told her that we were planning to marry she wanted to know if I would ask Ratna to convert to Islam, and when I said I wouldn't she looked long and hard into my eyes, then nodded once very slowly and ever so faintly. She didn't say anything but I got the distinct feeling that she didn't disapprove, and she happily went across to Laxmi Sadan and asked Dina for her daughter's hand. We didn't consider any engagement necessary, we had pledged ourselves to each other long ago.

Wedding plans were afoot when nature reiterated, as if reiteration was needed, the absolute truth of how much an actor, to be effective in a film, depends on his performance being orchestrated right by the director. Even though I had managed not to disgrace myself recreating a few Shammi Kapoor songs for a film called *Situm*, it was as obvious as the nose on my face that I was just not the right material for this kind of thing. But there was also the nagging suspicion that I hadn't yet been cast right. Esmayeel Shroff, who had made some slightly unusual but highly successful films and who had long said he wanted us to work together, offered me the leading part in a film called *Dil Aakhir Dil Hai*, yet another of the kind of romantic films I had always been allergic to. I could not for a second see myself in the part but thinking I had everything to gain—three songs to sing, thus the chance to atone for *Sunaina*—and the fact that I was paired with not one but two gorgeous leading ladies, Rakhee and Parveen Babi, both major-league stars then, made me promptly accept.

Simultaneously a failed actor called Shekhar Kapur, who I had known till then only as Shabana's boyfriend, came asking if I would act in a film he was planning to make. He said he was adapting the story from a paperback by Erich Segal which he handed me and which I abandoned after Chapter Two, but the premise was interesting and I thought that if well made it had half a chance; besides it was to be shot in the delicious Delhi winter and partly in my old school, St Joseph's, Nainital. I had begun to enjoy Shekhar's company and when we discussed the shoot, even though he seemed to know what he was talking about, I went along feeling somewhat uncertain, half fearing this would be another of those annoying family melodramas in which the children could give you diabetes. I have to say I did not entertain the highest hopes for it. A very big lesson was in the offing.

Shekhar said from the start that he didn't want me to be a 'character', he wanted me to be myself, an instruction I found reassuring. I had so far mostly been told what the character is an analogy to, or representative of or a personification of. For the first time since *Sparsh* I was being told that it was my behaviour and my reactions that were needed, not those of an imaginary person. Despite not knowing Shekhar well I immediately felt in a comfort zone with him and, as earlier with Sai, enjoyed the same kind of freedom in revealing myself on camera. I felt trusted and appreciated; the film-maker seemed to know my strengths and weaknesses and would very gently nudge me back on to the right track when needed. It was astonishing sometimes, the way the subtext miraculously appeared in scenes that would be maudlin in the hands of a less perceptive director, and as in *Sparsh* I was helped enormously by a wonderful script. From the moment the first shot was taken it was clear that Shekhar knew his onions and he cared deeply for the performances. I stayed completely stress-free, and apart from giving the production department some anxious moments by developing food poisoning in mid-shoot, I don't think I gave anyone any trouble at all though at times I did feel like throttling the child lead. Shekhar however was patient and constantly caring, and with unending calm and affection managed to coax out of all of us what I still consider rather good performances.

This film, *Masoom*, has introduced me to three generations of children and not only holds pride of place in my memories, it is one film which everyone everywhere seems to have seen, whereas the other one on which I had pinned not a few hopes and which I shot for just before going to Delhi and had to shoot for immediately on returning, is buried in a grave without a marker and deservedly so. A cloying moronic piece of fluff, in which situations of conflict were created only because 'dramatic' solutions had been thought of beforehand, it pretended to tackle a progressive subject but pusillanimously conformed to all the tried and tested formulae, without a clue as to what had made those clichés work in the first place. I never saw it, I didn't need to; even though this time I hadn't tried to be real and followed to a T every instruction about plastering myself in make-up, keeping hair in place, no creases in clothes etc., I knew that my performance was another huge embarrassment. I was given the kind of moustache I'd never ever have in real life and I had to enact situations I wouldn't have expected to in my wildest dreams, among them romantic scenes in bed with both these ladies and songs where I resemble a marionette whose strings are being pulled by an inebriated puppeteer. Hardly anyone saw it and the couple of loyal friends who did assured me it was so excruciating to watch, *Sunaina* was great cinema in comparison.

This has occurred not a few times in my career and it has taken me a while to figure out that in these films the behavioural references of the actors must not be to real life but to other films. I had absorbed nothing of the Hindi-film acting style at all; and, in fact, despite greatly admiring and imitating many actors, had absorbed nothing lasting from any of them, except Mr Kendal, and I had outgrown most of that as well. My dictionary of references was from life, not from Hindi films in which the incidents are neither close to life nor the result of either the writer's or the director's empathetic resources but the bastard child of an earlier filmic experience. Every scene felt like a rehash of stuff that had worked well before in another context; I could feel no connection to these scenes, even the originals of which I hadn't liked and had in fact rewritten in my head when I saw the movies. I couldn't find a smidgen of truth in anything; and not having the fondest affection for the kind of acting in popular Hindi cinema and nothing of a grasp of it, I could not bring an iota of conviction to the part. This nearly apocalyptic choice, the mention of which stumps even trivia buffs, wrote 'finis' to my stint as a leading man in mainstream cinema for many years, whereas *Masoom*, about which I had been initially quite condescending invariably finds first mention among my films almost thirty-five years after it was made. As Grotowski had said in another lifetime, 'there is no such thing as talent but there is such a thing as lack of talent, and lack of talent occurs when one is not in one's right place'. Finding my 'spot' has taken me well-nigh forty years but I think I have spent at least some of that time in the right place.

Whether as husband and father I would be in my right place was a question that did give me some anxious moments until it finally happened, and I think I acquitted myself in both roles with not a little credit. Ratna and I didn't get married by the sea, the registrar not being willing to travel all the way to

Madh Island, but in Dina's home—for sentimental reasons also. As soon as the vows were taken in the presence of only immediate family, we spent the rest of the day carousing with a few friends on the beach, innocently believing life is perfect until we got to the Khar subway that day on our way home.

When about a year later Heeba finally arrived to live with us, I did what I could to repair the breach. The memory of the childhood in Iran, when it is discussed, still seems to distress her. She seldom talks about it and I have to kill the urge to enquire into what was probably a delicate and difficult time. Purveen, Heeba and Bushra, Heeba's half-sister, were in Iran through the turmoil of Ayatollah Khomeini's return and the revolution, which forced the Shah (no relation!) to flee. Both girls had probably been subjected to a rigid orthodox upbringing, they both always wore a chador covering their hair and ears, a sartorial custom which to our combined relief she abandoned almost as soon as she moved in to live with us. Namaaz continued for a few days but then that too quickly went by the board.

Purveen had evidently turned into quite a fundamentalist herself shortly before embarking on her travels; probably the reason Iran was chosen as a destination. Heeba had never been to school and spoke only Farsi then but, having spent the first couple of years of her life in England, had probably learnt to speak English first. Though out of practice, she understood it well, and it came back very quickly indeed. She was fourteen and I don't know too many fourteen-year-olds who could so gracefully handle the ignominy of being admitted in Class 6 with children much younger. She went on to graduate and study drama in Delhi and is now a well-adjusted, contented working actor, an asset to our company and an inspiringly positive influence on her two half-brothers. But though I have to live with the knowledge that the scar tissue of my earlier indifference will never disappear, I wouldn't think she has too many complaints now. The credit for her rehabilitation goes entirely to Ratna.

I wish I could say we all lived happily ever after but life is too complicated for such a smug summing up. And anyway, that is another story.

Epilogue

Ever since I was fifteen years old, following my triumphant turns as Shylock and Lear in school, when I actually began to dare to think of myself as an actor I have always had this waking nightmare: one day I meet up with a wise old man who, after watching my work, says to me, 'Well . . . doubtless everyone has always said you are a very good actor but . . .' And I still have no clue what he says after the 'but'. My imagination doesn't exactly fail me at that point but it doesn't seem sure in which direction to head, and thus I have found many different directions, but never a resolution to the conversation.

This fear which over the years I have actually begun to enjoy living with, half fearfully half eagerly anticipating hearing the rest of what that old man has to say, has perhaps propelled me to take nothing whatsoever for granted and made me stumble upon answers when I wasn't even looking for them. The old man himself has not shown up to this day. But he has manifested himself in several ways and at the most unexpected times, and never in the garb I expected: sometimes a young Jesuit, sometimes a woolly-headed professor, sometimes a stoned companion, sometimes a beautiful woman and sometimes a guardian angel. I think I have reached the stage that when I look in the mirror I get a hazy glimpse of him and he's looking right into my eyes.